VOLUME 573

JANUARY 2001

THE ANNALS

of The American Academy *of* Political
and Social Science

ALAN W. HESTON, *Editor*
NEIL A. WEINER, *Assistant Editor*

CULTURE AND DEVELOPMENT:
INTERNATIONAL PERSPECTIVES

Special Editors of this Volume

CHRISTOPHER CLAGUE
SHOSHANA GROSSBARD-SHECHTMAN
San Diego State University
California

 Sage Publications, Inc. *THOUSAND OAKS   LONDON   NEW DELHI*

The American Academy of Political and Social Science

3937 Chestnut Street   Philadelphia, Pennsylvania 19104

Origin and Purpose. The Academy was organized December 14, 1889, to promote the progress of political and social science, especially through publications and meetings. The Academy does not take sides in controverted questions, but seeks to gather and present reliable information to assist the public in forming an intelligent and accurate judgment.

Meetings. The Academy occasionally holds a meeting in the spring extending over two days.

Publications. THE ANNALS of the American Academy of Political and Social Science is the bi-monthly publication of The Academy. Each issue contains articles on some prominent social or political problem, written at the invitation of the editors. Also, monographs are published from time to time, numbers of which are distributed to pertinent professional organizations. These volumes constitute important reference works on the topics with which they deal, and they are extensively cited by authorities throughout the United States and abroad. The papers presented at the meetings of The Academy are included in THE ANNALS.

Membership. Each member of The Academy receives THE ANNALS and may attend the meetings of The Academy. Membership is open only to individuals. Annual dues: $65.00 for the regular paperbound edition (clothbound, $100.00). For members outside the U.S.A., add $12.00 (surface mail) or $24.00 (air mail) for shipping of your subscription. Members may also purchase single issues of THE ANNALS for $20.00 each (clothbound, $30.00).

Subscriptions. THE ANNALS of the American Academy of Political and Social Science (ISSN 0002-7162) is published six times annually—in January, March, May, July, September, and November. Institutions may subscribe to THE ANNALS at the annual rate: $375.00 (clothbound, $425.00). Add $12.00 per year for subscriptions outside the U.S.A. Institutional rates for single issues: $70.00 each (clothbound, $75.00).

Periodicals postage paid at Thousand Oaks, California, and at additional mailing offices.

Single issues of THE ANNALS may be obtained by individuals who are not members of The Academy for $30.00 each (clothbound, $40.00). Single issues of THE ANNALS have proven to be excellent supplementary texts for classroom use. Direct inquiries regarding adoptions to THE ANNALS c/o Sage Publications (address below).

All correspondence concerning membership in The Academy, dues renewals, inquiries about membership status, and/or purchase of single issues of THE ANNALS should be sent to THE ANNALS c/o Sage Publications, Inc., 2455 Teller Road, Thousand Oaks, CA 91320. Telephone: (805) 499-9774; FAX/Order line: (805) 375-1700. *Please note that orders under $30 must be prepaid.* Sage affiliates in London and India will assist institutional subscribers abroad with regard to orders, claims, and inquiries for both subscriptions and single issues.

Printed on recycled, acid-free paper

THE ANNALS

Editorial Office: 3937 Chestnut Street, Philadelphia, PA 19104.

For information about membership (individuals only) and subscriptions (institutions), address:*

SAGE PUBLICATIONS, INC.
2455 Teller Road
Thousand Oaks, CA 91320

Sage Production Staff: MARIA NOTARANGELO, KATE PETERSON, and ROSE TYLAK

From India and South Asia,
write to:
SAGE PUBLICATIONS INDIA Pvt. Ltd
P.O. Box 4215
New Delhi 110 048
INDIA

From Europe, the Middle East,
and Africa, write to:
SAGE PUBLICATIONS LTD
6 Bonhill Street
London EC2A 4PU
UNITED KINGDOM

Please note that members of The Academy receive THE ANNALS with their membership.
International Standard Serial Number ISSN 0002-7162
International Standard Book Number ISBN 0-7619-2394-2 (Vol. 573, 2001 paper)
International Standard Book Number ISBN 0-7619-2393-4 (Vol. 573, 2001 cloth)
Manufactured in the United States of America. First printing, January 2001.

The articles appearing in THE ANNALS are abstracted or indexed in *Academic Abstracts, Academic Search, America: History and Life, Asia Pacific Database, Book Review Index, CAB Abstracts Database, Central Asia: Abstracts & Index, Communication Abstracts, Corporate ResourceNET, Criminal Justice Abstracts, Current Citations Express, Current Contents: Social & Behavioral Sciences, e-JEL, EconLit, Expanded Academic Index, Guide to Social Science & Religion in Periodical Literature, Health Business FullTEXT, HealthSTAR FullTEXT, Historical Abstracts, International Bibliography of the Social Sciences, International Political Science Abstracts, ISI Basic Social Sciences Index, Journal of Economic Literature on CD, LEXIS-NEXIS, MasterFILE FullTEXT, Middle East: Abstracts & Index, North Africa: Abstracts & Index, PAIS International, Periodical Abstracts, Political Science Abstracts, Sage Public Administration Abstracts, Social Science Source, Social Sciences Citation Index, Social Sciences Index Full Text, Social Services Abstracts, Social Work Abstracts, Sociological Abstracts, Southeast Asia: Abstracts & Index, Standard Periodical Directory (SPD), TOPICsearch, Wilson OmniFile V,* and *Wilson Social Sciences Index/Abstracts,* and are available on microfilm from University Microfilms, Ann Arbor, Michigan.

Information about membership rates, institutional subscriptions, and back issue prices may be found on the facing page.

Advertising. Current rates and specifications may be obtained by writing to THE ANNALS Advertising and Promotion Manager at the Thousand Oaks office (address above).

Claims. Claims for undelivered copies must be made no later than six months following month of publication. The publisher will supply missing copies when losses have been sustained in transit and when the reserve stock will permit.

Change of Address. Six weeks advance notice must be given when notifying of change of address to ensure proper identification. Please specify name of journal. **POSTMASTER:** Send address changes to: THE ANNALS of the American Academy of Political and Social Science, c/o Sage Publications, Inc., 2455 Teller Road, Thousand Oaks, CA 91320.

THE ANNALS

of The American Academy *of* Political *and* Social Science

ALAN W. HESTON, *Editor*
NEIL A. WEINER, *Assistant Editor*

─────────────── **FORTHCOMING** ───────────────

SUPREME COURT'S FEDERALISM:
REAL OR IMAGINED?
Special Editor: Frank Goodman

Volume 574   March 2001

CHILDREN'S RIGHTS
Special Editor: Jude L. Fernando

Volume 575   May 2001

COURTHOUSE VIOLENCE:
PROTECTING THE JUDICIAL WORKPLACE
Special Editors: Victor Flango
and Don Hardenbergh

Volume 576   July 2001

See page 2 for information on Academy membership and
purchase of single volumes of **The Annals.**

CONTENTS

BOOK DEPARTMENT CONTENTS

SOCIOLOGY

ECONOMICS

The origin of this special issue of *The Annals* on cultural capital and development lies in a June 1999 conference on the interaction between economics and other disciplines held under the auspices of the Society for the Advancement of Behavioral Economics at San Diego State University. One example of fruitful interaction between economics and other disciplines is found in the study of economic development and cultural institutions such as language, prescribed gender roles, and ethnic identity. This preface and the following articles offer fresh perspectives on the possible effects of cultural institutions on economic performance and politics. Many of the articles also investigate reasons why particular institutions arise and, in particular, how economic development affects cultural institutions.

To the extent that a cultural institution, such as a particular language or a division of labor between the genders, generates future benefits to a society, and that creating or maintaining this institution is costly, that institution can be viewed as a form of cultural capital. We are following sociologist Pierre Bourdieu in viewing culture as a form of capital in which people and societies invest their time and material resources. However, we tend to use the word "culture" in a broader sense than Bourdieu, as broadly as anthropologist Bronislaw Malinowski. In his article on culture in the *Encyclopedia of the Social Sciences* (1931), Malinowski stated that "culture comprises inherited artefacts, goods, technical processes, ideas, habits, and values."[1] Our concept of cultural capital incorporates and expands on Bourdieu's concepts of cultural capital (Bourdieu 1979, 1998) and symbolic capital (Bourdieu [1980] 1990). Among the groups most likely to invest in their cultural capital are business firms, whose cultural capital is similar to what John Tomer (1987) has called "organizational capital." Whenever firms consciously change their rules or procedures, or invest in their workers' identification with the firm's culture, they can be viewed as investing in cultural capital.

Even if they do not perform well according to widely accepted indicators such as per capita income, nations tend to be slow at changing their cultural institutions. We hope that by pointing out some of the benefits of particular cultural institutions and some of the mechanisms influencing culture, the articles in this volume will encourage policymakers to think further in the direction of alleviating poverty via investments in cultural capital.

THE EVOLUTION OF DEVELOPMENT ECONOMICS

From the beginnings of the separate field of economic development, most scholars recognized that important institutional and cultural differences existed between the advanced "industrial" countries and the "underdeveloped" countries. However, although a few economists in the 1950s and 1960s thought seriously about cultural differences as an explanatory factor in underdevelopment, for the most part these differences were not integrated into economic analysis. There are several reasons why economists in that period tended to ignore culture as a determinant of economic development. First, the recognition of cultural heterogeneity challenged the assumptions omnipresent in traditional economic models: rationality, perfect information, and utility maximization. Economists sometimes consider it their raison d'être to find an explanation of phenomena consistent with rational calculation, selfishness, and foresight. A cultural explanation of an economic phenomenon was seen as a possible contradiction of the accepted views on *Homo economicus*.

A second reason why economists tended to ignore culture is that cultural variables are not easy to measure. Thinking about the measurement of cultural variables is not part of the tradition of economics.[2] Third, even if differences in culture can be observed, through survey instruments or by seeing differences in patterns of behavior in similar circumstances, it is still very difficult to sort out cause and effect. Economists pride themselves on the construction of models with clearly defined exogenous and endogenous variables, and economics at that time lacked the tools for incorporating cultural variables into such models.

In the early postwar years, there was intense disagreement on the applicability of neoclassical economics to the problems of underdevelopment. Some economists took the view that the principles of utility and profit maximization, supply and demand, comparative advantage, and the efficiency of markets were applicable to all economies. Others, in the new field of development economics, argued that a new style of economic analysis was needed, but few of the proponents of the new development economics took institutions, politics, or culture very seriously. Their models of big push, balanced growth, unlimited supplies of labor, and the virtues of economic planning have not stood up well to subsequent experiences. To the contrary, recent experience has reinforced the traditional economist's view that well-functioning markets are essential for development. A good deal of research has shown that market-friendly policies of governments promote economic progress. With the growth in consensus on this issue, attention has turned to the determinants of the adoption of such policies. This has led economists to study the institutions that underlie well-functioning market economies, such as property rights and contract enforcement mechanisms.

At the same time that the experiences of less developed countries were inducing economists to study these market-supporting institutions, some advances in the discipline itself were making the task easier. The traditional domain of economics has been the study of human behavior in markets, typically under the assumption that the institutions supporting a market economy, such as property rights and contract enforcement, were in place. In recent decades, economics has broadened its subject matter to include topics formerly considered the exclusive province of other disciplines (Hirschleifer 1985; Grossbard-Shechtman 2001; Grossbard-Shechtman and Clague in press). These topics include crime, fertility, marriage, voting, the law, political and bureaucratic behavior, and the internal functioning of firms and other organizations. At the same time as this expansion of the subject matter of economics, and partly as a result of this expansion, some of the core areas of the discipline have changed. The traditional assumptions regarding *Homo economicus*, while proving useful in exploring new areas, were found to be quite inadequate in accounting for some behavior in these new areas, unless they were modified to take account of the limits on human capacities to process and retain information and of human propensities to form bonds of affection and trust (see the work summarized in Schwartz 1998). These modifications have turned out to be very useful in explaining some of the core areas in economics, such as the way firms interact in markets (Hirschleifer 1985).

Thus, as economists working on problems of less developed countries turned their attention from the effects of economic policies (dirigisme versus liberalization) toward the institutional foundations of market economies, they have been able to draw on recent developments in economic theory, including in particular the New Institutional Economics (North 1981, 1990). In the New Institutional Economics, institutions are visualized as the outcome of games of social interaction, in which individuals rationally choose their actions, according to their mental models of the world, their information sets, and the behavior of other players in the game. This intellectual framework, which grew out of economic history and the advances in game theory and information theory, has been applied to puzzles in economic development (for example, Nabli and Nugent 1989; North 1990; Lin and Nugent 1995; Clague 1997; Olson 2000). Cultural norms and beliefs can be seen as the deepest level of institution (Feeny 1993), and thus the same framework can illuminate the role of cultural differences in economic performance.[3]

Are differences in cultural capital the major explanation of the vast differences in productivity and income between nations? Some scholars think so (Landes 1998; Harrison and Huntington 2000). In analyzing this question, we can make use of the important distinction between personal culture and civic culture (Olson 1996). Personal culture (or marketable human capital) is what the individual carries with him as a result of being brought up in a particular culture. It is what differentiates an immigrant from the natives of a country. There is abundant evidence that immigrants tend to adopt the behavior patterns of their new homelands, at least in their economic decisions. In this sense, personal culture is typically not a major obstacle to immigrants' prosperity. Migrants from poor countries to the United States, for example, rather quickly earn wages much closer to the American average than to the average in their home countries (Chiswick and Sullivan 1995). In contrast to Olson's personal culture, his concept of civic culture is the set of norms, attitudes, and values of an entire community. This concept is similar to what we call societal cultural capital. This cultural capital affects the incentives of individuals in ways that the new institutional theories illuminate. Thus it is perfectly consistent to believe that incentives matter greatly for economic behavior, and that individuals from different cultures would respond in similar ways to the same incentives, while recognizing that differences in institutions and cultural capital can account for vast differences in productivity.

This issue of *The Annals* offers new perspectives on various aspects of culture related to politics and the economy, including democracy, corruption, women's rights, wedding expenditures, and ethnic cleansing. The articles show that the analyses of economists can be useful in these new areas of application. To the extent that these are empirical analyses, research by economists does not necessarily differ from that performed by political scientists or sociologists studying similar issues. Some of the contributions to this volume show that even though they were developed in the West, some of the ideas found in economic theories are applicable universally and can help us understand cultural institutions.

CULTURE AND POLITICS

In their article on democracy in poor countries, Christopher Clague, Suzanne Gleason, and Stephen Knack present a statistical study of the prevalence of democratic political institutions in the postwar period. A frequent observation by social scientists is that the likelihood of democracy in a country is strongly influenced by the level of economic development. Yet there are striking exceptions to this generalization, and when one begins to explore other determinants, the level of economic development loses a good deal of its explanatory power. This study finds an important role for variables that can be given a cultural interpretation, such as experience as a British colony, the penetration of the English language under British colonial rule, Islam as a dominant religion, and the percentage of the population that is of European extraction.

The topic of corruption also needs to be analyzed in the context of related political and cultural institutions, as is done in the second article in this special issue. After many decades of polite neglect, corruption has become a very hot topic in research on economic development. Omar Azfar, Young Lee, and Anand Swamy describe some research showing that countries with higher levels of corruption have lower rates of investment and economic growth. This cross-country evidence is buttressed by micro-level surveys revealing that business people in selected countries complain strongly about corruption and indicate that they would be willing to pay substantial sums to be free of it. The article also reports on the authors' interesting finding—based on a survey in newly independent Georgia and a cross-country study—that, relative to men, women are less inclined to be corrupt.

EXPLAINING COMMITMENT TO
FAMILIES AND OTHER COLLECTIVES

Richard Ball's contribution to this special issue examines interrelationships between economic development and an important dimension of cultural differences between societies: individualism-collectivism, or the degree to which people constrain the pursuit of individual goals in order to further collective goals. With regard to the effects of individualism and collectivism on economic development, a long literature contends that economic development is impeded by traditional collectivism and enhanced by individualism, but another strand of literature describes circumstances in which the opposite is true. As to the effects of economic development on this cultural trait, some authors suggest that economic development makes people more individualistic, while others show ways in which it fosters collectivism. The discussion reveals, first, that an important dimension of this cultural trait is the size of the group with which individuals identify and, second, that appropriate social institutions can substitute for collectivist norms and also enhance collectivist identification with larger groups.

Groups and organizations differ not only in size but also in purpose. One of the most important and universal organizations is the family. In the context of poor Indian villages, observers often wonder why families spend high portions of their income on festivals and wedding celebrations. In the next article in this volume, Vijayendra Rao incorporates a cultural lens into an economic framework to understand why the poor incur these (for them) large expenditures. The article explains how culturally defined notions of identity, individuality, and civic life shape preferences, and culturally determined rules and social obligations affect constraints, and how these in turn interact with economic incentives to determine behavior. The article does this both in terms of theory—by mixing anthropological and economic conceptual frameworks—and empirics—by mixing qualitative data with the econometric analysis of specially designed sample surveys. The article finds that festivals and marriages are arenas where reputations are built and managed and that these reputations play a crucial role in determining people's identities, preserving their networks, and giving them higher social status. Whether these expenditures are regarded as wasteful or productive depends on the degree to which they enhance relative position or build social cohesion and the capacity for collective action—part of what we call cultural capital. This insight suggests promoting development policies that privilege collective over individual action, which interventions such as micro-credit programs and social funds are attempting to do.

GENDER ROLES

All cultures prescribe roles for men and women, and these prescriptions often vary dramatically from society to society. These roles in turn influence individual propensities to engage in work, home production, and politics. While economists usually assume that gender roles are given, they can also analyze variations in these gender roles (see Grossbard-Shechtman and Neuman 1998). The next article in this special issue examines a number of cultural prescriptions regarding gender roles. Using Indian district-level data, Suzanne Gleason investigates variation in female political participation and female child survival. The evidence indicates that female voter participation is higher in districts with higher literacy rates and in more urban districts, but, somewhat surprisingly, female labor force participation appears to have a negative effect on female voter participation. The article also reports that, relative to male child survival, female child survival is higher in districts with higher female literacy and labor force participation, but it is apparently not affected by female political participation.

ETHNICITY AND ETHNIC CONFLICTS

Ethnic groups are another type of group that invests in cultural capital. The degree to which neighboring ethnic groups cooperate and get along with each other is a very interesting question that has intrigued many social scientists and on which Murat Somer's article in this volume offers a novel economic perspective. Somer interprets the sudden explosion of ethnic violence in Yugoslavia in terms of a cascade model and in so doing challenges the view that enduring hatreds were the main cause. He observes that levels of ethnic toleration were fairly high in Tito's Yugoslavia, as evidenced by surveys of ethnic identity and rates of ethnic intermarriage. The cascade model helps explain why the process of polarization occurred so rapidly, contrary to the expectations of the most knowledgeable observers at the time. Somer's article illustrates that behavior that seems to be the result of enduring cultural attitudes may be strongly influenced by temporary, situational factors. At the same time, the article argues that ethnic behavior responds to long-term institutional incentives, which in the Yugoslav case restricted public expression of ethnic hostilities without sufficiently encouraging the enhancement of ethnic brotherhood in private.

HINDU CULTURE AND DEVELOPMENT

In the last article in this collection, John Adams shows how the views of sociologist Max Weber and others on the incompatibility between Hindu culture and economic progress have not stood up well to subsequent analysis. He also criticizes the views of those who deny that features of Hindu culture, such as the caste system, have powerful impacts on economic behavior. He argues for a sophisticated middle way, based on careful social science research, which recognizes that Indian culture continues to shape attitudes and behavior and has both positive and negative effects on social well-being.

IMPLICATIONS FOR DEVELOPMENT POLICY

While the articles in this collection indicate that applying economic analysis to the study of culture is a productive avenue for research, this special issue raises more questions than it answers. We are still very far from understanding why cultures differ so dramatically. There is room for much further research into the multiple interrelationships between various economic, political, and cultural institutions. In this endeavor, we may benefit not only from more economic analysis but also from sociological and anthropological analysis and from cooperation between the disciplines. In this light, one could examine whether, as suggested by Adams in his article, there is an affinity between Indian culture and participatory democracy.

We also need more studies of investments in cultural capital by individuals, firms, families, and other groups, in part because such studies can help us design strategies and policies that work effectively to promote economic and social development. We hope that this volume helps readers realize that it has become inevitable for scholars to deal with cultural differences between countries and cultural changes over time.

CHRISTOPHER CLAGUE
SHOSHANA GROSSBARD-SHECHTMAN

Notes

1. By "inherited" we mean inherited by an individual who either is born into a group (the customary sense of "inherited") or joins a group and accepts the culture ruling that group. A group's cultural capital is the sum of the cultural capital embodied in the members of that group.

2. That is why the work of Adelman and Morris (1967) was praised when it came out but then was largely ignored until the late 1990s.

3. It is interesting that some of the important advances in information theory emerged from the work of economists (especially Akerlof [1970] and Stiglitz [1974]) in contemplating problems of less developed countries.

References

Adelman, Irma and Cynthia Taft Morris. 1967. *Society, Politics, and Economic Development: A Quantitative Approach*. Baltimore, MD: Johns Hopkins University Press.

Akerlof, George. 1970. The Market for Lemons: Quality, Uncertainty, and the Market Mechanism. *Quarterly Journal of Economics* 84:488-500.

Bourdieu, Pierre. 1979. *La distinction: Critique sociale du jugement*. Paris: Editions de Minuit.

———. [1980] 1990. *The Logic of Practice*. Stanford, CA: Stanford University Press. (Originally published in French.)

———. 1998. *La domination masculine*. Paris: Seuil.

Chiswick, Barry R. and Teresa A. Sullivan. 1995. The New Immigrants. In *State of the Union: Americans in the 1990s*, ed. Reynolds Farley. Vol. 2. New York: Russell Sage.

Clague, Christopher, ed. 1997. *Institutions and Economic Development: Growth and Governance in Less-Developed and Post-Socialist Countries*. Baltimore, MD: Johns Hopkins University Press.

Feeny, David. 1993. The Demand for and Supply of Institutional Arrangements. In *Rethinking Institutional Analysis and Development: Some Issues, Choices, and Alternatives*, ed. Vincent Ostrom, David Feeny, and Hartmut Picht. San Francisco: Institute for Contemporary Studies.

Grossbard-Shechtman, Shoshana, ed. 2001. *On the Expansion of Economics*. Armonk, NY: M. E. Sharpe.

Grossbard-Shechtman, Shoshana and Christopher Clague. In press. What Is Economics? *Journal of Socioeconomics*.

Grossbard-Shechtman, Shoshana and Shoshana Neuman. 1998. The Extra Burden of Moslem Wives—Insights from Israeli Women's Labour Supply. *Economic Development and Cultural Change* 46:491-517.

Harrison, Lawrence and Samuel Huntington. 2000. *Culture Matters: How Values Shape Human Progress*. New York: Basic Books.

Hirschleifer, Jack. 1985. The Expanding Domain of Economics. *American Economic Review* 75:53-68.

Landes, David. 1998. *The Wealth and Poverty of Nations*. New York: Norton.

Lin, J. Y. and Jeffrey Nugent. 1995. Institutions and Economic Development. In *Handbook of Development Economics*, ed. Jere Behrman and T. N. Srinivasan. Vol. 3. Amsterdam: North-Holland.

Nabli, Mustapha and Jeffrey Nugent. 1989. The New Institutional Economics and Economic Development. *World Development* 17:1333-47.

North, Douglass C. 1981. *Growth and Structural Change*. New York: Norton.

———. 1990. *Institutions, Institutional Change, and Economic Performance*. New York: Cambridge University Press.

Olson, Mancur. 1996. Distinguished Lecture on Economics in Government: Big Bills Left on the Sidewalk: Why Some Nations Are Rich, and Others Poor. *Journal of Economic Perspectives* 10(2):3-24.

———. 2000. *Power and Prosperity: Outgrowing Communist and Capitalist Dictatorships*. New York: Basic Books.

Schwartz, Hugh. 1998. *Rationality Gone Awry? Decision Making Inconsistent with Economic and Financial Theory*. Westport, CT: Praeger.

Stiglitz, Joseph. 1974. Incentives and Risk-Sharing in Sharecropping. *Review of Economic Studies* 41:219-55.

Tomer, John F. 1987. *Organizational Capital*. New York: Praeger.

ANNALS, *AAPSS*, **573**, January 2001

Determinants of Lasting Democracy in Poor Countries: Culture, Development, and Institutions

By CHRISTOPHER CLAGUE, SUZANNE GLEASON,
and STEPHEN KNACK

ABSTRACT: This article presents a statistical study of the determinants of democracy in the postwar period. Important variables are found to be former status as a British colony, island status, the share of the population professing Islam, the share of the population that is of European descent, penetration of the English language during British colonial rule, and a measure of ethnic homogeneity. The evidence suggests that cultural beliefs and institutional inheritances are important determinants of the viability of democracy in poor countries, even when controlling for literacy and socioeconomic development.

Christopher Clague is professor emeritus of economics from the University of Maryland, where he was director of research for the Center for Institutional Reform and the Informal Sector from 1990 to 1997. He is now a lecturer at San Diego State University.

Suzanne Gleason is an instructor of radiology and economics at the Harvard Medical School (MGH Decision Making and Technology Assessment Group). Her research interests include institutions, health care, and the role of government in affecting personal well-being.

Stephen Knack is a senior research economist at the World Bank. His current work focuses on the impact of institutions and social capital on economic development and the role of foreign aid in promoting good governance.

NOTE: The authors thank John Adams for detailed comments on an earlier draft of this article.

ONE of the most widely recognized and empirically documented findings in social science is the association between a country's level of economic development and the democratic character of its political institutions. This association is a prominent feature of the modernization school of political science and sociology, which developed explanations primarily of the causal chain from economic development to democratic and participatory political institutions.

Nevertheless, the correlation of democracy with economic development is far from perfect. A surprising number of very poor and underdeveloped countries exhibit democratic political institutions. The existence of these economically underdeveloped democracies provides support for another strand in the literature on democracy, one that emphasizes sequential and institutional development. Historically, contestation with a restricted franchise has almost always preceded inclusive democratic institutions. Theory and history support the proposition that the institution of electoral contestation for power is initially a fragile plant but one that develops strong roots when permitted a period of continuous functioning. The question posed in this article is, Under what conditions is democratic evolution likely in an underdeveloped country?

Our concern is particularly with the conditions under which a *lasting* democracy is likely to emerge. Clearly, a democracy that fails to last does not protect the political and civil rights of its citizens. Moreover, recent research has found that lasting democracies enjoy better protection of contract and property rights, even at the same level of income, than countries with either stable autocracies or unstable democracies (Clague et al. 1996). Along with sound economic policies, these economic rights are highly important for economic performance (Clague et al. 1996; Knack and Keefer 1995). It would be very desirable to have a deeper understanding of why some societies, even at low levels of income, develop this beneficial combination of political and economic institutions.

An association between British colonial rule and democracy has been noted by several observers (Weiner 1987; Lipset, Seong, and Torres 1993; among others). This variable is not decisive, since there are many British former colonies that have not become democratic. What is there about British rule that is conducive to the evolution of democracy? Does the association hold when other relevant variables are taken into account?

Small states and island states are more likely to be democratic. Do these associations derive from size and island status, or are they the result of associations of these variables with other country characteristics that influence democracy? Societies in which Islam is the dominant religion are less likely to be democratic than other societies. Is this association the product of the cultural heritage of Islam or the by-product of its association with other variables?

Here we explore these and other hypotheses about the determinants of democracy, using a large sample of countries in the postwar period. We focus on the degree of democratic practice over the whole period, rather than on the determinants of transitions from autocratic to democratic rule or on the breakdown of democracy. Our research design permits us to investigate the relationship between enduring country characteristics and fairly long-term experiences with democracy. This approach affords a different window on the determinants of democracy from research strategies that focus on changes in democratic status. The next section reviews some of the literature on the determinants of democracy and presents our theoretical framework. The following section (section 2) discusses various hypotheses that lend themselves to empirical tests. Section 3 describes our measure of democracy, and section 4 presents the multivariate analysis. The last section offers some interpretation of the results.

1. THEORETICAL FRAMEWORK

Our definition of democracy is a conventional one. The chief executive and the legislature must be selected by public elections that are freely contested under conditions of freedom of speech and organization, and the legislature must have a significant share of political power. This definition emphasizes contestation rather than inclusion (Dahl 1971); thus we consider polities to be democratic before the extension of the franchise to the entire adult population.[1]

A prominent theory of the emergence and maintenance of democracy is the modernization school, of which Lipset (1959) is the leading example (see Diamond 1992 for a recent restatement). This theory predicts a strong relationship between measures of economic and social development (including literacy, level of education, urbanization, and industrialization) and the presence of democratic regimes. In this view, economic development undermines authoritarian rule and facilitates the emergence and survival of democracy not only by these structural changes associated with development but also by increasing the level of rationality in individual decision making, by inducing greater toleration of opposing points of view, and by attenuating the struggle over economic resources. Strong versions of the theory claim that democracy is an aberration at low levels of socioeconomic development and becomes increasingly probable as development reaches high levels.

The modernization school has been criticized for not spelling out the precise mechanisms by which economic development leads to democracy and for not providing persuasive evidence for the mechanisms mentioned. Rueschemeyer, Stephens, and Stephens (1992) have developed a theory based on the balance of class power, which they argue changes during the course of economic development so as to create conditions under which democracy becomes more likely. This theory is developed from, and applied to, countries in Europe, Latin America, and the British settler colonies in North

America and Australasia. In these cases it is remarkably insightful. It has not been applied to Africa, Asia, and the Middle East, where it may also provide insights but where other important factors are at work. Another strand of literature contends that the emergence of democracy requires special circumstances, in which the elites calculate that their interests are better served by agreeing to rules of peaceful contestation than by their separate attempts to control the state. Thus the circumstances require that no single contender for power be able to achieve the preferred outcome of autocratic rule. Prominent statements of this institutionalist, or path-dependent, view are in Rustow 1970, Dahl 1971, and more recently Olson 1993. In this vein, Higley and Burton (1989) and the authors in Higley and Gunther 1992 have stressed the importance of the emergence of elite consensus for the stability of democratic regimes. Lijphart's (1977) concept of consociational democracy leaves ample room for political leadership, as does the "voluntaristic" framework of O'Donnell and Schmitter (1986). Przeworski (1991) has described the strategic choices open to political forces during the breakdown of authoritarian regimes and the transition to democratic institutions. In all of these accounts, the institutions of contestation can take root and grow strong, even before the society becomes highly educated, urbanized, or "modern." Moreover, economic development does not automatically lead to the emergence and strengthening of these political institutions.

The choices of elites take place in a cultural context. Attempts to introduce foreign institutions such as elections, legislatures, and judicially enforced rule of law may succeed in one society and fail in another because of deep-seated cultural attitudes and expectations about how political authority should and will be used. Such cultural attitudes may be reflected in a society's religion and its degree of ethnic diversity and ethnic tension. They may be influenced by the presence of some fraction of the population of European descent, which may have brought cultural attitudes favorable to democracy. Our empirical analysis enables us to throw light on the effects of some of these variables; our hypotheses are described in the next section.

2. HYPOTHESES

This study uses data on the political regimes of 146 countries during the 1960-94 period. For countries that became independent after 1960, the period starts with the date of independence. For each year, each country is classified as a democracy or an autocracy (or assigned to an intermediate category in a few cases where the data were not clear). The main dependent variable is the fraction of years during the period that a country is a democracy. We use as a check on our results the Freedom House data on political rights for the 1972-90 period (Freedom House various years). To alleviate problems of reverse causation, we use as inde-

pendent variables country characteristics at the beginning of the period,
that is, around 1960 (or the date of
independence).

2.1. Economic development

The prior empirical literature on
the effects of socioeconomic development on democracy is summarized
by Hadenius (1992); Sirowy and
Inkeles (1990); and Diamond (1992).
Democracy is correlated with measures of economic development such
as income per capita, the share of the
labor force in agriculture, urbanization, and educational attainments.
Recent literature has become more
careful about the direction of causation in the relationship of development and democracy; several recent
studies find a fairly strong causal
effect of an increase in income on the
emergence or sustainability of
democracy (Barro 1997; Helliwell
1994; Burkhart and Lewis-Beck
1994). Our study is not designed to
test these timing effects, since our
dependent variable is the level of
democracy over the 1960-94 period.
However, in order to test hypotheses
related to variables other than economic development, it is necessary to
control for the level of development.
For this purpose, we use the share of
the labor force in agriculture in 1960
(or the year of independence if that is
later). The share of the labor force in
agriculture is a conceptually better
measure of economic development
for purposes of the modernization
thesis than per capita income, particularly for mineral-rich countries.
Some countries have very high
incomes but lack the other characteristics of economic development and

modernization that theorists had in
mind in describing the association of
development with democracy.

Literacy and life expectancy are
other concomitants of economic
development, and they are also quite
plausibly causal determinants of
democracy. However, it is very plausible that the causation also runs
from democratic political institutions to higher levels of literacy and
life expectancy. Moreover, the extent
of literacy, primary education, and
health services probably reflects cultural attitudes toward social equality, which in turn affect the likelihood
of democracy. Although many studies
have found literacy and life expectancy to be highly correlated with
democracy, these variables may not
be causal factors. We shall explore
the role of these variables below, but
we do not include them in our basic
regressions.

2.2. Ethnic diversity

Divisions within society based on
ethnicity, language, and religion
have important effects on political
outcomes, including the emergence
and maintenance of democratic political institutions. Such divisions are
more prevalent, or more intensely
felt, in the less developed countries
(LDCs) than in the developed democracies. These social divisions are
commonly thought to be an obstacle
to the establishment and preservation of democracy in the Third World,
but the measurement of such diversity is complicated; even the theoretical effects of social diversity on
democracy are far from straightforward. At the theoretical level, the
structure of divisions based on

ethnicity, language, and religion may affect the evolution of democracy. The structure of divisions refers to the shares of social groups: for example, a large group comprising more than 90 percent of the population, or two equally sized groups, or a multitude of groups with none holding more than 20 percent. Logically prior to such an analysis is the definition of the groups: should the analysis focus on ethnic categories, language, religion, or a combination of characteristics?

Country histories show that the politically relevant dimensions of cleavage can be any or all of these three characteristics (Horowitz 1985). Where several different languages are spoken, language may not be the politically relevant cleavage, as in the Philippines, where one's identity is closely tied to language but political parties organize across language groups. The same is true of ethnic and religious divisions, even where these divisions are very prominent in nonpolitical contexts. Yet each of these divisions can serve as the basis for political polarization, leading to such consequences as group hegemony, separatist movements, and intergroup tension. Thus we are led to define the groups according to the politically relevant dimensions of cleavage. Sullivan (1991) characterizes the structure of groups according to the dimensions of cleavage that are politically relevant in each country. Another variable is based on language alone. Muller (1964) reports the number of people who are native speakers of each language in each country. From this information we construct the

population share of native speakers of the most commonly spoken language. This variable is designated MULLER. Finally, we experiment with the widely used index of ethnolinguistic fractionalization (FRACTION) compiled in the *Atlas Naradov Mira* (USSR [1964] 1972).

There remains the issue of how to construct an index of homogeneity or diversity. The index of ethnolinguistic fractionalization is 1 minus the Herfindahl index of the group shares: 1 minus the sum of the squares of the group shares. For the purposes of explaining the emergence and maintenance of democracy, this statistical measure is not necessarily the appropriate one. Consider a society with two groups, one of which contains 55 percent of the population and the other, 45 percent. If voting is along group lines, the minority group may calculate that it will never participate in government, and its commitment to democracy will be accordingly diminished. It might therefore resort to a coup and rule by force.[2] In a society where no group contains more than 20 percent of the population, all groups may calculate that they have a chance of participating in the majority coalition at least part of the time. In such cases, greater diversity could be more, rather than less, favorable to democracy.[3]

Another deficiency of a Herfindahl index of group shares is that it takes no account of which group is dominant in the society. Consider two societies in each of which there is a majority group containing 90 percent of the population and a minority group with 10 percent. In the first society, the majority is economically and politically dominant, while in the second, the minority rules over the majority. In the first society, the degree of ethnic diversity would not pose a serious obstacle to the establishment and maintenance of democracy. Examples of countries (and minority groups) that seem to fit this pattern are New Zealand (Maoris), the United States (African Americans), Norway (Laplanders), and Japan (Ainu). In the second society, on the other hand, the ruling ethnic minority would not stay in power if it permitted free and fair elections with a universal franchise, and this minority can be expected to resist establishing fully democratic institutions. Two cases might be distinguished here. In one, the ruling ethnic minority has already established institutions of electoral representation with a franchise limited to its ethnic group.[4] Examples would be South Africa until 1992 and Rhodesia from 1965 to 1978. The ruling group certainly did resist expansion of the franchise, but this stance proved untenable in the ideological climate of the postwar period.

In the second case, the dominant ethnic minority has not been selecting its political leaders through fair elections but, rather, by authoritarian means. Examples are Syria, Iraq, Burundi, and Taiwan. The prospects for transition from autocracy to democracy seem to be particularly unfavorable in such countries, precisely because of ethnic tensions. The dominant minority has reason to fear loss of its privileges and perhaps even vindictive assaults on its property if the subordinate majority comes to power.

Thus the structure of groups is an inadequate guide to the prospects for democracy in a society; one must consider the power relationships between the groups. We shall use a variable called SULLIVAN,[5] which is the population share of the largest group in society, according to the group definitions devised by Sullivan (1991, 252-53). In conjunction with this variable, we shall use a dummy variable, MINORITY RULE, which takes on a value of unity for the four cases of minority rule identified previously, namely, Syria, Iraq, Burundi, and Taiwan.

2.3. Island status and size of population

The association of democracy with island status and with very small population size has been noted in the literature (Dahl and Tufte 1973; Ebel 1972; Ostheimer 1975; Weiner 1987; Hadenius 1992). Are these associations the product of other variables, and, if not, what are the causal mechanisms? We hypothesize that island status itself (for which we created the variable ISLAND) increases the probability of lasting democracy. Let us start by thinking of an island that is not a colony. The government is initially autocratic, run for the benefit of the autocrat's clique or social class. An autocratic ruler has an incentive to expand his domain in order to increase tax revenues and to improve his defensive position against threatening powers (North 1981). For these purposes, he needs a strong military establishment. Now an island polity has a natural boundary, namely, the water. The benefit-risk ratio for the ruler from expanding his domain is less favorable for an island state, and the degree of threat from external powers is less. For both reasons, the military establishment is smaller and less influential in island states. This decentralizes power among the contenders and makes it likely that an agreement on rules of contestation will emerge. This account has plausibility as applied to the first modern democracy, Great Britain.

Most of the islands in our sample of 146 countries have been colonies of another power. Thus the preceding line of reasoning cannot explain the initiation of democratic rule in these island polities. Still, the physical characteristics of these islands may contribute to the longevity of these democracies. Island states are more ethnically and linguistically homogeneous, and these characteristics tend to favor the emergence and maintenance of democracy. Historically, island peoples have been less subject to conquest and domination by alien people. According to this hypothesis, the introduction of our ethnic diversity variables should weaken the coefficient of island status in a regression explaining democracy.

Another variable clouding the interpretation of island status is the identity of the colonial power. There is a very strong correlation between ISLAND, which is a dummy variable taking on the value of 1 if the country is surrounded by water, and BRITISH, which is a dummy taking on the value of 1 if the colonial power

was Britain or one of its settler colony offshoots, the United States, Canada, Australia, and New Zealand. Weiner (1987) has suggested that the island effect is entirely due to its association with British colonial rule. To assess Weiner's conjecture, we include both BRITISH and ISLAND in our regressions.

ISLAND is also correlated with population size. Initially, we thought it was plausible that the small size of the population could be favorable to the emergence of agreement on rules of contestation. In very small states, political leaders often know one another through family and social connections, and this may facilitate a consensus on the rules of political competition. We used our statistical analysis to try to disentangle the effects of population size and ISLAND. We were surprised to find that dummies for small states and for ministates came in negative, and the inclusion of these dummies strengthened the positive effects of ISLAND (see section 4.2 below).[6]

2.4. Colonial history

Colonial experience may affect a country's prospects for democracy. The colonial power may or may not have transmitted its culture and language to the colony, and the mother country may not have been democratic itself during the period of colonial rule. Even if democratic itself, the mother country may not have given the colony experience with democratic political institutions under controlled conditions. The manner in which the colony gained its independence may also matter for democratic outcomes.

To address these issues, we define a series of dummy variables for the identity of the most recent colonial power. All countries are divided into one of the following categories: former colony of Great Britain or one of its settler colonies (United States, Australia, New Zealand), for which we created the variable BRITISH; former colony of France, for which we created the variable FRENCH; former colony of Spain or Portugal; former colony of another colonial power (Belgium, Netherlands, Italy, Japan); and countries that have never been colonized (the last three categories will not be treated in this article). BRITISH was the only dummy that was consistently significant (when each dummy was used alone). We constructed a variable for the length of democratic rule (called LENGTH), which is the number of years for which an ex-colony was ruled by a democratic country. This measure of cultural penetration by a democratic colonial power was not significant. Another measure of cultural penetration is the extent to which the colonial power's language came into common usage in the colony. Muller (1964) estimates the fraction of the population who are native speakers of each language, including the colonial power's language, in each country in 1960. This gives us a measure of language penetration (LANGPEN) by the colonial power. (This includes only native speakers, not those who learn the colonial power's language as a second language.) We can construct a variable that measures language penetration by a democratic colonial power (LANGDEM) and language pene-

tration by a British colonial power (LANGBRIT).

2.5. Religion and culture

Some cultures have been more receptive to democratic political institutions than others. Religion is one component of culture, and we constructed a variable for the proportion of the population that is Muslim (MUSLIM). Our results indicate a very strong negative effect of MUSLIM on the incidence of democracy. An issue is whether the negative coefficient on MUSLIM in our multivariate regressions reflects something in the religion itself or rather the particular history and culture of the countries in the Islamic heartland. To illuminate this issue, we have constructed a dummy variable for the Islamic heartland (called ARAB-PERSIA). Another way of trying to separate the different influences is to include a variable for the proportion of the population that is of European ancestry (EUROPE). This variable captures to some extent the diffusion of European culture. By holding this variable constant, we can see whether Islamic culture, as represented by MUSLIM, has a more negative effect on democratization than other non-European cultures in the Third World.

3. THE DATA

Clague et al. (1996, 1997) developed a classification of political regimes: I, autocracy; II, almost autocracy; III, intermediate category; IV, almost democracy; and V, democracy. Countries were put in one of these categories for each year from 1960 to 1994. The main data sources were the variables executive competitiveness from Gurr (1990) and executive selection and legislative effectiveness from Banks (1979 and updates from the author). The data were updated to 1994 by Suzanne Gleason from information in the *Europa Yearbook*. The dependent variable is the mean level of democracy, which is the fraction of years in the 1960-94 period (or the period of independence to 1994) that a country is classified as a democracy (category IV or V).

The data set consists of 168 independent countries, of which 17 were members of the Communist bloc until 1989. These 168 countries constitute essentially all the independent countries in the world. We do not include the 17 Communist states in our analyses; that leaves 151 countries for which we have data for our democracy classification. For data reasons, we eliminate 5 ministates: Tuvalu, Nauru, Micronesia, Marshall Islands, and Tonga. That leaves 146 countries, of which 20 are highly developed democracies.[7] Our sample of LDCs thus includes the remaining 126 countries.

A widely used alternative measure of democracy is the political rights index from Freedom House (Freedom House various years). This refers to the rights of all adults to vote and to compete for political office and the ability of elected representatives to have a decisive voice in public policy. Our data are averages over the years 1972 to 1990. The country-years are scored from 1 to 7, with higher scores representing stronger political rights (the reverse of the Freedom House scoring).

Some descriptive statistics for these democracy and autocracy variables are presented in Table 1. The first two rows show that islands are more democratic and less autocratic than the average LDC. The next two rows show that very small states are more democratic and less autocratic. Ministates are those with populations less than 500,000 (in 1960 or at independence). Microstates are those with populations less than 100,000. BRITISH and FRENCH refer to the ex-colonies of these powers, except that BRITISH includes the ex-colonies of the United States, Australia, and New Zealand. "LA" designates the former Spanish and Portuguese colonies in the Western Hemisphere. "ARAB-PERSIA" refers to the countries in the Islamic heartland from Morocco to Iran. British ex-colonies are more democratic and less autocratic than the average LDC; the contrast is especially pronounced for the dummy for lasting democracies. French ex-colonies are remarkably undemocratic (only Lebanon contributes a positive score to the mean level of democracy) and remarkably autocratic. LA displays considerable years of democracy but is remarkably low in the variables for lasting democracy (only Costa Rica and Venezuela appear here); it is also low in measures of continuous autocracy (entries here are Mexico, Panama, and Paraguay). ARAB-PERSIA, by contrast, is not only very low in democracy (Lebanon here again) but very high in continuous autocracy. Sub-Saharan Africa is also quite low in democracy (entries

TABLE 1
MEANS OF VARIOUS SAMPLES OF LDCs

	Panel A: Democracy and Autocracy					
	Mean Level of Democracy	Pure Democracy Dummy	Freedom House Political Rights	Pure Autocracy Dummy	Autocracy 70%	Number of Observations
All LDCs	0.3425	0.2222	3.4758	0.2540	0.5873	126
Islands	0.6702	0.5667	4.8186	0.0667	0.3000	30
Ministates	0.5005	0.4063	4.4269	0.1875	0.4688	32
Microstates	0.5619	0.4000	4.6303	0.1000	0.4000	10
BRITISH	0.5361	0.4407	4.0854	0.1864	0.4407	59
FRENCH	0.0234	0.0000	2.1348	0.5000	0.9545	22
LA	0.4175	0.1111	4.4064	0.0000	0.2778	18
ARAB-PERSIA	0.0226	0.0000	2.3436	0.5789	0.9474	19
Sub-Saharan Africa	0.1267	0.0714	2.2036	0.4048	0.8810	42
Caribbean	0.7006	0.5714	5.5178	0.0714	0.2143	14
Pacific islands	0.9360	0.6000	5.6175	0.0000	0.0000	5

	Panel B: Independent Variables: Means by Country Categories					
	Island	MUSLIM	Agricultural Labor Force Share	EUROPE	LANGBRIT	SULLIVAN
All LDCs	0.2381	0.2991	0.6320	0.0865	0.1089	0.6573
Islands	1.0000	0.1462	0.5686	0.0674	0.3186	0.8110
Ministates	0.6250	0.2592	0.5535	0.0463	0.2781	0.7350
Microstates	0.9000	0.1950	0.5887	0.0141	0.3684	0.8633
BRITISH	0.4068	0.2934	0.5766	0.0474	0.2304	0.6862
FRENCH	0.0909	0.5876	0.7549	0.0077	0.0060	0.5224
LA	0.0000	0.0000	0.5117	0.2550	0.0000	0.7139
ARAB-PERSIA	0.0526	0.8346	0.4964	0.0167	0.0070	0.6600
Sub-Saharan Africa	0.0714	0.3102	0.8021	0.0118	0.0695	0.4858
Caribbean	0.7143	0.0247	0.5176	0.0371	0.5716	0.7893
Pacific islands	1.0000	0.0000	0.6752	0.0182	0.2308	0.7138

NOTES: The Pure Democracy (Autocracy) dummy takes a value of 1 for countries that are democratic (autocratic) over the entire period, and zero otherwise. The table shows the mean value of these dummy variables. The Autocracy 70% dummy takes a value of 1 if the country is autocratic during 70 percent or more of the period.

here include Botswana, South Africa, and Zimbabwe) and quite high for continuous autocracy.

4. MULTIVARIATE ANALYSIS

The mean level of democracy (M6094) is a variable that lies in the (0,1) interval with many observations at the two end points. The appropriate statistical technique for this type of variable is a two-sided tobit regression (Rosett and Nelson 1975).

4.1. Main results

Table 2 displays our initial regressions.[8] The first two columns are for the sample of 126 LDCs; the last two are for the entire sample of 146

TABLE 2
BASIC REGRESSIONS

	Sample			
	(1) LDC	(2) LDC	(3) All	(4) All
Intercept	0.5333	−0.0773	1.3261	0.1657
	(2.472)	(0.311)	(6.395)	(0.647)
BRITISH	0.7350	0.8133	0.6618	0.8026
	(4.635)	(5.250)	(3.796)	(5.051)
	0.364	0.368	0.324	0.446
ISLAND	0.3524	0.4050	0.3418	0.4706
	(2.047)	(2.485)	(1.782)	(2.802)
	0.187	0.203	0.172	0.272
MUSLIM	−1.11509	−0.9611	−1.4367	−0.9757
	(−5.171)	(−4.620)	(−5.485)	(−4.513)
	−0.362	−0.267	−0.452	−0.389
AGRI-LF	−0.7568	−0.3266	−1.7297	−0.4950
	(−2.499)	(−1.063)	(−5.293)	(−1.553)
	−0.174	−0.068	−0.368	−0.130
EUROPE		0.9896		1.4491
		(3.144)		(5.002)
		0.259		0.408
Sigma	0.6223	0.5794	0.7236	0.6066
(Standard error)	(0.675)	(0.070)	(0.089)	(0.073)
Number of observations	126	126	146	146

NOTES: Dependent variable is the mean level of democracy. t-statistics are listed below coefficients; marginal effects are listed below t-statistics.

countries, including the 20 highly developed democracies. We focus primarily on the LDC sample. The cells for the variables of interest contain three entries. The top one is the coefficient in the tobit regression; below that is the t-ratio of the coefficient, and below that is the marginal effect of the variable on the probability of democracy.[9] Thus in regression (2), being a former colony of Britain or one of its four settler colonies increases the probability of democracy by 0.368; being an island increases it by 0.203; and increasing the Muslim share in the population from 10 percent to 90 percent decreases the probability by 0.267.

The European fraction of the population strongly influences the probability of democracy. In part, this variable works in the LDC sample because it picks up five countries (Spain, Portugal, Greece, Cyprus, and Malta) that are physically in or near Europe and hence are subject to the strong economic incentive to become part of the European Union, which is open only to democracies. Another four LDCs have European populations greater than 50 percent: Costa Rica, Argentina, Chile, and

Uruguay. However, even if these nine countries are omitted from the LDC sample, the European fraction comes in very strongly, and the other variables are not much affected.

The level of economic development, as measured by the proportion of the labor force that works in agriculture (AGRI-LF), strongly affects the probability of democracy. The exception to this occurs when the European share of the population is also in the regression; in that case, it becomes insignificant.

Table 3 introduces variables representing the degree of cultural penetration of the colonial power, as measured by the fraction of the population who are native speakers of the colonial power's language. The language penetration variable is significant; this reflects the Spanish American ex-colonies, which tend to be more democratic than other LDCs. Introduction of this variable reduces the marginal effect of MUSLIM from -0.27 to -0.23, but MUSLIM remains highly significant. This result indicates that part of the negative effect of MUSLIM on democracy can be attributed to the resistance of these countries to cultural penetration from Europe, as measured by this language variable.

The variable representing the cultural penetration by a democratic colonial power (LANGDEM) falls short of significance at conventional levels. But LANGBRIT comes in more strongly and is significant; this captures the effect of British cultural penetration. Not surprisingly, the introduction of LANGBRIT weakens BRITISH, but both remain significant, indicating that BRITISH has an influence even when the local population does not produce many native English speakers.[10]

Table 4 introduces the SULLIVAN measure of ethnic homogeneity. We lose three observations in these regressions, two because of missing data and one because of South Africa, where the democratic regime applies only to the minority population. SULLIVAN does not represent the ethnic composition of that minority. SULLIVAN works quite well; it works even better in the total sample than in the LDC sample but is significant in both cases. The MINORITY RULE dummy has the correct sign but is generally not significant. The addition of EUROPE weakens SULLIVAN considerably, but the latter remains significant. These results indicate that ethnic homogeneity is a significant determinant of democracy. Interestingly, the addition of SULLIVAN substantially weakens ISLAND, indicating that one of the reasons why islands are more democratic than non-islands is that they are more ethnically homogeneous. The addition of SULLIVAN does not weaken MUSLIM in regressions that already contain EUROPE.

The language homogeneity variable MULLER does not work very well. It does best in the regressions omitting LANGBRIT and EUROPE, but even there, although it has the expected sign, it is insignificant. These results indicate that language alone does not provide a particularly good way to measure ethnic homogeneity. There seems to be a good deal to be gained by making the judg-

TABLE 3
LANGUAGE PENETRATION VARIABLES

	Sample					
	(1) LDC	(2) LDC	(3) LDC	(4) All	(5) All	(6) All
Intercept	−0.3131 (−1.103)	−0.0479 (−0.198)	−0.0556 (−0.233)	−0.0301 (−0.105)	0.1489 (0.594)	0.1581 (0.641)
BRITISH	0.8401 (5.546) 0.418	0.6990 (4.424) 0.347	0.6312 (4.105) 0.314	0.8113 (5.126) 0.457	0.6840 (4.131) 0.393	0.6129 (3.710) 0.357
ISLAND	0.4078 (2.593) 0.225	0.3094 (1.860) 0.166	0.2824 (1.737) 0.151	0.4818 (2.891) 0.283	0.3853 (2.253) 0.226	0.3589 (2.147) 0.212
MUSLIM	−0.6780 (3.189) −0.231	−0.8298 (−3.999) −0.268	−0.7724 (−3.810) −0.251	−0.8236 (−3.590) −0.344	−0.8524 (−3.934) −0.372	−0.7940 (−3.743) −0.361
AGRI-LF	−0.0945 (−0.308) −0.022	−0.3183 (−1.062) −0.073	−0.3083 (−1.044) −0.070	−0.3957 (−1.233) −0.105	−0.4962 (−1.589) −0.135	−0.4882 (−1.585) −0.135
EUROPE	1.0213 (3.375) 0.291	1.0311 (3.370) 0.290	1.0195 (3.411) 0.288	1.5306 (5.197) 0.434	1.4550 (5.110) 0.415	1.4356 (5.138) 0.411
LANGPEN	0.5821 (2.730) 0.157			0.3158 (1.494) 0.093		
LANGDEM		0.6156 (1.728) 0.164			0.5986 (1.586) 0.177	
LANGBRIT			0.8559 (2.355) 0.236			0.8478 (2.198) 0.253
Sigma (Standard error)	0.5564 (0.056)	0.5650 (0.068)	0.5560 (0.066)	0.5992 (0.072)	0.5959 (0.072)	0.5857 (0.071)
Number of observations	126	126	126	146	146	146

NOTES: Dependent variable is mean level of democracy. t-statistics are listed below coefficients; marginal effects are listed below t-statistics.

ments that Sullivan made in determining the politically relevant ethnic groups.

Similarly, the index of ethnolinguistic fractionalization (FRACTION) is not very successful in explaining democracy. As in the case of MULLER, FRACTION works best when neither LANGBRIT nor EUROPE is in the regression. Because FRACTION is not available for many of our countries, the sample sizes are reduced to 96 and 116 (instead of 126 and 146) for the less

TABLE 4

SULLIVAN INDEX OF HOMOGENEITY

	Sample			
	(1) LDC	(2) LDC	(3) All	(4) All
Intercept	−0.0311 (−0.114)	−0.1983 (−0.726)	0.3654 (1.287)	−0.1076 (−0.380)
BRITISH	0.5137 (3.330) 0.280	0.5528 (3.687) 0.311	0.4434 (2.565) 0.249	0.5373 (3.401) 0.329
ISLAND	0.1269 (0.748) 0.071	0.1930 (1.174) 0.114	0.0876 (0.481) 0.050	0.2556 (1.511) 0.161
MUSLIM	−0.8097 (−4.104) −0.293	−0.6821 (−3.571) −0.263	−0.9769 (−4.352) −0.374	−0.6987 (−3.491) −0.316
AGRI-LF	−0.6914 (−2.504) −0.172	−0.3741 (−1.297) −0.097	−1.4347 (−4.980) −0.347	−0.5582 (−1.857) −0.158
LANGBRIT	0.6780 (1.910) 0.197	0.7764 (2.261) 0.235	0.6733 (1.708) 0.192	0.7679 (2.115) 0.240
EUROPE		0.7358 (2.449) 0.225		1.1466 (4.130) 0.350
SULLIVAN	0.8315 (3.065) 0.186	0.5644 (2.057) 0.130	1.1498 (3.775) 0.256	0.5872 (2.065) 0.147
MINORITY RULE	−0.7144 (−1.615)	−0.5327 (−1.282)	−1.0163 (−1.919)	−0.6065 (−1.354)
Sigma (Standard error) Number of observations	0.5507 (0.066) 123	0.5255 (0.063) 123	0.6230 (0.076) 143	0.5538 (0.067) 143

NOTES: Dependent variable is mean level of democracy. t-statistics are listed below coefficients; marginal probability effects are listed below t-statistics.

developed and total samples, respectively. In the basic regressions, this reduction in the sample size does not have much effect on any of the coefficients. When FRACTION is added to this basic regression, it has the correct negative sign, but it approaches significance only in the total sample. When SULLIVAN and MINORITY RULE are added, FRACTION reverses to the incorrect sign and becomes insignificant. SULLIVAN remains highly significant. Thus in this head-to-head contest, SULLIVAN does a better job of explaining democratization than FRACTION does.[11]

Our results support the following conclusions:

1. Being a former colony of Great Britain or of one of its settler colonies has a powerful positive effect on democracy in poor countries. There is an additional positive effect of British cultural penetration, as measured by the proportion of the population that speaks English.

2. There is a strong negative effect of Muslim culture on democracy.

3. Islands are more democratic than non-islands, holding constant the basic variables of BRITISH, MUSLIM, AGRI-LF, and EUROPE. The data suggest that the effect of a country's being an island is partly due to the greater ethnic homogeneity of island populations (as measured by SULLIVAN).

4. Ethnic diversity has some negative effect on democracy, but this effect is not strong. The SULLIVAN index of homogeneity acts positively, but this variable is to some extent endogenous to political outcomes. The other ethnic diversity variables, MULLER and FRACTION, do not explain democracy very well. Moreover, there are clear examples of ethnically diverse LDCs with persistent democracies: India, Malaysia, Mauritius, and Botswana.

Our next task is to see whether these conclusions (particularly the first three) stand up under more detailed analysis.

4.2. Robustness checks and additional variables

The results are only slightly affected by excluding 10 microstates with populations of less than 100,000. There are greater changes from excluding 34 ministates (32 of which are LDCs) with populations of less than 500,000. (These population figures are for 1960 or the year of independence; populations have grown since then.) This exclusion weakens the effect of island status substantially, as would be expected, since many of these small states are islands. The coefficient on LANGBRIT is reduced, and it becomes insignificant, but BRITISH remains highly significant. Thus the effect of BRITISH is not dependent on the inclusion of the ministates. The coefficient on MUSLIM is reduced somewhat but remains highly significant.

Another way of testing the sensitivity of the results to the inclusion of the ministates or the microstates is to put in dummy variables MICRO-DUMMY (for those with populations less than 100,000) or SMALL-DUMMY (for those with populations less than 500,000). Somewhat surprisingly, these dummies (entered singly) come in negative, while they strengthen the effect of island status and leave the other coefficients largely unaffected. This result suggests that small size itself is not conducive to democracy, while being an island is.[12]

This result is striking, because as Table 1 showed, ministates and microstates are on average more democratic than other LDCs. Moreover, on theoretical grounds, we expected to find that small size is conducive to democracy (see section 2.3 above). The negative coefficients on the size dummies may be a statistical artifact, as island status is highly collinear with these dummies; when island status is not in the regression, each dummy has a positive sign. In any case, the main conclusion is that the results for our basic variables hold when the presence of small states is taken into account.

In order to throw some light on the interpretation of the negative coefficient on MUSLIM, we introduced a dummy, ARAB-PERSIA, which corresponds closely to the Islamic heartland.[13] This dummy is very significant, and it cuts the coefficient on MUSLIM nearly in half, but the latter coefficient remains significant. The coefficient on MUSLIM is practically the same if the Arab-Persian countries are excluded from the sample. These results indicate that the negative effect of MUSLIM is not limited to the countries of the Islamic heartland, with their particular historical experience.

When we introduced various regional dummies into the basic regression, the only ones that were significant were those for sub-Saharan Africa (SSAFR) and Latin America (LA). SSAFR is negative and LA is positive, but the coefficients on the other variables are little affected, except that AGRI-LF becomes even less significant. The regional effects are not much altered by the inclusion of the size dummies, which themselves remain negative.

Barro (1999) introduced a dummy for oil-exporting countries, on the grounds that income generated from natural resource abundance generates less pressure for democratization than income generated from labor and capital. Because many of the oil exporters are Muslim countries, this variable may have an effect on the MUSLIM coefficient. It turned out, however, that the correlation of an oil dummy[14] and MUSLIM is only 0.44, and the effect of its introduction on the other coefficients is modest. In column 2 of Table 2, for example, the MUSLIM coefficient is reduced from -0.96 to -0.81, and it remains highly significant. A broader measure of natural resource abundance would have a smaller correlation with MUSLIM and a smaller effect on its coefficient.

We consider in Table 5 two variables that may be causes of democracy but are also quite plausibly effects of democracy and perhaps reflective of social attitudes conducive to democracy: literacy and life expectancy. The use of these variables forces a reduction in sample size, which may have an effect on the coefficients. In the case of life expectancy, the reduction in sample size from 126 to 113 has only modest effects on the coefficients, as can be seen by comparing column 4 of Table 5 with column 3 of Table 3. The introduction of life expectancy in column 5 of Table 5 renders ISLAND insignificant (and of the wrong sign). Thus life expectancy fully accounts in a statistical sense for the effect of island status on democracy. The other variables are little affected by the introduction of life expectancy.

We have two measures of literacy, one in 1960 or at independence (LIT60) and one in 1993 (LIT93). The use of LIT60 reduces our sample of LDCs from 126 to 106, and the sample effects weaken island status, lowering its marginal effect from 0.15 ($t = 1.74$) to 0.13 ($t = 1.34$) (from column 3 in Table 3 and from column 1

TABLE 5
LITERACY AND LIFE EXPECTANCY

	(1)	(2)	(3)	(4)	(5)
Intercept	0.1966	−0.5243	−0.1743	0.1368	−5.3665
	(0.779)	(−1.465)	(−0.350)	(0.609)	(−2.468)
BRITISH	0.5792	0.5729	0.6051	0.5998	0.6126
	(3.708)	(3.832)	(3.883)	(3.929)	(4.119)
	0.306	0.309	0.324	0.318	0.331
ISLAND	0.2374	0.0595	0.1768	0.3017	−0.0953
	(1.340)	(0.337)	(0.996)	(1.736)	(−0.514)
	0.131	0.032	0.097	0.172	−0.048
MUSLIM	−0.7309	−0.4652	−0.6730	−0.7461	−0.5888
	(−3.557)	(−2.244)	(−2.929)	(−3.865)	(−3.107)
	−0.246	−0.170	−0.231	−0.255	−0.211
AGRI-LF	−0.4604	0.0205	−0.2669	−0.3466	0.2972
	(−1.443)	(0.059)	(−0.724)	(−1.256)	(0.821)
	−0.108	0.005	−0.063	−0.082	0.071
EUROPE	0.9076	0.5954	0.8420	0.9171	0.6097
	(3.158)	(2.095)	(2.980)	(3.306)	(2.141)
	0.261	0.171	0.244	0.261	0.177
LANGBRIT	0.8087	0.8240	0.7153	0.6344	0.6230
	(1.786)	(1.816)	(1.649)	(1.677)	(1.712)
	0.235	0.247	0.209	0.181	0.181
LIT60		0.9780			
		(2.815)			
		0.284			
LIT93			0.3662		
			(0.880)		
			0.088		
Log life expectancy 1962					1.3147
					(2.556)
					0.282
Sigma	0.5227	0.4959	0.5092	0.5097	0.4884
(Standard error)	(0.065)	(0.061)	(0.063)	(0.062)	(0.059)
Number of observations	106	106	105	113	113

NOTES: All samples are of LDCs. t-statistics are listed below coefficients; marginal effects are listed below t-statistics.

in Table 5). The introduction of LIT60 in column 2 of Table 5 weakens island status still further, to 0.03, indicating that islands are not more democratic when account is taken of their higher levels of literacy. But their higher levels of literacy and life expectancy may have something to do with their island status, which may have had effects on the sense of community with fellow citizens.

The introduction of LIT60 also weakens MUSLIM, lowering its marginal effect from –0.25 to –0.17, indicating that part of the effect of Muslim heritage may be due to the failure of these societies to provide much primary education by 1960. However, when we introduce LIT93 rather than LIT60 into basically the same sample,[15] LIT93 is not significant and its effect on MUSLIM is very small (the marginal effect falls from –0.25 to –0.23). It seems that the modern world produces strong inducement toward literacy, but that is not sufficient to generate pressure for democracy in countries where the political culture and institutional inheritance do not support it. Most Muslim-dominated countries now have literacy rates well over 50 percent,[16] yet there is little evidence of evolution toward democracy in the Muslim world.

The other variable whose coefficient is strongly affected by the introduction of LIT60 but not by the introduction of LIT93 is island status. Introducing LIT93 reduces the marginal effect of island status from 0.13 to 0.10, as compared with the reduction from 0.13 to 0.03 when LIT60 is introduced. Again, we are led to the conclusion that LIT60 probably captures some country characteristics that are strongly related to democracy, but that increases in literacy after 1960 in countries without these characteristics do not have much positive effect on democracy.

Our finding that LIT93 is not significantly related to democracy parallels the findings of some researchers (for example, Pritchett 1996) that increases in levels of education are not associated with increases in growth rates or levels of total factor productivity. Evidently, the forces generating increases in education in the postwar period are not the same as those operating before World War II.

Finally, we note that the coefficient on BRITISH is not affected by the introduction of either measure of literacy. Thus former colonies of Britain or of its settler colonies are not more democratic because they were more literate at independence. The regression in note 17 shows that, given the level of the other variables, the level of literacy was not higher in former colonies of Britain or of its settler colonies than in colonies in general.[18]

Table 6 shows regressions using the Freedom House measure of political rights, averaged over the years 1972-90. The results are very similar for the Freedom House measure of civil liberties. In the basic regressions in columns 1 and 2, our main variables are highly significant, just as in our tobit regressions (see Table 2). The introduction of life expectancy in column 3 weakens the effect of island status (the regression coefficient falls from 1.19 to 0.63) and MUSLIM (from –1.07 to –0.54), but they remain marginally significant. The introduction of LIT60 lowers these coefficients dramatically, from 1.19 to 0.10 for island status and from –1.07 to –0.19 for MUSLIM, but

TABLE 6
FREEDOM HOUSE REGRESSIONS

	(1)	(2)	(3)	(4)	(5)
Intercept	4.5761	3.4991	−16.185	1.2824	1.7214
	(10.225)	(7.085)	(3.686)	(1.827)	(1.867)
BRITISH	0.5402	0.8044	0.6114	0.6302	0.7808
	(1.903)	(2.935)	(2.353)	(2.449)	(2.878)
ISLAND	1.0856	1.1857	0.6335	0.1049	0.8662
	(3.234)	(3.751)	(1.780)	(0.282)	(2.630)
MUSLIM	−1.4207	−1.0700	−0.5371	−0.1949	−0.7356
	(−4.164)	(−3.229)	(−1.669)	(−0.551)	(−2.065)
AGRI-LF	−1.8777	−0.9332	−1.3602	0.5051	−0.1213
	(−3.224)	(−1.576)	(−1.794)	(0.735)	(−0.175)
EUROPE		2.6314	1.3886	1.5220	2.3386
		(4.152)	(2.214)	(2.471)	(3.704)
Log life expectancy 1962			4.7298		
			(4.533)		
LIT60				3.3431	
				(4.812)	
LIT93					1.8482
					(2.335)
Number of observations	126	126	113	106	124
RBAR–squared	0.3375	0.4159	0.5049	0.4902	0.4333
(S.E.E.)	(1.446)	(1.358)	(1.211)	(1.1974)	(1.329)

NOTES: All samples are of LDCs. Dependent variable is the Freedom House measure of political rights.

the introduction of LIT93 has considerably smaller effects: it lowers island status from 1.19 to 0.87 and MUSLIM from −1.07 to −0.74, and both remain significant. This is similar to the pattern we observed in Table 5.

Our results on the roles of colonial heritage and religion are quite different from those of Barro (1997, 1999). He finds British colonial heritage to be insignificant and Islam to have only a very modest effect. In part, these findings are due to the statistical technique employed; Barro uses five-year averages in a panel format, in which the lagged value of democracy is an independent variable. Because the level of democracy is quite persistent, the lagged level takes on a good deal of explanatory power, leaving less to be explained by variables that do not change over time, such as colonial heritage and religion. In addition, Barro includes life expectancy and primary education variables, which tend to weaken the effect of Islam. Finally, Barro's sample is smaller than our basic sample, mainly because his schooling variables force the elimination of many small countries.

5. CONCLUDING OBSERVATIONS

Our empirical results indicate that the probability of democracy in the postwar period is strongly affected by country characteristics that reflect cultural and institutional inheritances. Demographic, economic, and sociological variables fail to account for some of the patterns of the spread of democracy around the world. Why are Muslim countries much less democratic than their levels of economic development would predict? Kuran (1997) reviews a number of explanations for Muslim resistance to Western ideas and practices. In a synthesis of explanations offered by Ibn Kaldun, Bernard Lewis, Avner Greif, and others, he contends that the poverty of public discourse has inhibited collective action to remedy social ills. His interpretation, along with that of many other authors,[19] stresses the role of perceptions and beliefs in the determination of institutional practices.

The institutions of electoral democracy emerged in Europe and in countries populated by Europeans. The important role of this cultural influence is suggested by a comparison of Latin America and the Muslim world in the nineteenth century and in the twentieth century up to World War I. In the former region, electoral institutions were beginning to

emerge, particularly in Argentina, Uruguay, Chile, Colombia, and Costa Rica. (Gasiorowski [1996] rates these countries as semi-democracies by 1914.) To be sure, electoral fraud was widespread and the franchise was restricted, but the institutions were beginning to take hold in some countries and represented middle-class aspirations in others. In the Muslim world, by contrast, in the two politically independent entities, the Ottoman Empire and Iran, elections were virtually unknown.

Under British rule, many colonies had experience with electoral, legislative, and judicial institutions. British colonial policy had long been very different in this respect from the French theory and practice, and while the French resisted decolonization after World War II, the British were much more willing to grant independence, especially when they could find domestic political groups that would support democratic governance.[20] It seems plausible to characterize much of the British influence as institutional rather than cultural. People understood how electoral institutions were supposed to operate, and these institutional rules may have provided a focal point for political leaders in the newly independent states, especially in the Caribbean and the Pacific islands and in India, Sri Lanka, Malaysia, and Mauritius. While British colonial rule probably did not particularly encourage social egalitarianism, it did support respect for individual freedoms and the rule of law. Caribbean intellectuals, such as Eric Williams, although strongly anticolonial and pro-socialist, cherished the political rights and civil liberties associated with British practice (Bell 1967; Dominguez 1993).

The high level of democracy in the Caribbean is fully explained by our regression, in that a dummy for the Caribbean countries is quite insignificant. Our variables capture the deep penetration of British influence, island status, and the relatively low degree of ethnic fragmentation (see the values of SULLIVAN in Table 1). The high level of democracy in the Pacific islands is partly explained by ethnic homogeneity, island status, and British influence, but the dummy for these islands is positive and approaches statistical significance.

British rule in sub-Saharan Africa did not produce conditions conducive to democracy. Much of this can be explained by the low levels of economic development and literacy and by ethnic fragmentation. Even with these and other variables in the equation, the dummy for sub-Saharan Africa is strongly negative (the marginal effect of the dummy is −0.217). The few sub-Saharan African countries with some democratic experience do have a British connection: Botswana, Zimbabwe, Gambia, and South Africa.

In conclusion, our results provide substantial evidence that British colonial experience and Muslim heritage have strong effects on the probability of democracy. Island status has a substantial statistical influence, which is largely mediated by ethnic homogeneity (SULLIVAN), life expectancy, and literacy in 1960. These variables themselves may be influenced, through historical processes, by island status.

Notes

1. In the postwar period, democracies with restricted franchises are quite rare, and thus our statistical analysis would be little affected by making a nearly universal franchise part of the definition of democracy, as many authors do. The distinction is, of course, very important for discussions of democracy in the nineteenth century.

2. The military coup in Fiji in 1987 might be an example of these forces at work.

3. Consider the example of the 13 former British colonies that joined to form the United States. On the basis of religion, this was a highly fractionated society. But because none of the religious groups was strong enough to have a realistic expectation of establishing itself as the state religion, it was mutually agreed to remove religion from government.

4. Note that if the electoral institutions of the ruling minority are counted as a democracy, then logically the community whose ethnic diversity is being measured is the ruling group itself (that is, the 10 percent of the population), not the whole country. It would be illogical to consider the society as homogeneous because there is a 90 percent majority if one is looking at the political arrangements within the 10 percent minority. For this reason, we exclude South Africa from regressions in which we use the SULLIVAN index of homogeneity.

5. We changed two values. Morocco was given a 0.63 instead of 0.99 (to reflect the Berber minority), and Cyprus was given a value of 1.00 instead of 0.78 (to reflect the fact that the polity we include in our regressions is the Greek part of the island).

6. Ebel (1972) contends that small size is conducive to authoritarianism in Latin America through several mechanisms, some of which are derived from dependency theory. Seligson (1987), citing Ebel, also supports this line of reasoning. We did not find these arguments theoretically persuasive.

7. The highly developed democracies with continuous democracy are Australia, Austria, Belgium, Canada, Denmark, Finland, France,

Germany, Iceland, Ireland, Italy, Japan, Luxembourg, the Netherlands, New Zealand, Norway, Sweden, Switzerland, the United Kingdom, and the United States.

8. Additional regressions and analysis are contained in the working paper version of the present article (Clague, Gleason, and Knack 1997).

9. The marginal effect of a variable on the probability of democracy is calculated as follows, taking BRITISH as an example in Table 2, column 2. First, the probability is calculated, using the sample means of all the other independent variables and a value of zero for BRITISH (prob = 0.085). This procedure is repeated, using a value of 1 for BRITISH (prob = 0.454). The marginal effect is the difference, $0.454 - 0.085 = 0.368$. For MUSLIM, the lower value is taken as 0.10, and the upper value is 0.90 (corresponding to 10 percent Muslim population and 90 percent Muslim, respectively). For the agricultural labor force, the lower value is one standard deviation below the sample mean (0.403), and the upper value is one standard deviation above the sample mean (0.861). The same procedure is used for literacy and life expectancy. For the other variables (EUROPE, LANGPEN, SULLIVAN), the lower value is zero and the upper value is 0.50.

10. Note that LANGPEN is the fraction of the population who are native speakers of the colonial power's language. It would be desirable to have a measure of the fraction of the population who have become reasonably fluent in the colonial power's language, even though they are not native speakers, but this information is not available on a systematic basis. Estimates of the fraction of the population in India who are reasonably fluent in English are remarkably small: 3.0 percent in 1960 (Muller 1964, 8) and 3.3 percent in 1995 (*Encyclopedia Britannica*, 15th ed.).

11. Although FRACTION strongly negatively affects growth performance in a cross-country study, Collier finds that this effect holds for dictatorships but not for democracies (see Collier and Gunning 1999, 67).

12. A category of ministates, the microstates, with populations in the thousands in parentheses, are Qatar (71), Kiribati (52), Maldives (97), Antigua and Barbuda (71), Dominica (76), Grenada (97), St. Kitts and Nevis (66), São Tomé and Principe (59), Sey-

chelles (42), and Vanuatu (80) (10 states). The next group, ministates with populations of 100,000 to 200,000, contains Iceland (176), Brunei (177), Bahrain (182), Bahamas (140), Cape Verde (197), Belize (121), Comoro Islands (195), Djibouti (108), St. Lucia (110), Solomon Islands (200), St. Vincent and the Grenadines (101), and Western Samoa (131) (12 states). The next category, ministates with populations of 201,000 to 500,000, contains Botswana (481), Gabon (460), Gambia (372), Swaziland (360), Kuwait (290), Luxembourg (315), Malta (329), Barbados (231), Suriname (290), Fiji (394), the United Arab Emirates (205), and Equatorial Guinea (272) (12 states).

13. The dummy variable includes Morocco, Mauritania, Algeria, Tunisia, Libya, Egypt, Jordan, Syria, Iraq, Iran, Saudi Arabia, Kuwait, Bahrain, Qatar, Oman, the United Arab Emirates, Yemen Arab Republic, and the People's Democratic Republic of Yemen. Excluded are Turkey, Sudan, and Afghanistan.

14. The countries included are Algeria, Nigeria, Iran, Iraq, Kuwait, Saudi Arabia, Trinidad, Venezuela, Oman, Indonesia, Libya, Brunei, the United Arab Emirates, Qatar, and Bahrain.

15. We lose an observation due to a missing value for LIT93.

16. Some examples of literacy rates in 1993: the United Arab Emirates (78 percent), Qatar (78 percent), Lebanon (92 percent), Bahrain (84 percent), Kuwait (77 percent), Jordan (85 percent), Syria (69 percent), and Saudi Arabia (61 percent). The rates in some democratic countries are as follows: India (51 percent), Botswana (68 percent), and Mauritius (82 percent).

17. LIT60 = 74.796 − 0.7680 BRITISH + 17.948 ISLAND − 23.824 MUSLIM − 0.5144 AGRI-LF + 30.153 EUROPE. The standard error of the coefficient for the intercept is 11.855; for BRITISH, 0.239; for ISLAND, 4.485; for MUSLIM, 5.579; for AGRI-LF, 6.676; and for EUROPE, 5.365. Number of observations = 126; RBAR-squared = 0.7671; S.E.E. = 16.260.

18. In an interesting article, Grier (1999) argues that British colonies in Africa experienced higher growth rates in the postwar períod, largely because the British colonial authorities provided more primary education than their French counterparts did. Grier's observations on the differences between the colo-

nial policies of the two powers are well taken, but the differences in education policies are not sufficient to account for the differences in democratic outcomes.

19. See, for example, Lewis 1993; Pipes 1983; Waterbury 1994. More sociological interpretations can be found in Berger 1962; Gerber 1987; Hourani 1981; Rodinson 1973.

20. On British and French colonial policies, see Emerson 1962; Smith 1978; Flint 1983; Chamberlain 1985; Low 1988. See also Grier 1999 and n. 17 in the present article.

References

Banks, Arthur S. 1979. Cross-National Time Series Data Archive. Center for Social Analysis, State University of New York at Binghamton. Database.

Barro, Robert. 1997. *Determinants of Economic Growth: A Cross-Country Empirical Study*. Cambridge: MIT Press.

———. 1999. Determinants of Democracy. *Journal of Political Economy* 107(6, pt. 2):S158-S183.

Bell, Wendell. 1967. *The Democratic Revolution in the West Indies: Studies in Nationalism, Leadership, and the Belief in Progress*. Cambridge, MA: Schenkman.

Berger, Monroe. 1962. Social Basis of Political Institutions. In *Readings in Arab Middle Eastern Societies and Cultures*, ed. Abdulla M. Lutfiyya and Charles W. Anderson. The Hague: Mouton.

Burkhart, Ross and Michael Lewis-Beck. 1994. Comparative Democracy: The Economic Development Thesis. *American Political Science Review* 88:903-10.

Chamberlain, M. E. 1985. *Decolonization: The Fall of the European Empires*. New York: Basil Blackwell.

Clague, Christopher, Suzanne Gleason, and Stephen Knack. 1997. Determinants of Lasting Democracy in Poor Countries. IRIS working paper no.

209, Department of Economics, University of Maryland, College Park.

Clague, Christopher, Philip Keefer, Stephen Knack, and Mancur Olson. 1996. Property and Contract Rights Under Autocracy and Democracy. *Journal of Economic Growth* 1(June):243-76.

———. 1997. Democracy, Autocracy, and the Institutions Supportive of Economic Growth. In *Institutions and Economic Development: Growth and Governance in Less-Developed and Post-Socialist Societies*, ed. Christopher Clague. Baltimore: Johns Hopkins University Press.

Collier, Paul and Jan Willem Gunning. 1999. Explaining African Economic Performance. *Journal of Economic Literature* 37(1):64-111.

Dahl, Robert A. 1971. *Polyarchy: Participation and Opposition*. New Haven, CT: Yale University Press.

Dahl, Robert A. and Edward R. Tufte. 1973. *Size and Democracy*. Stanford, CA: Stanford University Press.

Diamond, Larry. 1992. Economic Development and Democracy Reconsidered. In *Reexamining Democracy: Essays in Honor of Seymour Martin Lipset*, ed. Gary Marks and Larry Diamond. Newbury Park, CA: Sage.

Dominguez, Jorge I. 1993. The Caribbean Question: Why Has Liberal Democracy (Surprisingly) Flourished? In *Democracy in the Caribbean: Political, Economic, and Social Perspectives*, ed. Jorge Dominguez, Robert Pastor, and R. Delisle Worrell. Baltimore, MD: Johns Hopkins University Press.

Ebel, Roland. 1972. Governing the City-State: Notes on the Politics of the Small Latin American Countries. *Journal of Interamerican Studies and World Affairs* 14(3):325-46.

Emerson, Rupert. 1962. *From Empire to Nation: The Rise to Self-Assertion of Asian and African Peoples*. Cambridge, MA: Harvard University Press.

Flint, John. 1983. Planned Decolonization and Its Failure in British Africa. *African Affairs* 82(328):389-411.

Freedom House. Various years. *Freedom in the World*. Westport, CT: Greenwood Press.

Gasiorowski, Mark J. 1996. An Overview of the Political Regime Change Dataset. *Comparative Political Studies* 29(4):469-83.

Gerber, Haim. 1987. *The Social Origins of the Modern Middle East*. Boulder, CO: Lynne Reiner.

Grier, Robin. 1999. Colonial Legacies and Economic Growth. *Public Choice* 98(3-4):317-35.

Gurr, Ted Robert. 1990. *Polity II: Political Structures and Regime Change, 1800-1986*. Ann Arbor, MI: Inter-University Consortium for Political and Social Research.

Hadenius, Axel. 1992. *Democracy and Development*. New York: Cambridge University Press.

Helliwell, John F. 1994. Empirical Linkages Between Democracy and Economic Growth. *British Journal of Political Science* 24:225-48.

Higley, John and Michael G. Burton. 1989. The Elite Variable in Democratic Transitions and Breakdowns. *American Sociological Review* 54(Feb.):17-32.

Higley, John and Richard Gunther, eds. 1992. *Elites and Democratic Consolidation in Latin America and Southern Europe*. New York: Cambridge University Press.

Horowitz, Donald L. 1985. *Ethnic Groups in Conflict*. Berkeley: University of California Press.

Hourani, Albert. 1981. *The Emergence of the Modern Middle East*. Berkeley: University of California Press.

Knack, Stephen and Philip Keefer. 1995. Institutions and Economic Performance: Cross-Country Tests Using Alternative Institutional Measures. *Economics and Politics* 7(3):207-27.

Kuran, Timur. 1997. Islam and Underdevelopment: An Old Puzzle Revisited. *Journal of Institutional and Theoretical Economics* 153:41-71.

Lewis, Bernard. 1993. *Islam and the West*. New York: Oxford University Press.

Lijphart, Arend. 1977. *Democracy in Plural Societies: A Comparative Exploration*. New Haven, CT: Yale University Press.

Lipset, Seymour Martin. 1959. Some Social Requisites of Democracy: Economic Development and Political Legitimacy. *American Political Science Review* 53(1):69-105.

Lipset, Seymour Martin, Kyoung-Ryung Seong, and John Charles Torres. 1993. A Comparative Analysis of the Social Requisites of Democracy. *International Social Science Journal* 36(May):155-75.

Low, Anthony. 1988. The End of the British Empire in Africa. In *Decolonization and African Independence: The Transfer of Power*, ed. Prosser Gifford and William Roger Louis. New Haven, CT: Yale University Press.

Muller, Siegfried H. 1964 *The World's Living Languages*. New York: Frederick Ungar.

North, Douglass. 1981 *Growth and Structural Change*. New York: Norton.

O'Donnell, Guillermo and Philippe C. Schmitter. 1986. *Transitions from Authoritarian Rule: Tentative Conclusions About Uncertain Democracies*. Baltimore, MD: Johns Hopkins University Press.

Olson, Mancur. 1993. Dictatorship, Democracy, and Development. *American Political Science Review* 87:567-86.

Ostheimer, John M. 1975. Are Islanders Different? A Survey of Theoretical Ideas. In *The Politics of the Western Indian Ocean Islands*, ed. John M. Ostheimer. New York: Praeger.

Pipes, Richard. 1983. *In the Path of God.* New York: Basic Books.

Pritchett, Lant. 1996. Where Has All the Education Gone? Policy research working paper no. 1581, World Bank, Washington, DC.

Przeworski, Adam. 1991. *Democracy and the Market: Political and Economic Reforms in Eastern Europe and Latin America.* New York: Cambridge University Press.

Rodinson, Maxime. 1973. *Islam and Capitalism.* New York: Random House.

Rosett, Richard N. and Forrest D. Nelson. 1975. A Probit Regression Model. *Econometrica* 43(Jan.):141-46.

Rueschemeyer, Dietrich, Evelyne Huber Stephens, and John D. Stephens. 1992. *Capitalist Development and Democracy.* Chicago: University of Chicago Press.

Rustow, Dankwart A. 1970. Transitions to Democracy: Towards a Dynamic Model. *Comparative Politics* 2:337-63.

Seligson, Mitchell. 1987. Costa Rica and Jamaica. In *Competitive Elections in Developing Countries*, ed. Myron Weiner and Ergun Ozbudun. Durham, NC: Duke University Press.

Sirowy, Larry and Alex Inkeles. 1990. The Effects of Democracy on Economic Growth and Inequality: A Review. *Studies in Comparative Institutional Development* 25(1):126-57.

Smith, Tony. 1978. A Comparative Study of French and British Decolonization. *Comparative Studies in Society and History* 20(1):70-102.

Sullivan, Michael J. 1991. *Measuring Global Values: The Ranking of 162 Countries.* New York: Greenwood Press.

USSR. State Geological Committee, Department of Geodesy and Cartography. [1964] 1972. *Atlas Naradov Mira.* In *World Handbook of Political and Social Indicators*, ed. Charles Lewis Taylor and Michael Hudson. New Haven, CT: Yale University Press.

Waterbury, John. 1994. Democracy Without Democrats? The Potential for Political Liberalization in the Middle East. In *Democracy Without Democrats: The Renewal of Politics in the Muslim World*, ed. Ghassan Salame. London: I. B. Tauri.

Weiner, Myron. 1987. Empirical Democratic Theory. In *Competitive Elections in Developing Countries*, ed. Myron Weiner and Ergun Ozbudun. Durham, NC: Duke University Press.

ANNALS, *AAPSS*, **573**, January 2001

The Causes and
Consequences of Corruption

By OMAR AZFAR, YOUNG LEE, and ANAND SWAMY

ABSTRACT: In recent years, economists have come to recognize that corruption is not just an aberration or a nuisance; it is a systemic feature of many economies, which constitutes a significant impediment to economic development. The authors present an overview of the literature on the causes and consequences of corruption and briefly comment on some policy issues, drawing on recent research, including their own.

Omar Azfar is assistant research scientist and Young Lee is research associate at the IRIS Center, University of Maryland at College Park. Anand Swamy is an assistant professor in the Economics Department at Williams College in Massachusetts.

E CONOMISTS have long debated the policies and institutions that best promote economic development. The appropriate policies with regard to trade, macroeconomic policy, and the extent of government involvement in economic activity, among others, have all been sources of controversy. Often, the arguments have been between those who believe that markets, left to themselves, deliver desirable outcomes, and others who believe that the functioning of markets can be improved via extensive governmental intervention. Both schools of thought, however, often assume that there exist widely recognized norms, standards, and legal arrangements that govern economic transactions and that governments and citizens are usually confident that these rules will be obeyed. Of late, this assumption is increasingly being questioned. It is now generally acknowledged that violations of these rules, of which corruption in government is a prominent example, are pervasive in many economies and that this has a profound impact on economic outcomes.

Consider, for instance, the issue of whether a government should impose a tariff on the import of a commodity. Proponents might argue that the tariff protects a vulnerable industry and that it brings in revenues for the government. Critics may assert that it inhibits competition and hurts consumers. However, both arguments begin with the premise that the tariff will actually be collected as specified and that the revenues will accrue to the government. But what if the tariff becomes an opportunity for bribery? On the one

hand, it creates uncertainties for the traders, who do not know quite how much they have to pay; on the other hand, it reduces the revenues accruing to the government. The outcome can be dramatically different from textbook accounts of deadweight losses due to the tariffs as well as descriptions of the benefits from protection of infant industries.

To be sure, economists have long been aware of "rent-seeking" (Krueger 1974) and other corrupt activities. For decades, some very visible political leaders, such as General Mobutu of (then) Zaire and Ferdinand Marcos of the Philippines, have been known to have misappropriated huge amounts of public funds. Still, until recently, corruption was viewed as a second-order problem. Indeed, some prominent social scientists, notably Huntington (1968) and Leff (1964), even suggested that when inappropriate economic policies are in place, corruption can be welfare enhancing. Recent events and research on the impact of corruption have, however, led to a change of heart.

By the early 1990s, a consensus had formed, at least among the main Western international development agencies in Washington (the so-called Washington Consensus), on the economic policies that would best promote economic development. These included openness to trade, privatization of publicly owned firms, and prudent fiscal policies, with public investments being concentrated in high-return areas such as education. However, by the mid-1990s, it had become clear that many developing and transition countries

that had adopted the policies advocated by the Washington Consensus
had not grown as rapidly as expected.
Even more dramatically, incomes
actually declined during the
post-Communist transition, instead
of converging to Western levels, as
expected.

Many observers argued that key
reform initiatives, such as privatization, had been distorted due to
large-scale corruption. There were
also allegations of misuse of large
sums of Western aid. The concern
with corruption was reinforced by
the financial crisis that began in East
Asia; in several countries, exces-
sively cozy relationships between
banks, firms, and the government
were seen to be an important aspect
of the problem of financial misman-
agement (Lanyi and Lee 1999). As a
result, the analysis of corruption and
efforts to find ways to combat it have
now moved to center stage. Our purpose in this article is to provide the
nonspecialist reader an overview of
this discussion, drawing on recent
research, including our own.

The remainder of this article is
organized as follows. We begin briefly
with definitions. We then discuss
theoretical perspectives on the consequences of corruption. The next
two sections examine empirical evidence regarding the impact of corruption on economic growth and
development. Section 4 uses micro-
data, mostly from the Republic of
Georgia, and section 5 focuses on
cross-country evidence. Section 6 discusses the causes of corruption and
potential remedies. The final section
presents a summary and conclusion.

DEFINING CORRUPTION

A reasonable definition of the term
"corruption" is provided by Klitgaard
(1988): "[A corrupt official] deviates
from the formal duties of a public role
because of private-regarding (personal, close family, private clique)
pecuniary or status gains; or violates
rules against the exercise of certain
private-regarding behavior" (23).
Can we always unambiguously identify corruption? In some countries
and cultures, when a public official
provides a service, it is common to
respond with a gift or a tip. At what
point does a gift or a tip become a
bribe? One indicator could be the
amount; a tip or a gift, if given in
response to a service provided by a
public official, is usually quite a
small sum. Another indicator could
be the timing of the transaction; the
provision of the service is not conditional on the gift or tip, which is usually given later (Rose-Ackerman
1999, 91-111). Still, this raises the
issue of the extent to which the definition of corruption is culture specific
and whether international comparisons are meaningful.

There are other dimensions, too,
where the boundary between corruption and other activities may be
blurred. Can election campaign
finance be a form of corruption? To
proponents of campaign finance
reform, current campaign practices
in America may appear to serve the
same purposes as corruption in other
countries. Others may argue that so
long as campaign finance remains
within the boundaries of existing law,
it cannot be considered a corrupt

activity, even if it is of dubious moral or social value. The public-private distinction can also complicate the definition of corruption. Suppose, for instance, the principal of an elite private school takes a bribe for admitting a child. Many would consider this corruption; however, most researchers who have studied corruption (including the authors of this article) have focused exclusively on transactions in which at least one party is in government.

These considerations notwithstanding, the available evidence suggests that there is considerable agreement across cultures with respect to what is considered corrupt behavior. In a survey conducted at the Internet site of Göttingen University, respondents from various countries were asked to evaluate countries (those regarding which they were knowledgeable) on the propensity for bribe taking by public officials.[1] The responses from Western and non-Western residents were very similar.[2] It also appears to be the case, based on a survey conducted by Kaufmann (1997, 125), that elites from across the developing world and transition economies view public sector corruption as a serious obstacle to economic development. Despite the ambiguity in its definition, there does appear to be a broadly similar understanding of the term "corruption" across the world, and a concern with its consequences.

THEORETICAL PERSPECTIVES

It is certainly possible, at least in theory, to think of scenarios in which corruption can be socially advantageous. Suppose, for instance, that government employees are paid very low wages and are unmotivated. A citizen who approaches a government official might get tardy service. A bribe may expedite matters. In this incarnation as speed money, bribery may be, if not highly beneficial, at least relatively innocuous. Imagine further a scenario in which foreign exchange controls and quotas are in place. Which firm should get the foreign exchange? Presumably, the one that will use it most productively. One might expect that this firm will offer the highest bribe; thus corruption will introduce an element of competition and lead to efficient allocation of a scarce resource.[3]

Arguments to the contrary, which emphasize the harmful effects of corruption, are, if anything, more numerous and convincing. An environment in which speed money is widely used can become one in which public officials practice extortion; service will be provided only if bribes are paid. As far as resource allocation is concerned, the highest bribe may be paid by a low-cost and low-quality producer, not necessarily the one who is most efficient. It has also been suggested that when bribery is rampant, regulations are put in place in order to create opportunities for rent seeking (Kaufmann 1997, 116). Moreover, funds may be diverted away from the most socially useful projects, toward those that are beneficial to bribers and corrupt public officials.[4] It is also hard to see, for instance, the advantages of the transfer by Haiti's "Baby Doc" Duvalier of huge sums to foreign banks; the funds for antipoverty programs being appropriated by the rich; payment by developing countries of inflated sums for their weapons purchases; or the failure of governmental health programs due to misappropriation of funds.[5]

Perhaps even more damaging is the fact that when corruption becomes endemic, it can threaten the basic rule of law, property rights, and enforcement of contracts. As Olson (1996), North (1981, 1990), and others have emphasized, the benefits of markets can be realized only if they are supported by the appropriate institutions. For instance, if capital is to go from those who have it to those who would use it best, a well-functioning legal system is necessary to assure the lender that his or her money will be returned. Further, capital accumulation requires a judiciary that will competently and fairly judge disputes between investors and firms or project managers (Azfar, Matheson, and Olson 1999). Similarly, a peasant who is contemplating investment on his or her land must have the confidence that the land will not be confiscated. Corruption in the legal system can therefore threaten the prospects for economic development.[6]

In sum, though governments sometimes set up harmful and intrusive regulations, economic development needs to be supported by a credible state. The necessary functions of a state include, among other things, the formulation and enforcement of sensible laws to underpin the functioning of markets and other social institutions. Corruption undermines respect for all law, good and bad; it thereby weakens the state and undermines the prospects for economic development.

There are at least two ways of empirically evaluating the impact of corruption on economic development. One possibility is to work with micro-data, that is, information on individual units such as firms, households, or government departments. An alternative is to work with national-level data: provided there exist internationally comparable measures of corruption at the national level, we can compare the economic performances of countries with different levels of corruption. The cross-country comparisons will not merely serve as a check on the micro-level analysis; they are substantively important in themselves, in that they can give us an approximate estimate of the impact of corruption on national economies.

THE CONSEQUENCES OF
CORRUPTION: MICRO-EVIDENCE

In 1996, the president of the World Bank offered to support member countries' efforts to reduce corruption. Georgia was among the first to accept the offer. To this end, the World Bank developed a set of diagnostic surveys focusing on corruption in the public sector, targeted at households, enterprises, and public officials. We were fortunate to be given access to the data collected in these surveys, which were implemented in 1998 and covered 802 households, 350 enterprises, and 206 public officials. Much of this section of the article is based on these data.[7]

Our first piece of evidence relates to one of the earliest debates in the literature on corruption. As mentioned earlier, in an overregulated economy with an unmotivated bureaucracy, bribery may merely expedite the bureaucratic process; that is, corruption may be speed money. If this were the case, we would expect households and firms to be reasonably satisfied with the outcomes of their corrupt transactions. However, Georgian enterprise managers said they would be willing to pay, on average, as much as 22.5 percent of their official revenues to eliminate corruption. This suggests that corruption is a serious obstacle to doing business and involves more than just speed money. Our private conversations with businessmen in Pakistan suggested they, too, would be willing to pay a similar percentage to get rid of corruption. Enterprises in Cambodia are also willing to pay a significant amount, on average 6.5 percent of their revenues, to eliminate corruption, according to the World Bank Governance and Anti-Corruption Survey from Cambodia.

The surveys from Georgia also revealed that corruption is disproportionately present in the law enforcement sectors—the police and the judiciary. The police, the traffic police, and the judiciary are all in the bottom third of institutions rated for honesty by households, enterprises, and public officials in Georgia. Households rated the police, local public prosecutors, local courts, and the traffic police as the four worst government agencies in terms of quality. Unfair decisions by judges were cited as a very important reason for not using courts by 37 percent of Georgian firms and 39 percent of households. Only 6 percent of households reported using courts to resolve disputes after being defrauded; another 10 percent used arbitrators; and most did nothing (Anderson et al. 1999, fig. 15).[8] If the intuition of North (1990), Olson (1996), and others who have highlighted the importance of contract enforcement is correct, it is likely that corruption in the legal system is an impediment to economic development in Georgia.

Government procurement often provides lucrative opportunities for corruption. This was documented at least as early as the seventeenth century. Samuel Pepys, a man many regard as the founder of the British Navy, recorded in his diary in 1664 that he received a payment of 300 pounds (10 times the salary of an unskilled worker) as a bribe for issuing a contract for the supply of victuals for Navy men. He protests even to himself that this bribe was received at "no cost to the King," but an earlier entry in his diary clearly indicates that he agreed to a higher price because it would allow him to get a larger bribe. The defense of a bribe taker has often involved the claim that the crime is victimless, but in this case there is clear evidence of cost to the exchequer (Noonan 1984, 366-87).

This practice seems equally prevalent today. In the Georgia surveys, over 50 percent of enterprise managers reported that the need to give bribes was "a very important reason" for not participating in procurement that was relevant to their business.

The government will receive a good price if there are a large number of competing bidders; it is likely that, in Georgia, corruption in procurement is costly to the exchequer not only because of the direct drain of resources but also because it reduces competition.

Another harmful aspect of corruption is its regressive nature. Data from Georgia, Ecuador, and Cambodia consistently show that low-income households bear a larger burden of corruption, as measured by the bribes/income ratio. This regressive nature of the corruption burden appears to be due to pervasive corruption in basic public services, education, and health.

An indication that corruption has become endemic is when government jobs begin to be sold. The price of the job then depends on its remuneration, including bribes. This not only ensures that merit plays little role in job allocation; it also forces the new hire to be corrupt to recover the initial payment.[9] Furthermore, to the extent such a market for jobs emerges, it can encourage the formulation of regulations that will create opportunities for bribery. The argument that regulations may be created to help extract rents may seem implausible because the person formulating the regulations is typically not the same as the person extracting the bribes. However, if jobs can be sold by those who set up the regulatory apparatus to those who extract bribes, the market can close this gap.

In Georgia we see an interesting relationship between the average amount of bribes given by households to an agency and the percentage of officials who paid for their jobs. This clear pattern ($R^2 = .84$) in Figure 1 shows how well the market works. Georgian officials also reported that, in 64 percent of the cases, bribes were shared with superiors (Anderson et al. 1999, 22). This may induce senior officials to create opportunities for rent seeking. A similar relationship between purchase of jobs and bribe taking was also found in the data collected by the World Bank's Governance and Anti-Corruption Survey in Ecuador.

Does this corruption we observe at the micro-level affect aggregate national-level outcomes? Evidence is mounting that it does. A variety of economic outcomes are being studied even as this paper is being written. The most researched issue to date is the impact of corruption on economic growth, which we discuss in the next section.

THE CONSEQUENCES OF CORRUPTION: EVIDENCE BASED ON NATIONAL-LEVEL DATA

How do we measure the level of corruption in a country as a whole? Even though there are conceptual problems associated with the measures economists have traditionally used (gross domestic product [GDP], for instance), one can, at least in principle, outline well-defined methodologies for computing them. We cannot do this for our measures of corruption, at least not yet. The available measures of the level of corruption in a country are all based on the perceptions of observers and participants. In that sense, they are all subjective measures; two well-

FIGURE 1
THE VICIOUS CIRCLE: BUYING JOBS AND EXTRACTING BRIBES

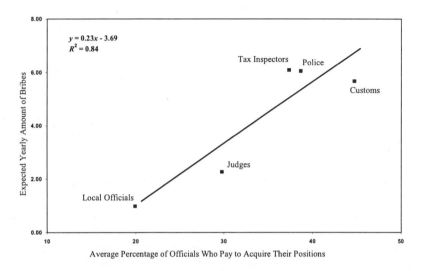

trained economists looking at the same scenario might come up with different measures of corruption. This is a matter of concern to many researchers. However, it is very reassuring that the measures produced by different agencies and organizations are strongly correlated. Moreover, the widely used measure of corruption developed by Transparency International, which we will discuss further, combines numerous surveys, which reduces the probability that a single idiosyncratic survey will unduly influence the index of corruption.

One of the early papers that studied the impact of corruption using cross-country data was by Mauro (1995), who relied on a measure of corruption produced by a company called Business International, which was later incorporated into the Economist Intelligence Unit. The company's correspondents evaluated countries in terms of a large number of risk factors and sold these evaluations to banks, multinational corporations, and other international investors. Mauro worked with three indices, one for "corruption" ("The degree to which business transactions involve corruption or questionable payments"), another for "bureaucracy and red tape" ("The regulatory environment foreign firms must face when seeking approvals and permits. The degree to which it represents an obstacle to business"), and a third for the quality of the legal system ("Efficiency and integrity of the legal environment as it affects business, particularly foreign firms"). Countries were ranked on a scale of zero to 10 for each index, with a higher number indicating a better performance. Since these indices are strongly correlated, inclusion of each of them separately as explanatory variables in a regression model would make it difficult to disentangle their effects because of multicollinearity. Therefore, Mauro used a simple average of these three measures to construct an index of bureaucratic efficiency.

Mauro then estimated numerous regression models in which the dependent variable was either the ratio of investment to GDP (1960-85) or per capita GDP growth (1960-85); the index of bureaucratic efficiency was introduced as an explanatory variable, along with other controls. He found that bureaucratic inefficiency reduced GDP growth mainly via its negative impact on the rate of investment. A sense of the magnitude of this effect can be obtained from the following illustrative calculation he presents:

If Bangladesh were to improve the integrity and efficiency of its bureaucracy to the level of Uruguay (corresponding to a one-standard deviation increase in the bureaucratic efficiency index), its investment rate would rise by almost five percentage points, and its yearly GDP growth rate would rise by over half a percentage point. (1995, 705)

Some researchers have argued that corruption is especially harmful because of the element of unpredictability it introduces into business transactions. To investigate this hypothesis, the World Bank, for its 1997 issue of the *World Development Report*, conducted a survey of 3700 companies in 69 countries and asked questions regarding the extent of corruption as well as its predictability. Using these data, Campos, Lien, and Pradhan (1999) find that, even controlling for the extent of corruption, the less predictable corruption is, the lower the rate of investment.

Several other studies have also found a negative relationship between GDP growth and corruption. Steve Knack and Philip Keefer (1995) introduced into the literature measures of institutional quality developed by Political Risk Services, a private firm that sought to provide its clients measures of the risks associated with international business. Political Risk Services produced a rating system, which they called the International Country Risk Guide (ICRG), in which countries were evaluated on 24 dimensions of political, financial, and economic risk, one of which was corruption. Knack and Keefer created a composite index, combining the ICRG scores on quality of bureaucracy, corruption, rule of law, risk of expropriation of private investment, and risk of repudiation of contracts by government, and they found that better institutional quality had a strong positive relationship with GDP growth. In subsequent work, Olson, Sarna, and Swamy (2000) have shown that better institutional quality (one measure of which is lower levels of corruption) can also promote economic growth via its impact on the rate of the growth of productivity.

One mechanism by which corruption may impede development is by distorting public expenditure priorities. Mauro (1998) finds that corruption may lead to the underfunding of education, which provides fewer opportunities for bribery than more procurement-intensive activities. Several other studies that analyze the impact of corruption on determinants of economic growth such as education and foreign investment are surveyed by Lambsdorff (1999).

The cross-country research has quickly produced interesting results, which support the view that corruption is detrimental to economic growth. Still, there are several difficult statistical issues on hand, because of which we need to be cautious in drawing conclusions. First, it is important to note that various measures of institutional quality tend to move together very closely. For instance, a country that has a low level of corruption also probably has higher rule obedience in general, better-defined property rights, and so forth. Due to this multicollinearity, it is difficult to separate the effects of various institutional characteristics. The fact that each institutional characteristic is difficult to measure also creates the possibility that the impact of one (badly measured) characteristic can be picked up by another variable. Perhaps the best way to view the existing cross-country evidence is that it establishes the importance of good governance as a whole, one aspect of which is reducing the level of corruption. On the other hand, micro-evidence, such as our findings for Georgia, more specifically identifies the harmful effects of corruption.

Another difficult statistical issue in the cross-country literature is determining the direction of causality. It is easy to conceive of situations in which there is feedback from the level of economic activity to the extent of corruption, so it is not always clear exactly how to interpret the observed correlation.[10] This problem can, in principle, be addressed by finding suitable instruments, that is, variables that affect the level of corruption but not the dependent variable in the regression model. Convincing instruments are, however, often difficult to find. Problems in inferring causality trouble the cross-country corruption literature as they do much of the other macroeconomics literature that is based on cross-country regressions.

CAUSES AND REMEDIES

Why does corruption exist, and what can be done about it? As Klitgaard (1998, 46) puts it, "Corruption is a crime of calculation, not passion." When will the calculations work out in favor of a public official's being corrupt? Presumably, when the potential benefits of being corrupt are high (for example, the official has the sole discretion to provide an essential license or permit), the probability of being caught is small, or the official's wage is low.[11] It follows that corruption should decline if regulatory reform reduces the monopoly and discretionary power of officials, if greater transparency increases the probability of being caught, and if higher pay or better working conditions for officials increase the pecuniary benefits of being honest.

The precise set of policies required to reduce corruption will, of course, vary from country to country. Doig and Riley (1998) argue that in Mali and Senegal, trade liberalization helped reduce customs fraud, when combined with high salaries for customs officials and other institutional reforms. On the other hand, in Tanzania, corruption appears to have increased during the period of liberalization, and a high-level commission recommended strengthening of enforcement agencies and campaigns to promote public awareness. One country in which corruption has decreased dramatically over time is Hong Kong. Part of the success came from the formation of the autonomous Independent Commission Against Corruption, which was given sweeping powers and was able to staff itself without relying on existing enforcement agencies, whose integrity was suspect. Some researchers at the World Bank (Kaufmann 1998) have suggested that survey-based evidence on the sources and consequences of corruption be widely disseminated as part of a broader effort to involve the public, media, parliament, and other stakeholders in anticorruption efforts.

Statistical evidence on the determinants of corruption is only beginning to emerge. Using cross-country data, Treisman (1998) has found some evidence that federal states are more corrupt than unitary states. The theory is that when both central and subnational officials can extract bribes, the total amount extracted will be high, because neither side will want to leave surplus for the other. Treisman also notes, however, the counterargument that, in a decentralized setup, competition between regions to attract enterprises may

lower the level of corruption. He also finds that former British colonies and countries with a larger percentage of Protestants have lower levels of corruption. There is mixed evidence on the issue of whether higher government wages reduce the level of corruption. Some researchers have argued that a free press is likely to reduce the incidence of corruption, and there is some cross-country evidence to support this.[12] As researchers across the world continue to collect and analyze data on corruption, we hope to see stronger statistical evidence on these issues.

A rather unusual policy to combat the problem of corruption has recently been implemented in Mexico City and in Lima, Peru (Moore 1999; McDermott 1999). In both places, the city administration has decided to replace male traffic police with female traffic police, on the grounds that women are less likely to be corrupt. Swamy et al. (1999) take a close look at this issue: is there any evidence that greater participation by women in public life leads to lower levels of corruption? They do not suggest that the ethical standards of men and women are fundamentally different in some suprahistorical sense; rather, they seek to evaluate whether, at this point in history, whatever the underlying reasons, men and women approach corruption differently.

Swamy et al. first use data on attitudes toward corruption reported in the World Values Survey, a survey of norms and attitudes in a large number of developed and developing countries.[13] The central finding, based on data from 43 countries surveyed in 1991, is that 28 percent of men felt that accepting bribes was sometimes justified, but only 23 percent of women felt the same way. The gender differential was robust in controlling for other factors, such as age, marital status, devotion to religion, and so on. The analysis was then carried out separately for each country, and a statistically significant gender differential (women being less tolerant of corruption) was found in most of them.

While the aforementioned evidence pertained to a difference in attitudes, it was necessary to ask whether this translated into a difference in behavior. Using the survey of firms in Georgia discussed earlier, Swamy et al. found that while firms owned or managed by women gave bribes on approximately 5 percent of the occasions they came in contact with a government agency, the percentage was more than twice as high for men, at 11 percent. Again, the gender differential was robust regarding the inclusion of other factors that might affect the incidence of corruption.

The final step was to assess whether these differences at the micro-level might have any national-level consequences. Swamy et al. used the index of corruption developed by Transparency International (TI), in which countries are ranked on scale of zero to 10, with 10 representing a corruption-free country. They found that countries in which the percentage of women in parliament is higher tend to have lower levels of corruption (higher levels of the TI index). A standard deviation increase in the percentage of the lower house of parliament that is women is associated with an increase of approximately 0.6 in the TI index value for 1998; this is a substantial effect, given the mean of the TI index value for 1998 is 4.9. These results are consistent with the expectation that, at least in the short run, a greater presence of women in public life will reduce corruption.

The preceding discussion notwithstanding, we do not mean to suggest that reducing or eradicating corruption is a simple or straightforward matter. The measures that have been discussed, ranging from civil service reform to democratization, all require political and popular will; we do not yet have a theory of why some polities are more tolerant of corruption than others. In the absence of commitment at the highest levels of government and support from the public, there is no guarantee that civil service reform or the establishment of, for example, a Hong Kong–style independent anticorruption agency will have the desired effects. There is also no consensus on the appropriate prioritization and sequencing of reforms; although research on these subjects is ongoing, as yet questions outnumber persuasive answers.

CONCLUSION

As the preceding discussion indicates, the emerging consensus among policymakers and researchers is that corruption is usually harmful to economic development. The focus is now on efforts to reduce corruption; this is still work in progress. While there is agreement on some general principles such as the need for transparency, accountability, and public participation in anticorruption efforts, much remains to be done at both policy and research levels. There is need for researchers, policymakers, activists, and the public to pool resources and information. It is appropriate, therefore, that we conclude this article by pointing out that several forums for such information pooling now exist. In addition to the World Bank, the United Nations, and other established international organizations, several international organizations focusing specifically on corruption have come into being, including Transparency International (http://www.transparency.de/) and the Anti-Corruption Network for Transition Economies (http://www.nobribes.org/).

Notes

1. At www.uni-goettingen.de/~uwvw.

2. For more details, see Lambsdorff 1999, fn. 4. Of course, this evidence is not decisive, because an Internet survey in which the respondents are self-selected does not provide a random sample.

3. Klitgaard (1988, chap. 2) neatly summarizes the competing views on the consequences of corruption.

4. Augustine Ruzindana, member of parliament and chairman of the public accounts committee in Uganda, argues that all over Africa there are abandoned roads, factories, and other projects that were constructed primarily because they provided an opportunity for corruption (Ruzindana 1998, 137).

5. Ugandan president Yoweri Museveni (cited in Ruzindana 1998, 135) describes how the dilution of drugs by corrupt medical staff led to the development of disease-resistant microbes.

6. Corruption in the judiciary has long been regarded as harmful to social welfare. In a landmark attempted-murder trial, *Cluen-*

tius v. *Oppianicus* in 74 B.C., where both sides may have bribed the judges, Oppianicus' lawyer Quinctius declared, "This touches all of us, the courts are nullities, no one who has a rich enemy can be safe." Despite the irony that the author of the statement was a rich man's lawyer, in a trial where his side had probably bribed the judges first, the point remains valid (Noonan 1984, 32-39).

7. We are extremely grateful to the World Bank, especially to Amitabha Mukherjee and Randi Ryterman, for making available the Georgia corruption survey.

8. Another 25 percent used friends and relatives, and 4 percent used threats (Anderson et al. 1999, fig. 15).

9. Like many other aspects of corruption, the sale of jobs has ancient beginnings. The Byzantine emperor Justinian lamented the practice in A.D. 535 and noted that he who pays for a job must sell his services. The Catholic Church sold priesthoods in medieval times. The East India Company famously sold customs posts, and local government positions were sold in nineteenth-century America. The need to be corrupt on the job is further increased if officers borrow to purchase jobs, of which there are historical instances (Noonan 1984, 111, 292).

10. A nice example is provided in Chand and Moene 1999, fn. 4. In Sierra Leone, when, in the last quarter of 1986, wages of public servants were fixed and the exchange rate was floated, the price of imported staples such as rice increased by a factor of seven. Following the decline in the real wages of customs officials, the level of corruption increased, plausibly due to the decline in the real wage. This is a scenario in which economic outcomes affected the level of corruption.

11. Klitgaard (1988) provided the following widely cited formula: corruption = monopoly + discretion − accountability.

12. For discussion of this and the previous point, and the relevant citations, see Lambsdorff 1999.

13. Inglehart, Basanez, and Moreno (1998) provide details on the procedures followed in the various surveys in the 1990s. The surveys in the Western countries were carried out by experienced survey organizations, many linked with the Gallup chain. In other countries, they were carried out by academies of science or by university-based institutes.

Inglehart et al. write, "In most countries stratified multistage random sampling was used, with samples selected in two stages. First a random selection of sample locations was made ensuring that all types of location were represented in proportion to their population. Next, a random selection of individuals was drawn up" (471).

References

Anderson, James, Omar Azfar, Daniel Kaufmann, Young Lee, Amitabha Mukherjee, and Randi Ryterman. 1999. Corruption in Georgia: Survey Evidence. World Bank. Mimeographed.

Azfar, Omar, Thornton Matheson, and Mancur Olson. 1999. Market-Mobilized Capital. Working paper, IRIS Center, University of Maryland, College Park.

Campos, J. E., D. Lien, and S. Pradhan. 1999. The Impact of Corruption on Investment: Predictability Matters. World Development 27(6):1059-67.

Chand, Sheetal K. and Karl O. Moene. 1999. Controlling Fiscal Corruption. World Development 27(7):1129-40.

Doig, A. and S. Riley. 1998. Corruption and Anti-Corruption Strategies: Issues and Case Studies from Developing Countries. In Corruption and Integrity Improvement Initiatives in Developing Countries, ed. Sahr J. Kpundeh and Irene Hors. New York: United Nations Development Program.

Huntington, Samuel. 1968. Political Order in Changing Societies. New Haven, CT: Yale University Press.

Inglehart, R., M. Basanez, and A. Moreno. 1998. Human Values and Beliefs: A Cross-Cultural Source Book: Political, Religious, Sexual, and Economic Norms in 43 Societies: Findings from the 1990-93 World Values Survey. Ann Arbor: University of Michigan Press.

Kaufmann, D. 1997. Corruption: The Facts. Foreign Policy, Summer:114-31.

———. 1998. Challenges in the Next Stage of Anti-Corruption. In New Perspectives on Combating Corruption. Washington, DC: Transparency International and the World Bank.

Klitgaard, Robert. 1988. Controlling Corruption. Berkeley: University of California Press.

———. 1998. International Cooperation on Combating Corruption. In New Perspectives on Combating Corruption. Washington, DC: Transparency International and the World Bank.

Knack, Stephen and Philip Keefer. 1995. Institutions and Economic Performance: Cross-Country Tests Using Alternative Institutional Measures. Economics and Politics 7(3):207-27.

Krueger, A. O. 1974. The Political Economy of a Rent-Seeking Society. American Economic Review 64:291-303.

Lambsdorff, J. G. 1999. Corruption in Empirical Research: A Review. Available at http://www.transparency.de/documents/work-papers/lambsdorff_eresearch.html.

Lanyi, Anthony and Young Lee. 1999. Governance Aspects of the East Asian Financial Crisis. Working paper, IRIS Center, University of Maryland, College Park.

Leff, Nathaniel. 1964. Economic Development Through Bureaucratic Corruption. American Behavioral Scientist 8:8-14.

Mauro, Paolo. 1995. Corruption and Growth. Quarterly Journal of Economics 110:681-712.

———. 1998. Corruption and the Composition of Government Expenditure. Journal of Public Economics 69: 263-79.

McDermott, Jeremy. 1999. International: Women Police Ride in on a Ticket of Honesty. Daily Telegraph (London), 31 July.

Moore, Molly. 1999. Mexico City's Stop Sign to Bribery: To Halt Corruption,

Women Traffic Cops Replace Men. *Washington Post*, 31 July.

Noonan, John T. 1984. *Bribes*. New York: Macmillan.

North, Douglass. 1981. *Structure and Change in Economic History*. New York: Norton.

———. 1990. *Institutions, Institutional Change, and Economic Performance*. New York: Cambridge University Press.

Olson, Mancur. 1996. Big Bills Left on the Sidewalk: Why Some Nations are Rich and Others Poor. *Journal of Economics Perspectives* 10:3-24.

Olson, Mancur, Naveen Sarna, and Anand Swamy. 2000. Governance and Growth: A Simple Hypothesis Explaining Cross-Country Differences in Productivity Growth. *Public Choice* 102(3-4):341-64.

Rose-Ackerman, Susan. 1999. *Corruption and Government: Causes, Consequences, and Reform*. New York: Cambridge University Press.

Ruzindana, Augustine. 1998. The Importance of Leadership in Fighting Corruption in Uganda. In *Corruption and the Global Economy*, ed. Kimberly Ann Elliot. Washington, DC: Institute for International Economics.

Swamy, Anand, Stephen Knack, Young Lee, and Omar Azfar. 1999. Gender and Corruption. Working paper, IRIS Center, University of Maryland, College Park.

Treisman, Daniel. 1998. The Causes of Corruption: A Cross-National Study. Department of Political Science, University of California, Los Angeles. Mimeographed.

ANNALS, *AAPSS*, **573**, January 2001

Individualism, Collectivism, and Economic Development

By RICHARD BALL

ABSTRACT: This article investigates how the prevalence of collectivism or individualism in a society relates to the economic development of the society. The central premise of the article is that causality runs in two directions: the collectivist or individualist character of a society will influence the course of economic development, and simultaneously economic growth and changes in economic structure will alter the orientation of the society toward individualism or collectivism. The recognition of this two-way causality suggests four broad hypotheses concerning the interaction between economic and cultural factors: (1) economic development is impeded by collectivism and facilitated by individualism; (2) economic development is facilitated by collectivism and impeded by individualism; (3) economic development promotes collectivism and erodes individualism; and (4) economic development erodes collectivism and promotes individualism. The arguments and evidence that have been marshaled in support of each of these hypotheses are examined, and the general themes and implications that emerge are discussed.

Richard Ball is an associate professor of economics at Haverford College. His research has focused on formal political economy models, empirical work on the political economy of development, and, most recently, the relative roles of formal institutions and informal norms in the creation and maintenance of economic prosperity and social harmony. In 1982-83 he spent a year as a visiting student at the University of Sierra Leone, in 1985-86 he worked in Chad as a famine relief and rural development field-worker for CARE, and in 1987 he worked as a summer intern for the Ford Foundation in Cairo.

THE social psychologist Harry Triandis (1990) has argued that "perhaps the most important dimension of cultural difference in social behavior, across the diverse cultures of the world, is the relative emphasis on individualism versus collectivism" (42). In more individualistic societies, people tend to behave like *Homo economicus*: they choose actions that maximize their private material self-interest. In more collectivist societies, people tend to behave like *Homo sociologicus*: their actions are conditioned by the norms, expectations, and interests of the social groups of which they are part. According to Triandis,

In individualist cultures most people's social behavior is largely determined by personal goals that overlap only slightly with the goals of collectives. . . . When a conflict arises between personal and group goals, it is considered acceptable for the individual to place personal goals ahead of collective goals. By contrast, in collectivist cultures social behavior is determined largely by goals shared with some collective, and if there is a conflict between personal and group goals, it is considered socially desirable to place collective goals ahead of personal goals. (42)

This article investigates how the prevalence of collectivism or individualism in a society relates to the economic development of the society. The central premise of the article is that causality runs in two directions: the collectivist or individualist character of a society will influence the course of economic development, and simultaneously economic growth and changes in economic structure will alter the orientation of the society toward individualism or collectivism. The recognition of this two-way causality suggests four broad hypotheses concerning the interaction between economic and cultural factors: (1) economic development is impeded by collectivism and facilitated by individualism; (2) economic development is facilitated by collectivism and impeded by individualism; (3) economic development promotes collectivism and erodes individualism; and (4) economic development erodes collectivism and promotes individualism. Various aspects of these hypotheses have been studied by a diverse array of authors—from Adam Smith and other classical political economists to contemporary scholars interested in social capital and civil society, including many schools and individuals in between, representing all the social sciences.

This article examines the array of arguments and evidence that have been marshaled in support of each of these hypotheses, and the conclusion discusses the general themes and implications that emerge. One lesson is that the level of economic development that a country has achieved, and the state of its economic and political institutions, have a large effect on the nature of the interactions between economic and cultural factors. That is, the applicability of each of the hypotheses to be explored depends on initial conditions. Second, the way in which collectivism affects economic performance depends on dimensions of the concept that are not specified in Triandis's definition. In particular, the size of the group to which collectivist feelings and behavior extend, and the degree to which collectivism depends on personal relationships and ties versus the degree to which collectivism exists among individuals with no direct personal connections, have important implications for the way in which collectivism influences economic development. Finally, theoretical and empirical evidence indicates that processes involving behavior based on social norms generally possess multiple equilibria. The existence of multiple equilibria makes social and economic development a precarious undertaking: depending on the sequence of events, the process can lead to very attractive outcomes, or it can lead to collapse.

1. ECONOMIC DEVELOPMENT IS IMPEDED BY COLLECTIVISM AND FACILITATED BY INDIVIDUALISM

The classical expression of the idea that the unbridled pursuit of self-interest—the individualistic society—is good for economic performance is found in Adam Smith's notion of the invisible hand (with its modern formulation in the First Theorem of Welfare Economics).[1] The essence of the argument is that if people are allowed to engage in voluntary exchange, they will do so until all possible gains from trade have been exhausted. The fact that no further mutually beneficial exchanges remain to be made between any parties means that an efficient allocation of resources has been achieved.

Of course, as Adam Smith was well aware (and as careful expositions of the First Welfare Theorem make explicit), a system of voluntary exchange motivated by individual

self-interest can be counted on to yield an efficient result only when markets exist and function perfectly. Much of economic theory and policy analysis is driven by the question of how free enterprise operates in the absence of well-functioning markets. Of particular relevance for this article is the class of market failures that fall under the rubrics of prisoners' dilemmas, collective action problems, and public goods. These problems are central to the discussion in section 2 on how a collectivist culture can be beneficial for economic development.

Max Weber (1930) also saw a constructive role for individualism in the development of the English economy. Weber argued that one of the critical ingredients in the rise of capitalism in England, which he dated to the sixteenth century,[2] was the spread of Calvinism, which emphasized "individualistic motives of rational legal acquisition by virtue of one's own ability and initiative" and "had the psychological effect of freeing the acquisition of goods from the inhibitions of traditionalistic ethics" (Weber 1930, 179 and 171, quoted in Macfarlane 1979, 47). By favoring rational thought over superstition and magic, and the pursuit of individual interests over communal ties, Protestantism helped to "shatter the fetters of the kinship group" (quoted in Bendix 1962, 139; Macfarlane 1979, 50) and unleash the spirit of individual enterprise that—following Adam Smith's notion of the invisible hand—is the basis of a market economy.

A number of early contributors to modern development economics, writing in the years following World War II, echoed Weber's notion of "fetters of kinship" as an impediment to economic development. Bauer and Yamey (1957) argued that "the extended family . . . is an example of an institution which has many advantages in one stage of economic achievement, but which may later become a drag on economic development" (64). The advantage of an extended family in a poor society is that it provides informal insurance; the disadvantage as a society begins to develop economically is that obligations within an extended family may dull individual incentives to invest and accumulate wealth, both because one can rely on relatives for economic support and because any accumulated wealth will have to be shared with many kin. Lewis (1955) expressed a similar point of view:

The extended family system has tremendous advantages in societies living at a subsistence level, but it seems not to be appropriate to societies where economic growth is occurring. In such societies it is almost certainly a drag on effort. For growth depends on initiative, and initiative is likely to be stifled if the individual who makes the effort is required to share the reward with many others whose claims he does not recognize. (114)[3]

In recent work, Platteau (forthcoming, chap. 5) similarly argues that traditional social networks provide informal insurance against crop loss, natural disasters, and other hazards. Norms of sharing and egalitarianism prevent individuals from accumulating sufficient wealth to self-insure and opt out of the insurance networks, which must have a large number of members to be efficient.

Strong ties to family or community members can also interfere with the functioning of the economy by contributing to bureaucratic corruption. Rather than allocating resources and jobs according to social objectives, bureaucrats bound by obligations to traditional networks may engage in favoritism and nepotism. This idea can be found in Lewis (1955, 114) and is central to a recent paper on corruption by Tanzi (1994). Tanzi argues that bureaucratic decisions should be made on the basis of "the principle of the arm's length relationship," which "requires that personal relationships should play no role in economic decisions" (1). In societies in which people feel bound by a network of social relationships, "the government employee, just like any other individual, would be expected to help relatives and friends with special treatment or favors even if, occasionally, this behavior might require bending, or even breaking, administrative rules and departing from 'universalistic principles' " (5). Platteau (1994, 798) cites a description of precisely this problem offered by an Indian psychoanalyst:

Although the Indian professional or bureaucrat may agree with his western counterpart that . . . the criterion for appointment or promotion to a particular job must be objective, decisions based solely on the demands of the task and "merits of the case," he cannot root out the cultural conviction that his *relationship* to the individual under consideration for the position is the single most important factor in his decision. . . . Allegiance to *impersonal* institutions and *abstract* moral concepts is without precedent in individual development experience. . . . Guilt and its attendant inner anxiety are aroused only when individual actions go against the primacy of relationships, not when foreign ethical standards of justice and efficiency are breached. (Kakar 1978, 125-26, emphasis added by Platteau)

The arguments considered to this point have all centered on how collectivist norms shape individual behavior and how this collectively oriented behavior impedes economic development. Several recent authors, using formal equilibrium analysis, have studied somewhat more subtle dynamics, in which collectivist norms shape the development of institutions, and the character of the institutions then influences the course of economic development. These studies follow the work of North (1981, 1989, 1990), whose pioneering studies emphasized the interplay of economic forces with institutions during the process of economic development.

Greif's (1994, 1997) work on the Maghribi (eleventh century) and Genoese (twelfth and thirteenth century) traders takes this institutional perspective. The common organizational problem that both of these societies had to solve was how to monitor the behavior of agents charged with executing foreign trade in distant lands on behalf of principals located at home. Greif shows historical evidence that both societies relied on some form of reputation effects to enforce faithful behavior by the agents. The difference in the institutions that developed was that the (collectivist) Maghribis engaged in collective punishment of agents who had cheated—no other Maghribi principal would engage an agent who had cheated any one Maghribi trader—whereas in the (individualistic) Genoese society, errant agents were punished unilaterally by the cheated principal. Both of these enforcement mechanisms successfully resolved the agency problem, but they differed in one crucial way: although the collectivist Maghribi system was self-enforcing, the Genoese system of unilateral sanctions was credible only when supported by "an external mechanism—such as a legal system backed by the state—that restricts agents' ability to embezzle merchants' capital." The reliance of the Genoese on "formal organizations to support agency and exchange" led them to develop "an extensive legal system for the registration and enforcement of contracts," and "the customary law that governed relations among Genoese traders was codified as permanent courts were established." In contrast, the Maghribis still "entered contracts informally, used or adopted an informal code of conduct, and attempted to resolve disputes informally" (1997, 75-76). The Genoese adoption of a formal legal system and contracts then facilitated further institutional innovations that promoted development of the commercial economy, including bills of lading for foreign trade and the sale of shares in family businesses. Through this chain of events, the individualistic culture of the Genoese induced a series of institutional innovations conducive to further economic development.

Kranton (1996), also building on North's work on the role of institutions in economic development, has studied the evolution of an economy from a personalized system of exchange based on reciprocity to anonymous market exchange. One scenario that emerges from her model captures the idea that trade sustained by personal relationships of reciprocity can impede the development of a market economy.[4] Her argument is based on search costs: if most people engage only in reciprocal exchange, the potential number of partners for market exchange will be small, and the search costs involved in finding a partner will be high. Dense personal networks can thereby crowd out the development of impersonal markets. As an example, Kranton (1996, 845) cites a study of markets in Cairo, Egypt, in which "people use connections to obtain goods and services, [and in so doing] they exacerbate the conditions that support the use of connections." Kranton cites the observation made in that study, that "because some people obtain jobs or laundry soap through informal networks, others are denied them when bureaucrats decide that the civil service cannot absorb any more new entrants or when the supply of soap has run out at the local cooperative" (Singerman 1995, 139). Commenting on Kranton's analysis and similar examples, Dasgupta (2000, 388-90) argues that "networks can be destructively competitive with

markets if they are involved in the production and exchange of 'marketable' goods through communitarian arrangements, such as those operating on the basis of norms of reciprocity." His general conclusion is that "past accumulation of certain kinds of social capital can act as a drag on economic development, by preventing more efficient institutions from spreading."

2. ECONOMIC DEVELOPMENT IS FACILITATED BY COLLECTIVISM AND IMPEDED BY INDIVIDUALISM

In contrast to all the literature mentioned previously regarding how individualism is good for economic performance and how collectivism can be an impediment, the recent burgeoning literature on social capital and trust mainly takes the opposite view, namely, that thick social networks and trust are good for, even a fundamental determinant of, economic performance. Frequently cited in this literature is Arrow's (1972) comment that "virtually every commercial transaction has within itself an element of trust, certainly any transaction conducted over a period of time. It can be plausibly argued that much of the economic backwardness in the world can be explained by the lack of mutual confidence" (357).

A unifying element in the various arguments for how and why collectivism facilitates economic development is the premise that economic transactions are pervaded by prisoners' dilemmas, collective action problems, and public goods. These related and overlapping[5] phenomena, which will be referred to collectively as social dilemmas, have a common structure: each of two or more people must choose to "cooperate" or "defect";[6] in terms of material self-interest, defecting is a dominant strategy for each individual; each individual's payoff is increasing in the number of other individuals who cooperate; and the unique Pareto efficient outcome is for every individual to cooperate.[7] Situations possessing this structure include the management of common property resources such as common grazing areas or fisheries, the construction and maintenance of irrigation facilities, the execution of multiparty business enterprises and employment relationships, and the exertion of public pressure for growth-enhancing government policies.[8] Such social dilemmas represent an important class of market failures, and in their presence Adam Smith's invisible hand argument, that the pursuit of individual self-interest will lead to an efficient allocation of resources, does not apply.

How to induce individuals to behave cooperatively in the presence of social dilemmas has been a central problem in philosophy and the social sciences. A variety of solutions has been proposed: Hobbes's Leviathan, a state with coercive power to enforce cooperative behavior; the Coasean notion of defined and protected property rights; and repeated interactions, where reputation effects, trigger strategies, and tit-for-tat play can lead to cooperative behavior. None of these solutions is perfect. Abuse of power by the state, or government failure, can be as socially costly as the market failures the state was intended to correct; the definition of property rights yields an efficient outcome only if negotiation costs are small; and with repeated play, universal cooperation is at best one equilibrium out of many, and universal defection is still always an equilibrium.

This section considers a different solution to the problem of social dilemmas: how and to what extent can social norms induce people to behave in ways that are socially beneficial when such behavior does not maximize their material self-interest? Social norms offer at best another imperfect mechanism for inducing cooperation—indeed, in some ways social norms may be an especially delicate mechanism—but they are of interest because conforming to a social norm of cooperation when faced with a social dilemma corresponds precisely to Triandis's (1990) notion of collectivist culture, in which "social behavior is determined largely by goals shared with some collective, and if there is a conflict between personal and group goals, it is considered socially desirable to place collective goals ahead of personal goals" (42). Conversely, defecting in a social dilemma corresponds precisely to Triandis's conception of individualistic culture, where "it is considered acceptable for the individual to place personal goals ahead of collective goals" (42).

Social norms dictating individual sacrifice for the good of the group are one facet of Coleman's (1990) conception of social capital: "A prescriptive norm that constitutes an especially important form of social capital within a collectivity is the norm that one should forgo self-interests to act in the interests of the collectivity."[9] And Coleman is explicit about the role that collective norms have to play in resolving social dilemmas:

A norm of this sort . . . is the social capital which builds young nations (and which dissipates as they get older), strengthens families by leading members to act self-lessly in the family's interest, facilitates the development of nascent social movements from a small group of dedicated, inward-looking, and mutually rewarding persons, and in general leads persons to work for the public good. . . . norms of this sort are important in overcoming the public-good problem that exists in conjoint collectivities. (311)

Arrow (1971, 22, quoted in Elster 1989, 107-8) has a similar view of the role of "norms of social behavior." He "suggest[s] as one possible interpretation that they are reactions of society to compensate for market failure. It is useful for individuals to have some trust in each other's word. In the absence of trust, it would become very costly to arrange for alternative sanctions and guarantees, and many opportunities for mutually beneficial cooperation would have to be forgone."[10]

Norm-based behavior, in which individuals sacrifice their private self-interest for the good of the collective, is guided by nonmaterial motivations, including psychological and social feelings about fairness, reciprocity, altruism, and morality. Platteau (1994) uses the term "moral norms" in reference to such behavioral prescriptions:

Moral norms [are] understood as rules that are at least partly internalised by the agents . . . and . . . prompt them to take others' interests into account. . . . [They] are followed even when violation would be undetected, and therefore unsanctioned, because the moral act—which appears to be in conflict with the immediate or direct interests of the actor himself—is valued for its own sake. (766)

This moral or psychosocial basis of norms contrasts sharply with the other major solutions to social dilemmas, which rely on the realignment of material incentives to induce self-interest maximizers to behave in a socially desirable way: a state enforces prescribed behavior through threat of material sanctions; models of Coasean bargaining assume people accept only materially advantageous trades; and equilibria involving universal cooperation in repeated games are still noncooperative in the sense that they are self-enforcing with respect to private material payoffs.

The assumption that people are motivated by concerns other than material self-interest is a departure from pure neoclassical economic theory,[11] but it has been gaining acceptance both in the growing field of behavioral economics, which focuses particularly on departures from a narrow construction of rational behavior, and in the mainstream of the economics profession.[12] A large experimental literature has accumulated strong evidence that human behavior is influenced by altruism, feelings of fairness, and various other psychosocial motivations.[13] In one seminal study, Guth, Schmitt-berger, and Schwarze (1982) asked pairs of subjects to play an "ultimatum game," in which one subject proposed a division of a fixed sum of money between the two players, and the second either accepted, and both received the proposed shares, or rejected, and both received nothing. Although a self-interest–maximizing respondent would accept any positive offer,[14] respondents in this experiment tended to refuse offers when their shares were much below 40 percent of the sum to be divided. This willingness to forgo a material reward in order to obstruct an inequitable outcome implies that respondents were motivated by feelings of fairness or equity. Another set of well-known experiments has shown that in simulated public goods settings, individuals choose to make positive contributions even when contributing nothing is a dominant strategy from the point of view of self-interest maximization.[15] A subset of these public goods experiments has shown that people tend to make large contributions when they believe others are also making large contributions, and they tend to make small contributions when they believe others are not contributing much (Marwell and Ames 1979; Croson 1998). This behavior is described as conditional cooperation or reciprocal altruism.

Rabin (1993) has made a prominent contribution toward incorporating the kinds of behavioral regularities observed in this experimental literature into internally consistent theoretical models. Rabin proposes a fairly general[16] solution concept for

games called "fairness equilibrium," in which considerations of fairness play a part (along with material incentives) in determining people's behavior. In particular, the key behavioral assumption in the model is that people are motivated by the kind of reciprocal altruism observed by Marwell and Ames (1979) and Croson (1998): "People like to help those who are helping them, and to hurt those who are hurting them" (Rabin 1993, 1281). An important property of a fairness equilibrium—and one that carries over generally in models in which behavior is motivated by fairness or norms of reciprocity—is that multiple equilibria can arise. In a game of chicken, for instance, it is a fairness equilibrium for both parties to back down, because the mutual goodwill that such behavior generates can override the material temptation to play tough when your opponent backs down. It is also a fairness equilibrium, however, for both parties to play tough, because the antipathy generated by this interaction overrides the material incentive to back down when your opponent plays tough.[17] A norm of fairness or reciprocity can thus lead both to socially desirable and to socially undesirable outcomes. But Rabin's fairness equilibrium concept does at least admit universal cooperation in a prisoners' dilemma as one possible outcome.

A prominent contribution to the empirical literature on the benefits of social capital is Putnam's (1993) work on civic traditions in Italy. He studies the economic and political performance of 20 regions in Italy following the devolution of authority from the central government in Rome to local governments in each of the regions. His primary finding is that although the formal institutions created in each region were nearly identical, the economic and political performance of the regions varied greatly depending on their social and political history. Regions with strong civic traditions—characterized by "active engagement in community affairs, by egalitarian patterns of politics, by trust and law abidingness"—performed significantly better than regions lacking those traditions—in which "political and social participation was organized vertically . . . [m]utual suspicion and corruption were regarded as normal . . . [i]nvolvement in civic associations was scanty . . . [and] [l]awlessness was expected" (182). His general conclusion is that

success in overcoming dilemmas of collective action and the self-defeating opportunism that they spawn depends on the broader social context within which any particular game is played. Voluntary cooperation is easier in a community that has inherited a substantial stock of social capital, in the form of norms of reciprocity and networks of civic engagement. (167)

Although Putnam (1993) emphasizes how social capital can lead to desirable political and economic outcomes, he also recognizes the problem of multiple equilibria. He states,

Stocks of social capital, such as trust, norms, and networks, tend to be self-reinforcing and cumulative. Virtuous circles result in social equilibria with high levels of cooperation, trust, reciprocity, civic en-

gagement, and collective well-being. . . . Conversely, the absence of these traits in the uncivic community is also self-reinforcing. Defection, distrust, shirking, exploitation, isolation, disorder, and stagnation intensify one another in a suffocating miasma of vicious circles. (177)

Banfield (1958) gives a detailed account of a community in southern Italy caught in such a miasma—an equilibrium of low trust and low social capital, and consequently a low level of political and economic development. According to his observations during a year of fieldwork, the people of the Montegrano district[18] acted according to a norm he calls "amoral familism." This principle prescribes that one should "[m]aximize the material, short-run advantage of the nuclear family; assume that all others will do likewise" (85). Banfield (chap. 5) lists a number of the social and economic consequences of this amoral familism, including the following representative selections: "In a society of amoral familists, no one will further the interest of the group or community except as it is to his private advantage to do so"; "for a private citizen to take a serious interest in a public problem will be regarded as abnormal and even improper"; "organization (i.e., deliberately concerted action) will be very difficult to achieve and maintain." Although the norm of amoral familism entails a limited collectivism among immediate family members, these passages indicate that, with respect to all other social groups, it epitomizes an individualistic culture. Banfield argues that, by preventing the community from developing any political capacity for animating collective action, this amoral familism contributed to the region's economic stagnation.

The problem of forming cooperative relationships between members of a social group larger than the family is central to Fukuyama's (1995) study of the role of trust in "the creation of prosperity." His thesis is that in collectivist cultures it is possible to form economic enterprises of greater size and complexity than is possible in individualistic societies where trust cannot be placed in anyone outside the family. The ability of "business organizations to move beyond the family rather rapidly and to create a variety of new, voluntary social groups that were not based on kinship" has been a necessary condition for the development of the "large, modern, rationally organized, professionally managed corporations" (57). He supports his thesis with detailed analyses of Japan and Germany[19]—which he classifies as relatively collectivist and economically successful—and China, Italy, France, and Korea—which he classifies as relatively familistic and less successful at large and complex economic enterprises requiring cooperation among non-kin. Like Putnam, he stresses the importance of informal voluntary organizations, even nonprofit ones like schools, hospitals, churches, and charities, in forming the social capital upon which the creation of formal economic enterprises depends.

Like the studies of Putnam, Banfield, and Fukuyama, most of the empirical work on the economic benefits of collectivism or social capital

has been based on single cases or analyses of a small number of countries. A recent article by Knack and Keefer (1997), however, tests the ideas from this literature using cross-country data. Their study uses data from the World Values Survey, a set of interviews administered to thousands of respondents in each of a large sample of both industrialized and developing countries. The survey contains hundreds of items related to attitudes about family life, work, religion, and other personal values. The main item that Knack and Keefer use as a measure of a country's social capital is the proportion of subjects in a country responding yes to the question, "Generally speaking, would you say that most people can be trusted, or that you can't be too careful in dealing with people?"[20] Knack and Keefer are duly cautious about problems of endogeneity and causality, but for the 29 market economies included in the study they find that, controlling for levels of income, education, and private investment, their measure of trust is positively related to growth in per capita income. They find that

a ten-percentage point increase in [trust] is associated with an increase in growth of four-fifths of a percentage point. A one standard deviation change in trust (14 percentage points) is associated with a change in growth of more than one-half (.56) of a standard deviation, nearly as large as the standardized coefficient for primary education (.64). (1260)

This statistical evidence complements the previous case study work on social capital and begins to answer Solow's critique that "if social capital is to be more than a 'buzz-word' its stock 'should be somehow measurable, even inexactly' " (Knack and Keefer 1997, 1255, quoting from Solow 1995).

3. ECONOMIC DEVELOPMENT PROMOTES COLLECTIVISM AND ERODES INDIVIDUALISM

The preceding sections have examined how the collectivist or individualist nature of a society affects economic performance, for good or ill. This section and the next consider the opposite direction of causality, how economic performance—particularly growth in income and development of a capitalist market economy—affects cultural values and social norms related to collectivism and individualism.

Despite the widespread notion that the development of a market economy tends to promote individualistic behavior, there are several strands of literature that take just the opposite view. Hirschman (1977, 1982) reviews the history of an idea he dubs the "*doux-commerce* thesis." Hirschman cites several eighteenth-century political economists and philosophers—including Montesquieu, William Robertson, Condorcet, Thomas Paine, and Adam Smith—who all saw the spread of commerce as a force for improvement in human behavior. Paine's words are representative of this point of view: "[Commerce] is a pacific system, operating to cordialise mankind, by rendering Nations, as well as individuals, useful to each other. . . . The invention of commerce . . . is the greatest approach towards universal

civilization that has yet been made by any means not immediately flowing from moral principles" (Paine [1792] 1951, 215, quoted in Hirschman 1982, 1465). Hirschman (1982) sums up the point of view that

a society where the market assumes a central position . . . will produce not only considerable new wealth because of division of labor and consequent technical progress, but would generate as a by-product, or external economy, a more "polished" human type—more honest, reliable, orderly, and disciplined, as well as more friendly and helpful, ever ready to find solutions to conflicts and a middle ground for opposed opinions. . . . capitalism . . . would create, in the course of time and through the very practice of trade and industry, a set of compatible psychological attitudes and moral dispositions, that are both desirable in themselves and conducive to the further expansion of the system. (1465-66)

Hirschman (1982, 1465) points out, however, that proponents of the *doux-commerce* thesis offered scant explanation of the "precise mechanisms" through which "expanding commerce [would] have such happy effects." In particular, it is not clear whether commerce makes people more "polished" because it makes them truly more collectivist—willing to forgo some personal gain for the benefit of the community—or whether, under the system of capitalism, it is simply in people's self-interest to be "honest, reliable, orderly, and disciplined." The arguments seem to imply, however, that it is mainly self-interest, rather than a genuine internalized morality, that leads people to behave well in a market society. Hirschman (1982, 1465) quotes Samuel Ricard's (1781, 463) statement that a person of commerce,

sensing the necessity to be wise and honest in order to succeed, . . . flees vice, or at least his demeanor exhibits decency and seriousness so as not to arouse any adverse judgement on the part of present and future acquaintances; he would not dare to make a spectacle of himself for fear of damaging his credit standing and thus society may well avoid a scandal which it might otherwise have to deplore.

Similarly, Rosenberg (1990), in a study of Adam Smith's views on markets and morality, argues that Smith believed that if businessmen act beneficently, it is because "beneficence *pays*" (6). Rosenberg (1990, 11) supports this view with a passage from Smith's *Lectures* (1978, 538-39):

Whenever commerce is introduced into any country, probity and punctuality always accompany it. . . . A dealer is afraid of losing his character, and is scrupulous in observing every engagement. When a person makes perhaps 20 contracts in a day, he cannot gain so much by imposing on his neighbors, as the very appearance of a cheat would make him lose. . . . Wherever dealings are frequent, a man does not expect to gain so much by any one contract as by probity and punctuality in the whole, and a prudent dealer, who is sensible of his real interest, would rather chuse to lose what he has a right to than give any ground for suspicion.

Rosenberg (1990, 7) cites another passage from Smith's *Theory of Moral Sentiments* (1976) that similarly argues that it is material inter-est, not moral sympathy, that underlies social cohesion:

Society may subsist among different men, as among different merchants, from a sense of its utility, without any mutual love or affection; and though no man in it should owe any obligation, or be bound in gratitude to any other, it may still be upheld by a mercenary exchange of good offices according to an agreed valuation.

As Rosenberg points out, these arguments bring to mind the modern theory of repeated games, in which reputation effects and related intertemporal strategic considerations can lead purely self-interested players to behave cooperatively. What the *doux-commerce* thesis seems to describe, therefore, is how the rise of commercial markets promotes cooperative behavior but not true collectivism in the sense of a willingness to forgo some private material gain for the sake of the community.

Even if commercial exchange initially induces cooperative behavior only by making it materially profitable, it is possible that over time the widespread practice of cooperation may imbue such behavior with normative content. Sugden (1989, 95-97) has analyzed how a convention that people follow at first just out of material expediency can eventually become a moral imperative. Once "probity and punctuality" have become standard practice, departures from such behavior will be seen as ethical transgressions—even if people originally began acting with probity and punctuality for entirely amoral reasons. The materially motivated cooperation promoted by capitalism may thus also generate a degree of genuine collectivism. This scenario, in fact, offers an example of what Hirschman (1982, 1465) found lacking in the writings on the *doux-commerce* thesis: a "precise mechanism" by which the introduction of impersonal market exchange leads to increased trust and cooperation (of the genuine kind, as opposed to the expedient kind).

A related question is how a rise just in income, holding constant economic structure and distribution, affects the degree of collectivism or individualism in a society. One possibility is that as people become better off, they may in some sense be able to afford to act more on the behalf of the communal good. More precisely, suppose that people are motivated both by their private material self-interest and by psychosocial motivations.[21] When they optimize over this two-part utility function, they will equate the marginal private benefits of their actions with (their valuation of) the marginal social costs. If people's preferences exhibit diminishing marginal utility, then an increase in their private material wealth will lead to an increase in the level of their socially motivated behavior. As Galbraith (1971, quoted in Lane 1991, 342) put it, "The paradox of pecuniary motivation is that, in general, the higher the amount, the less its importance in relation to other motivations."[22]

The empirical question is whether people's preferences for wealth really do exhibit diminishing marginal utility. As people get richer, do further increments in wealth matter less and less to them? Although we do not

have direct measures of individuals' marginal utilities, there are several sources of indirect evidence on the question. Kuznets (1955, 21), in his celebrated work on changes in income distribution during economic growth, pointed out that wealthier countries tend to implement more redistributive policies like progressive taxation and public assistance to the poor. This aggregate behavior is consistent with the idea that individuals are willing to contribute more to the social good as they become better off (at least to the extent that the observed redistributive policies reflect the preferences of the relatively well-off individuals). A number of studies[23] have investigated the relationship between income and happiness using individuals' subjective reports of their sense of well-being. Reviewing those studies, Lane (1998, 471) observes that

almost all the evidence from economically advanced countries shows that although more money to the poor decreases their unhappiness and increases their satisfaction with their lives, above the poverty line this relationship between level of income and level of subjective well-being is weak or non-existent. (471)

He concludes, "Apparently, the law of diminishing returns applies to money as it does to everything that money buys" (484).

The idea that people place greater weight on nonmaterial values as they become wealthier has received extensive study and support from Inglehart (1997; see references therein for numerous earlier works by Inglehart and colleagues). That work is based on the World Values

Survey, discussed earlier in reference to the Knack and Keefer (1997) study. A principal objective of that multicountry survey of social attitudes was to examine how personal values change as economic status changes. Using data from the survey, Inglehart identifies what he calls a shift from "Modernization" to "Postmodernization" and, as one dimension of that transition, a shift from "Materialist" to "Postmaterialist" values. Like Lane, Inglehart (1997) attributes "this change in direction" to "the principle of diminishing marginal utility" (27). According to Inglehart, the "motivating force behind the whole process" of Modernization was that "industrialization was a way to get rich." This prospect was "compellingly attractive" to preindustrial society because "by getting rich, one could dispel hunger, acquire military strength, and obtain a number of other desirable things, including a much longer life expectancy" (24). But once people feel secure in their economic and physical security, there is a shift in their values from "giving top priority to physical sustenance and safety, toward heavier emphasis on belonging, self-expression, and the quality of life." Inglehart supports this hypothesis with data from the World Values Survey confirming the expectation that "societies with high *levels* of economic development should have relatively high *levels* of Postmaterialist values, and societies that have experienced relatively high rates of economic *growth* should show relatively large *differences* between the values of younger and older generations" (131).

These arguments concerning the diminishing marginal utility of income and the shift from Modernization to Postmodernization are consistent with the hypothesis that—at least in societies that have achieved a certain degree of economic and physical security—increases in economic prosperity tend to decrease people's concern with their own material welfare and increase their concern with nonmaterial values. In relation to the hypothesis being explored in this section—that increases in prosperity tend to strengthen the collectivist values of a society—the relevant question is then whether these nonmaterial values toward which economically secure people tend to turn are more collective—a concern for other members of society, social justice, cooperation, and self-sacrifice—or more individualistic—individual liberty, self-expression, and unfettered freedom of choice in important life decisions. Inglehart (1997) does not address this question in precisely these terms, and the evidence he presents is mixed. Of the items that people with higher incomes tend to endorse more strongly, some are clearly collectivist (like "Progress toward a less impersonal and more humane society"), some are more individualistic ("Protecting freedom of speech"), and others are ambiguous ("Progress toward a society in which ideas count more than money").

What we can conclude is that the arguments based on Postmaterialist values and the diminishing marginal utility of material wealth present a plausible scenario by which increasing material prosperity can lead to increased collectivism. But it does not necessarily imply that prosperity fosters collectivism: people's Postmaterial concerns might be highly individualistic. The support that the *doux-commerce* thesis offers for the idea that growth—in particular the rise of commercial markets—fosters collective values is also limited. Markets may just make it individually profitable for people motivated by individualistic values to refrain from antisocial behavior.

4. ECONOMIC DEVELOPMENT ERODES COLLECTIVISM AND PROMOTES INDIVIDUALISM

The idea that the development of markets and commerce undermines collectivist cultural values is prevalent in popular thought and also has a long tradition in several branches of social science. Arrow's (1972) characterization of this negative view of the market is representative:

The picture of a society run exclusively on the basis of exchange has long haunted sensitive observers, especially from the early days of capitalist domination. The ideas of community and social cohesion are counterposed to a drastically reduced society in which individuals meet only as buyers and sellers of commodities. (346)

This observation is made in reference to a classic study by Titmuss (1971) illustrating how market exchange can undermine prosocial or cooperative norms of behavior. Titmuss compared the blood supply system of the United States, which relied to an important degree on cash payments to donors and the sale of blood products,

to the system in the United Kingdom, which was entirely voluntary. Titmuss documented not only that the voluntary system of the United Kingdom was more efficient and safer by several objective measure, but also that

the commercialization of blood and donor relationships [in the United States] represses the expression of altruism, erodes the sense of community, lowers scientific standards, limits both personal and professional freedoms, sanctions the making of profits in hospitals and clinical laboratories, legalizes hostility between doctor and patient, subjects critical areas of medicine to laws of the marketplace, places immense social costs on those least able to bear them—the poor, the sick, and the inept—increases the danger of unethical behavior in various sectors of medical science and practice, and results in situations in which proportionately more and more blood is supplied by the poor, the unskilled, the unemployed, Negroes and other low-income groups, and categories of exploited human populations of high blood yielders. (quoted in Arrow 1972, 344)

Another version of this idea is summed up by Triandis (1990), whose distinction between collectivist and individualistic culture frames the present article. In an argument that resonates with the individualistic dimension of the value changes that Inglehart (1997) observed in the World Values Survey, he states that

as the society gets to be more ... affluent, the advantages of group living are less clear. ... The advantages of groups, such as the greater probability of survival when both successful and unsuccessful hunters or food gatherers belong to the same food ingroup, need to be examined against the advantages of individualism in the form of freedom to do one's own thing and maximize pleasure, self-actualization, and creativity without having to pay penalties of doing one's duty to the collective, doing what the group expects, meeting one's obligations, and the like. (Triandis 1990, 70)

The logic in this observation is similar to the arguments discussed in section 1 on the role of collectivism in providing insurance in poor societies lacking formal insurance markets. Similarly, Macfarlane (1979), argues that the development of a cash economy increases the independence of one generation from its predecessor: "The growth of individual property rights and of wages for cash are among the factors that give the children some resources with which to withstand their father's commands" (27).

Kranton's (1996) formal analysis of reciprocal exchange, discussed earlier in section 1 on how collectivism impedes economic development, also includes a scenario in which economic development erodes collectivism. Just as Kranton's model has an equilibrium in which personalized reciprocal exchange crowds out market exchange, the presence of an extensive commercial market can undermine the foundation on which reciprocal exchange rests. Exclusion from future personal exchanges may be the only punishment that can be levied on an individual who cheats a partner in reciprocal exchange. But if a potential cheater knows that she will have access to an anonymous market, the threat of this punishment is diminished. Without a credible punishment for cheaters, opportunistic behavior will spread, and the system of reciprocal exchange will unravel. Kranton cites an anthropological study of the !Kung of the Kalahari Desert as an example. Between 1970 and 1975, the !Kung came into increasing contact with Bantu people from neighboring regions and began trading with them. "Traditional bows and arrows were still produced, but mostly for eventual sale on a worldwide curio market. The people wore mass-produced clothing instead of animal skins. . . . An influx of money and supplies had clearly played a large part in many of these changes" (Yellen 1990, 102). As a result, "long-standing !Kung values, such as the emphasis on intimacy and interdependence, were no longer guiding behavior as effectively as they once did" (Yellen 1990, 102B). "Soon they started hoarding instead of depending on others to give them gifts, and they retreated from their past interdependence. . . . Where once social norms called for intimacy, now there was a disjunction between word and action" (Yellen 1990, 105).

Yellen (1990, 102-5) also stresses the impact of the "ready access to wealth" and "the desire to have the material goods that became readily accessible" and argues that this "influx of money and supplies had clearly played a part" in the "cultural transition" away from collectivism. Ball (1999) has developed a theory that focuses on precisely this sort of dynamic—how an influx of wealth, or rapid economic growth, can undermine norms of cooperation. The economic model in that paper has the structure of a standard collective action problem or many-person prisoners' dilemma, but people are motivated by reciprocal altruism, so that if an individual believes that most others are cooperating, she will feel a psychosocial motivation to cooperate as well. A social norm of cooperation can therefore sustain an equilibrium of universal cooperation. This widespread cooperation then leads to economic growth. As the material wealth of the society grows, however, the returns to opportunistic behavior also grow, making it more tempting for people to defect from the norm of cooperation. As more and more people begin to defect, the norm that had sustained an equilibrium of universal cooperation is eroded. Widespread defection in turn undermines economic performance, and growth turns negative. Eventually, the society arrives at a miserable equilibrium in which defection is the norm, and income stagnates at a low level. This is the "miasma" that Putnam (1993) described and that Banfield's (1958) case study illustrates. The social and economic development of Nigeria since the oil boom of the 1960s also follows this pattern closely: a rapid influx of wealth; increasing social dislocation culminating in the Biafran civil war; and, finally, economic collapse and rampant corruption.

This self-destructive growth, however, is not the only possible scenario that emerges from the model. Under alternative assumptions, it is possible for a country to reach an equilibrium at a high level of wealth, with universal cooperation. The key parameter that determines whether such a happy equilibrium can be reached is the rate at which the economy grows. If growth is very fast, then the material temptations to defect become large before the society has had time to accumulate sufficient social capital to deter opportunistic behavior. On the other hand, slow growth allows time for the gradual accretion of social capital, so that by the time the returns to opportunism become large, a strong norm of cooperation has come into existence. This norm prevents widespread defection and allows the society to move toward the equilibrium with high income and widespread cooperation. The result that *rapid* growth leads to the erosion of collectivism is also consistent with the case of the Nigerian oil boom, as well as with many commodity booms in other countries. This scenario is much like the Dutch disease phenomenon, but the underlying mechanism is related not to appreciation of the real exchange rate and the loss of export competitiveness but to the effect of rapid increases in wealth on social norms.

A final implication of the model is that countries go through a particularly precarious period at middle levels of economic development. Societies at intermediate levels of development find themselves on a razor's edge, waiting to see which effect—the growth in the material stakes of the game and temptations to defect, or the accumulation of social capital and the norm of cooperation—dominates, thereby determining whether the society ends up in the miserable or the happy equilibrium. This precariousness is described in the classic study by Adelman and Morris (1967) of social and political factors in economic development. In their analysis of cross-country statistical evidence, they find that

countries at the intermediate levels of development . . . have one outstanding characteristic in common. They are without exception transitional societies in which the process of social, economic, and political modernization has proceeded far enough to disturb or even completely shatter traditional customs and institutions without, however, proceeding far enough to set them on the path of continuous and effective development. (203)

The result in Ball's (1999) model that economic growth can undermine collectivism, and thereby ultimately undo itself, has a number of intellectual antecedents. Hirschman (1982) dubs this idea the "self-destruction thesis," and reviews several of its incarnations. The notion that capitalist growth leads to some form of social breakdown that in turn undoes the very material progress that started the process of course brings to mind Marx. Although Hirschman argues that the "cornerstone" of Marx's thought on how capitalism "carries within itself 'the seed of its own destruction' " related primarily to class structure and the relations of production, rather than with the "moral foundations" of the system, he does point out that in "early writings, Marx and Engels make much of the way in which capitalism corrodes all traditional values and institutions such as love, family, and patriotism. Everything was passing into com-

merce, all social bonds were dissolved through capitalism" (1467).

Hirsch (1976) has developed a theory that Hirschman (1982) sees as a modern version of the self-destruction thesis. Hirsch argues that in rich societies, an individual's relative economic and social status may be more important than her absolute economic and social status. This can be true for purely psychological reasons: even well-to-do people may feel bad off if they envy others who have a little more. There can also be physical reasons why relative status matters: an individual might be happy driving a small car if everyone else does, but it may be dangerous to drive the same car if everyone else is driving a large car. Positional concerns may be most important in some subtler ways, of which education is a prime example: when a person looks for a job, what might matter most is not the absolute quality of her education but the quality of her education relative to other job seekers. The crux of Hirsch's argument is that positional concerns become more important as incomes rise. If my main concern is getting enough to eat, then my satisfaction from a meal is not diminished by my neighbor's consumption of another meal. But if I want to get a high-paying job on Wall Street, it matters a lot to me whether the college I attended was more or less prestigious than that of the next person in line for an interview. The increase of positional concerns that accompanies economic development can then foster competition and reduce people's incentives to behave cooperatively or engage in collective action.

Consequently, "as individual behavior has been increasingly directed to individual advantage, habits and instincts based on communal attitudes and objectives have lost out. The weakening of traditional social values has made predominantly capitalist economies more difficult to manage" (Hirsch 1976, 118, quoted in Hirschman 1982, 1466).

Another prominent version of a self-destruction hypothesis (although one not discussed by Hirschman) is presented in Olson's *Rise and Decline of Nations* (1982). According to Olson's theory, when an industrial society is stable for a long period, special interest groups have time to organize and implement the selective incentives necessary for successful collective action. But, in accordance with a central conclusion of Olson's *Logic of Collective Action* (1965), large groups with an interest in promoting general economic growth will be less successful than small groups with redistributive, efficiency-reducing objectives. Once they mature and coalesce, these "distributional coalitions slow down a society's capacity to adopt new technologies and to reallocate resources in response to changing conditions, and thereby reduce the rate of economic growth" (1982, 65). Long-term stability of an industrial economy carries within itself the seeds of its self-destruction.

Although Olson's theory clearly fits under Hirschman's rubric of a self-destruction hypothesis, it is not exactly an example of how economic prosperity erodes collectivism. In fact, Olson's arguments in both *The* *Rise and Decline of Nations* and *The Logic of Collective Action* are based on thoroughly individualistic behavior. People engage in collective action only when—because of the implementation of selective incentives, for instance—it is in their private material self-interest to do so. The scenario described in *The Rise and Decline of Nations* does not involve a breakdown in collective norms or cooperative behavior but a realignment of individual incentives—which are assumed to be purely private and individualistic throughout the process—in ways that eventually lead to economic stagnation.

GENERAL THEMES
AND IMPLICATIONS

Attempting to fashion a unified general theory of social and economic change from the mosaic of theories and evidence presented previously—or, for that matter, from any other raw material—is probably a fruitless endeavor. Hirschman, however, offers a useful perspective on how to make sense of the many, often contradictory, ideas that have been considered here. In his review of several theories of the effect of markets on social values and behavior, he expresses only "a moderate interest in the question as to which one is *right*. . . . however incompatible the various theories may be, each may still have its 'hour of truth' and/or its 'country of truth' as it applies in a given country or group of countries during some stretch of time" (1982, 1481). It is also possible for contradictory forces to be at work in the same time and place, and simply off-set each other to some degree. None-theless, we can draw some conclu-sions about the conditions under which the various forces and scenar-ios examined previously tend to be most important. We can also draw out some general lessons about the fundamental question motivating this article: how does the individual-ist or collectivist nature of a society interact with its economic development?

The initial conditions that influ-ence how culture and the economy interact include a country's level of material prosperity or income, as well as the robustness of its political, economic, and bureaucratic institu-tions. One generalization that emerges from the arguments exam-ined previously is that the effect of a society's degree of collectivism or individualism on economic develop-ment—whether that effect is salu-tary or deleterious—will tend to be greater when institutions are less developed. An overarching idea in section 2, which considered the bene-fits of collectivism for economic development, was that when formal institutions for resolving social dilemmas—contract law, courts, reg-ulatory bureaucracies—are absent or ineffective, social capital or trust can substitute for these institutions in the maintenance of social and eco-nomic cohesion. It follows that when effective formal institutions for cor-recting market failures exist, the need for collectivist social norms to solve those problems will be smaller.

Simultaneously, however, the potential for collectivism to place a drag on economic development, the subject of section 1, may also be greatest when formal institutions are poorly developed. Tanzi (1994) argues that favoritism in the alloca-tion of jobs and other resources over which bureaucrats have authority occurs when the "arm's length princi-ple" is violated. But the violation of this principle may be a result not only of a dysfunctional collectivism but also of an absence of personnel and accounting procedures with appropriate incentives and account-ability. Greif (1994, 1997) and Kranton (1996) both analyze ways in which collectivism can impede the creation of formal institutions—Kranton shows how collectivism can crowd out the formation of commer-cial markets, and Greif shows how individualism fostered the develop-ment of courts and of commercial institutions like bills of lading and the sale of shares in firms. But a soci-ety in which the market mechanism has been firmly entrenched, and in which courts and commercial con-tracting have become well estab-lished, will have moved beyond the stage at which such problems apply. The issue of collectivism's function-ing as an alternative to formal insur-ance markets—as discussed by Bauer and Yamey (1957) and Platteau (forthcoming)—is also one that arises when formal markets are absent. Some aspects of collectiv-ism will facilitate economic develop-ment, and others will impede it, but both of these effects will be strongest when formal institutions are less developed.[24]

The nature of the other direction of causality—how economic development affects a society's cultural orientation—will also depend on initial conditions. With some exceptions, the arguments considered previously on how economic development erodes collectivism have to do with dynamics that occur in early stages of economic development, in particular during the initial introduction or expansion of market exchange in societies where kin-based or reciprocal exchange had previously prevailed. Indeed, the decreased importance of personalized transactions between members of a well-defined collective is not merely a side effect of the rise of commercial markets but one of its essential characteristics. The diminishing role of collectivism in the economic sphere that accompanies the rise of markets, however, can spill over into decreasing collectivism in other realms of economic life. Yellen (1990), for instance, details how, when the !Kung economy was integrated with the wider Bantu market, not only did economic relations change but patterns of housing[25] and dispute resolution[26] were fundamentally altered as well. Macfarlane's (1979) observation that "the growth of individual property rights and of wages for cash . . . give the children some resources with which to withstand their father's commands" (27) describes a first-generation effect that similarly applies to societies in early periods of economic development. After the initial disruption of traditional collectivism, however, further economic development may help regenerate collectivist attitudes and practices. In particular, the diminishing marginal utility of

income and material goods, which Lane (1991) and Inglehart (1997) suggested can lead people to place increasing weight on nonmaterial objectives, will be observed only after people have attained a degree of security in their basic material needs.

Finally, some of the apparent contradictions in the hypotheses examined previously can be resolved if we consider different facets of the notion of collectivism. One issue is simply the extent and composition of the group to which collective feelings and responsibilities extend. In the region studied by Banfield (1958), for instance, there existed intense collectivism among immediate family members but not beyond this small circle. In practice, from the point of view of social interaction and economic exchange, this culture of "amoral familism" functioned as a highly individualistic culture, and it suffered economically and politically from the associated lack of general trust and cooperation. Although Banfield presented an extreme case, the general implication is that the kind of collectivism that impedes economic development consists of loyalty to a relatively small group of people. Moreover, intense loyalty to a small group may also entail "hostility to outsiders" (Macfarlane 1979, 31, discussing the work of Teodor Shanin [1972], 32-33, 39, 141), limiting the possibilities for gains from trade and specialization.

On the other hand, the authors who focused on the benefits of collectivism, notably Putnam (1993) and Fukuyama (1995), described the effects of intragroup trust and cooperation in larger social groups. In Fukuyama's analysis, the critical factor underlying the economic success of Japan and Germany, the countries he classifies as collectivist, was precisely that trust extended beyond people related by blood, so that complex modern corporations could be developed. Putnam stressed the importance of social capital as a stimulus for participation in civic life—which again implies engagement with a community beyond the immediate family. This distinction between the beneficial effects of collectivism spread throughout a wide community and the harmful effects of collectivism restricted to a small group is analogous to the contrast often drawn between the social benefits of collective action among a group of villagers managing a common property resource and the social harm done by cooperation by members of a cartel who restrict output for the purpose of propping up the price of their commodity.

A related but slightly more subtle issue is not simply the size of the collective group but the degree to which collectivism, trust, or social capital extends to people with whom one has no personal relationship. Even true moral norms—which, even without the threat of material sanctions, induce people to act at least partially for the good of a group rather than exclusively for their own self-interest—can extend just to people who have some personal relationships or connections or can apply generally to anyone a person might interact with. The more that norms or collectivism apply generally and without reference to personal relationships, the

greater will be their potential for facilitating collective action and promoting economic development. In the private sector, generalized collectivism will facilitate exchange between strangers who may engage just in one-shot transactions, and in the public sector bureaucrats will respect Tanzi's "arm's length principle."

So there are at least two ways to conceive of the degree of collectivism in a society. The first, which corresponds to Triandis's conception and can be called the strength of collectivism, has to do with how tightly individual actions are constrained by the force of social norms, or the degree to which group members feel socially obligated to forgo personal gains for the benefit of the collective. But the scope of collectivism also matters. This dimension has to do with the size of the group in which the feeling of collectivism has force, the group's composition (whether just among kin, members of an ethnic group,[27] a region, a nation, or all of humanity), and whether the sense of collectivism extends to people with whom one has no personal relationship. Events that occur with economic and social development—like the introduction of markets, advances in transport and communication, and increased educational opportunities—will influence both the strength and scope of collectivism. Even if the strength of collectivism tends to decrease as its scope increases, the widening of people's networks of interaction and exchange presents opportunities for social and economic progress. Granovetter (1973) has documented this kind of phenomenon in his analysis of the "strength of weak ties": as social distance between people increases, the ties between them may become weaker, but the social and economic importance of those ties may nonetheless increase.

The creation of generalized norms, or collectivism with a wide scope, presents one of the major cultural challenges faced by a society pursuing economic development. Establishing generalized norms may mean breaking traditional obligations based on a strong sense of (perhaps narrow) collectivism. This process entails throwing off Weber's "fetters of kinship." But unless these traditional ties are replaced by a new generalized collectivism, the breaking of traditional bonds leaves the society vulnerable to widespread defection and opportunism. The critical—even precarious—nature of this transition from one cultural regime to another is highlighted by the existence of multiple equilibria in norm-based systems. If all goes well and the development of impersonal markets is accompanied by a fast and robust enough spread of generalized norms, a society can reach an equilibrium in which people are rich and cooperative. But poverty and defection also can constitute an equilibrium, and that may be where a society ends up if the dissolution of personalized collectivism is not replaced by a collectivism that transcends personal relationships.

Notes

1. Hirschman (1977) traces the evolution of this idea among seventeenth- and eighteenth-century thinkers who preceded Smith.

2. Macfarlane's (1979) central argument, however, is that English rural society was characterized by a high degree of individualism much earlier than that, at least as early as the thirteenth century.

3. Platteau (forthcoming, chap. 5) quotes similar passages from Bauer and Yamey 1957 and Lewis 1955.

4. This is one scenario that emerges from Kranton's model, but it is not the only conclusion of her article. Section 4 of the present article discusses a very different scenario that also emerges from her model.

5. For descriptions and comparisons of these phenomena, see Ostrom 1990 (2-7) and Taylor 1987 (1-20).

6. In games in which people choose from a continuous set of actions, they decide to what degree they defect or cooperate.

7. Schelling (1978, chap. 7) presents a general analysis of problems with this structure.

8. The exertion of public pressure for redistributive, perhaps growth-reducing, public policies also has the structure of a collective action problem. Olson's (1982) analysis of such activity is discussed later in the present article, in section 4.

9. Coleman's (1990, chap. 12) general conception of social capital includes a variety of other social relations, including obligations and expectations, the transmission of information, authority relations, voluntary social organizations, and business organizations. Coleman attributes the term "social capital" to Loury (1977, 1987).

10. Elster (1989), however, is not convinced of this, and after citing this passage he presents several arguments against it.

11. Although to many social scientists and most ordinary people, this proposition is self-evident.

12. As evidence of this growing mainstream acceptance, see the articles in the *American Economic Review* by Akerlof (1991) and Rabin (1993), in the *Journal of Economic Literature* by Elster (1998) and Rabin (1998), and in the *Journal of Economic Perspectives* by Camerer (1997) and Elster (1989).

13. For a comprehensive survey of this literature, see Kagel and Roth 1995.

14. Anonymity was maintained so that individuals had no incentive to develop reputations for toughness.

15. Ledyard 1995 contains a comprehensive review of this research.

16. Although his analysis is restrictive in some ways. For example, it applies only to two-person games.

17. These statements about the equilibria that can be attained are true as long as the material payoffs of the game are not too large. When the stakes get too great, the fairness equilibrium predicts that they will swamp social motivations for reciprocal cooperation or retaliation, and behavior under the fairness equilibrium will be essentially identical to behavior predicted by the Nash equilibrium (which assumes purely self-interested behavior).

18. The name Montegrano is fictitious.

19. Fukuyama treats the United States as a special case but argues that, contrary to conventional wisdom, it should be classified as a relatively collectivist (and economically successful) country like Japan and Germany.

20. Using other questions from the World Values Survey, Knack and Keefer also construct a measure of "the strength of norms of civic cooperation." Results using this indicator are similar to results using the measure based on the question about trust.

21. An assumption of this kind is made by Rabin (1993) in his analysis of the fairness equilibrium. Other models in which people face trade-offs in their desire to promote their own material self-interest and their desire to contribute to some social objective include Akerlof 1980; Lindbeck, Nyberg, and Weibull 1999; Margolis 1982; Frey 1997; Ball 1999.

22. Although, by way of exception to this principle, we can all think of individuals who, despite having amassed impressive wealth, have lost none of their zeal for acquiring more.

23. Including Diener, Diener, and Diener 1995; Easterlin 1974; Veenhoven 1993.

24. This observation, however, does not imply that culture or norms are unimportant once a strong institutional framework has been established. For example, the Titmuss (1971) study of blood distribution in the United States and the United Kingdom examined two countries with well-developed institutions but found that social norms played a large role in how the systems functioned. Other studies of economic behavior in highly developed countries—such as Akerlof's (1980) study of social norms in the workplace, and the work of Roth and Scholz (1989) and Roth,

Scholz, and Witte (1989) on taxpayer compliance—have either taken as a reasonable assumption or shown empirically that people are influenced by factors like norms and social commitment.

25. "Until the early 1970's, the traditional !Kung camp was intimate: closely spaced huts roughly described a circle, and the entryways faced inward so that from a single vantage one could see many huts. Then the arrangements changed abruptly: the average distance between huts increased, and the circular arrangement yielded to linear and other private arrays" (Yellen 1990, 104).

26. "Meanwhile, the acquisition of goods limited mobility, . . . [which] fueled still more change, in part because the people could no longer resolve serious arguments in the traditional manner, by joining relatives elsewhere in !Kung territories. With the traditional means of settling disputes now gone, the !Kung turned to local Bantu chiefs for arbitration" (Yellen 1990, 105).

27. The role of ethnicity in the evolution of social groups and in the creation or destruction of a community's collectivism has been the subject of a large literature that the present article has not addressed. Hastings (1997) provides a good entrée into that literature. See also Somer (this volume).

References

Adelman, Irma and Cynthia T. Morris. 1967. *Society, Politics and Economic Development*. Baltimore, MD: Johns Hopkins University Press.

Akerlof, George. 1980. A Theory of Social Custom, of Which Unemployment May Be One Consequence. *Quarterly Journal of Economics* 94:749-75.

———. 1991. Procrastination and Obedience. *American Economic Review Papers and Proceedings* 81:1-19.

Arrow, Kenneth. 1971. Political and Economic Evaluation of Social Effects and Externalities. In *Frontiers of Quantitative Economics*, ed. M. Intriligator. Amsterdam: North-Holland.

———. 1972. Gifts and Exchanges. *Philosophy and Public Affairs* 1:343-62.

Ball, Richard. 1999. Norms of Cooperation and Temptations to Defect in an Evolutionary Model of Economic Development. Paper presented at the annual meeting of the Society for the Advancement of Behavioral Economics, San Diego.

Banfield, Edward. 1958. *The Moral Basis of a Backward Society*. Glencoe, IL: Free Press.

Bauer, Peter T. and Basil S. Yamey. 1957. *The Economics of Under-Developed Countries*. Chicago: University of Chicago Press.

Bendix, Reinhard. 1962. *Max Weber: An Intellectual Portrait*. Garden City, NY: Doubleday.

Camerer, Colin. 1997. Progress in Behavioral Game Theory. *Journal of Economic Perspectives* 11:167-88.

Coleman, James. 1990. *Foundations of Social Theory*. Cambridge, MA: Harvard University Press, Belknap Press.

Croson, Rachel. 1998. Theories of Altruism and Reciprocity: Evidence from Linear Public Goods Games. Department of Operations and Information Management, Wharton School, University of Pennsylvania. Manuscript.

Dasgupta, Partha. 2000. Economic Progress and the Idea of Social Capital. In *Social Capital: A Multifaceted Perspective*, ed. P. Dasgupta and I. Serageldin. Washington, DC: World Bank.

Diener, Ed, Marissa Diener, and Carol Diener. 1995. Factors Predicting the Subjective Well-Being of Nations. *Journal of Personality and Social Psychology* 69:851-64.

Easterlin, Richard. 1974. Does Economic Growth Improve the Human Lot? In *Nations and Households in Economic Growth*, ed. P. A. David and M. W. Reder. Stanford, CA: Stanford University Press.

Elster, Jon. 1989. Social Norms and Economic Theory. *Journal of Economic Perspectives* 3:99-117.

———. 1998. Emotions and Economic Theory. *Journal of Economic Literature* 36:47-74.

Frey, Bruno. 1997. *Not Just for the Money*. Cheltenham, UK: Edward Elgar.

Fukuyama, Francis. 1995. *Trust: The Social Virtues and the Creation of Prosperity*. New York: Free Press.

Galbraith, John Kenneth. 1971. *The Affluent Society*. 2d ed., rev. Harmondsworth, UK: Pelican.

Granovetter, Mark. 1973. The Strength of Weak Ties. *American Journal of Sociology* 81:1360-80.

Greif, Avner. 1994. Cultural Beliefs and the Organization of Society: A Historical and Theoretical Reflection on Collectivist and Individualist Societies. *Journal of Political Economy* 102:912-50.

———. 1997. On the Interrelations and Economic Implications of Economic, Social, Political and Normative Factors: Reflections from Two Late Medieval Societies. In *The Frontiers of the New Institutional Economics*, ed. J. Drobak and J. Nye. San Diego: Academic Press.

Guth, Werner, Rolf Schmittberger, and Bernd Schwarze. 1982. An Experimental Analysis of Ultimatum Bargaining. *Journal of Economic Behavior and Organization* 3:367-88.

Hastings, Adrian. 1997. *The Construction of Nationhood: Ethnicity, Religion, and Nationalism*. New York: Cambridge University Press.

Hirsch, Fred. 1976. *Social Limits to Growth*. Cambridge, MA: Harvard University Press.

Hirschman, Albert. 1977. *The Passions and the Interests: Political Arguments for Capitalism Before Its Triumph*. Princeton, NJ: Princeton University Press.

———. 1982. Rival Interpretations of Market Society: Civilizing, Destructive or Feeble? *Journal of Economic Literature* 20:1463-84.

Inglehart, Ronald. 1997. *Modernization and Postmodernization: Cultural, Economic, and Political Change in 43 Societies*. Princeton, NJ: Princeton University Press.

Kagel, John H. and Alvin E. Roth, eds. 1995. *The Handbook of Experimental Economics*. Princeton, NJ: Princeton University Press.

Kakar, Sudhir. 1978. *The Inner World*. New York: Oxford University Press.

Knack, Stephen and Philip Keefer. 1997. Does Social Capital Have an Economic Payoff? A Cross-Country Investigation. *Quarterly Journal of Economics* 112:1251-88.

Kranton, Rachel. 1996. Reciprocal Exchange: A Self-Sustaining System. *American Economic Review* 86:830-51.

Kuznets, Simon. 1955. Economic Growth and Inequality. *American Economic Review* 45:1-28.

Lane, Robert. 1991. *The Market Experience*. New York: Cambridge University Press.

———. 1998. The Joyless Market Economy. In *Economics, Values, and Organization*, ed. A. Ben-Ner and L. Putterman. New York: Cambridge University Press.

Ledyard, John O. 1995. Public Goods: A Survey of Experimental Research. In *The Handbook of Experimental Economics*, ed. J. H. Kagel and A. E. Roth. Princeton, NJ: Princeton University Press.

Lewis, Arthur. 1955. *The Theory of Economic Growth*. London: Allen & Unwin.

Lindbeck, Assar, Sten Nyberg, and Jorgen Weibull. 1999. Social Norms, the Welfare State, and Voting. *Quarterly Journal of Economics* 114:1-35.

Loury, Glenn. 1977. A Dynamic Theory of Racial Income Differences. In *Women, Minorities, and Employment Discrimination*, ed. P. A. Wallace and A. Le Mund. Lexington, MA: Lexington Books.

———. 1987. Why Should We Care About Group Inequality. *Social Philosophy and Policy* 5:249-71.

Macfarlane, Alan. 1979. *The Origins of English Individualism*. New York: Cambridge University Press.

Margolis, Howard. 1982. *Selfishness, Altruism, and Rationality*. Chicago: University of Chicago Press.

Marwell, Gerald and Ruth Ames. 1979. Experiments on the Provision of Public Goods. I: Resources, Interests, Group Size, and the Free-Rider Problem. *American Journal of Sociology* 84:1335-60.

North, Douglass. 1981. *Structure and Change in Economic History*. New York: Norton.

———. 1989. Institutions and Economic Growth: An Historical Introduction. *World Development* 17:1319-32.

———. 1990. *Institutions, Institutional Change, and Economic Performance*. New York: Cambridge University Press.

Olson, Mancur. 1965. *The Logic of Collective Action*. Cambridge, MA: Harvard University Press.

———. 1982. *The Rise and Decline of Nations*. New Haven, CT: Yale University Press.

Ostrom, Elinor. 1990. *Governing the Commons*. New York: Cambridge University Press.

Paine, Thomas. [1792] 1951. *The Rights of Man*. New York: E. P. Dutton.

Platteau, Jean-Philippe. 1994. Behind the Market Stage Where Real Societies Exist—Part II: The Role of Moral Norms. *Journal of Development Studies* 30:753-817.

———. Forthcoming. *Institutions, Social Norms and Economic Development*. Chur, Switzerland: Harwood Academic.

Putnam, Robert. 1993. *Making Democracy Work: Civic Traditions in Modern*

Italy. Princeton, NJ: Princeton University Press.

Rabin, Matthew. 1993. Incorporating Fairness into Game Theory and Economics. *American Economic Review* 83:1281-1302.

———. 1998. Psychology and Economics. *Journal of Economic Literature* 36:11-46.

Ricard, Samuel. 1781. *Traité Général du Commerce*. Amsterdam: Chez E. van Harrett et Soeters.

Rosenberg, Nathan. 1990. Adam Smith and the Stock of Moral Capital. *History of Political Economy* 22:1-17.

Roth, Jeffrey A. and John T. Scholz, eds. 1989. *Taxpayer Compliance*. Vol. 2, *Social Science Perspectives*. Philadelphia: University of Pennsylvania Press.

Roth, Jeffrey A., John T. Scholz, and Ann Dryden Witte, eds. 1989. *Taxpayer Compliance*. Vol. 1, *An Agenda for Research*. Philadelphia: University of Pennsylvania Press.

Schelling, Thomas. 1978. *Micromotives and Macrobehavior*. New York: Norton.

Shanin, Teodor. 1972. *The Awkward Class*. Oxford: Clarendon Press.

Singerman, Diane. 1995. *Avenues of Participation: Family, Politics and Networks in Urban Quarters of Cairo*. Princeton, NJ: Princeton University Press.

Smith, Adam. 1976. *The Theory of Moral Sentiments*. Ed. David D. Raphael and Alec L. MacFie. New York: Oxford University Press.

———. 1978. *Lectures on Jurisprudence*. Ed. Ronald L. Meek, David D. Raphael, and Peter Stein. New York: Oxford University Press.

Solow, Robert. 1995. But Verify. *New Republic* 11:36.

Sugden, Robert. 1989. Spontaneous Order. *Journal of Economic Perspectives* 4:85-97.

Tanzi, Vito. 1994. Corruption, Governmental Activities, and Markets. IMF Working Paper 94/99, International Monetary Fund, Washington, DC.

Taylor, Mark. 1987. *The Possibility of Cooperation*. New York: Cambridge University Press.

Titmuss, Richard. 1971. *The Gift Relationship: From Human Blood to Social Policy*. New York: Pantheon Books.

Triandis, Harry. 1990. Cross-Cultural Studies of Individualism and Collectivism. *Nebraska Symposium on Motivation, 1989* 37:41-133.

Veenhoven, Ruut, with the assistance of Joop Ehrhardt, Monica Sie Dhian Ho, and Astrid de Vries. 1993. *Happiness in Nations: Subjective Appreciation of Life in 56 Nations, 1946-1992*. Dordrecht, Holland: Reidel.

Weber, Max. 1930. *The Protestant Ethic and the Spirit of Capitalism*. London: G. Allen & Unwin.

Yellen, John. 1990. The Transformation of the Kalahari !Kung. *Scientific American* 262:96-105.

Poverty and Public
Celebrations in Rural India

By VIJAYENDRA RAO

ABSTRACT: This article examines the paradox that very poor house-holds spend large sums of money on celebrations. Using qualitative and quantitative data from South India, it demonstrates that expenditures on weddings and festivals can be explained by integrating an understanding of how identity is shaped in the Indian context with an economic analysis of decision making under conditions of extreme poverty and risk. It argues that publicly observable celebrations have two functions: they provide a space for maintaining social reputations and webs of obligation, and they serve as arenas for status-enhancing competitions. The first role is central to maintaining the networks essential for social relationships and coping with poverty, while the second is a correlate of mobility that may become more prevalent as incomes rise. Development policies that privilege individual over collective action reduce the incentives for the former while increasing them for the latter, thus reducing social cohesion while increasing conspicuous consumption.

Vijayendra Rao is an economist with an interest in anthropology. He received his Ph.D. in economics at the University of Pennsylvania, held postdoctoral positions at the Universities of Chicago and Michigan, and taught at Williams College before moving to the Development Research Group of the World Bank. He mixes the field-oriented collection of qualitative and quantitative data with economic methods to gain a more contextualized and grounded understanding of household behavior in poor communities.

NOTE: I am indebted to Sita Reddy for invaluable discussions and to Francis Bloch and Sonalde Desai for our joint work that informs part of the analysis in this article. I am grateful to Rama Ranee, A. C. Komala, and the National Council for Applied Economic Research for help with conducting the fieldwork and to Christopher Clague, Karla Hoff, Michael Woolcock, and an anonymous referee for constructive comments. The findings, interpretations, and conclusion of this article are those of the author and should not be attributed to the World Bank.

P ARADOXICALLY, families who earn barely enough to survive spend vast amounts of money on celebrations. In the rural South Indian data[1] I analyze in this article, a typical household spends approximately seven times its annual income on a daughter's marriage—on celebrating the wedding and on dowry transfers to the groom's family. Moreover, 15 percent of its expenditures, on average, are spent on celebrating village festivals. Poor households tend to find such large sums of money by going severely into debt at interest rates that range from 100 to 300 percent per year, which leads to chronic indebtedness and, sometimes, bonded labor. Despite the importance of these expenditures, the economics literature has largely ignored them, perhaps because they fall into the realm of nonrational behavior. However, given their pervasiveness, and the dominant role accorded to economics in the formulation of policy, this omission can have serious consequences for the design of policy interventions. Money spent on celebrations is, after all, money not spent on food, education, health, and other productive inputs.

What explains this paradox? Are celebrations wasteful? In this article, I will examine the factors underlying expenditures on festivals and weddings with qualitative and quantitative data from South India. In this introductory section, I sketch a general conceptual model of publicly observable events and the role they play in Indian village life. I will then illustrate this conceptual framework by examining aspects of wedding- and festival-related behaviors. While the article relies on fieldwork from the South Indian state of Karnataka, I believe that the analysis is applicable to other parts of South Asia. With changes in structure and context, the basic points are perhaps also relevant to human behavior in other non-Western societies. Working within a context with which I am relatively familiar, however, allows me to provide a more nuanced perspective on an important aspect of the cultural economics of behavior in poor households.[2]

In rural Indian life, celebrations tend to mark important transitions. A wedding marks the transition of a woman from daughter to wife and is the central event in her life cycle (Fruzzetti 1990). Festivals mark important events in the life cycle of a village—a religious event or a harvest (Fuller 1992). They are rituals, marking events that shape identity and meaning. They are also, necessarily, public. If they were private, the change in status would not be recognized, because others would not observe the ritual. The public nature of celebrations thus provides an opportunity for individuals to demonstrate, to signal,[3] to the world that an important time has arrived, an important transition completed. As public events, they also provide an opportunity for actions to be scrutinized and commented upon and for judgments to be made. Therefore, celebrations can be thought of as mechanisms where social and economic status is demonstrated, reified, and often enhanced.

How do public rituals shape identity and affect preferences? To understand this, it is necessary to understand anthropological conceptions of how Indians define their identities and shape their perceptions of themselves. In *Homo Hierarchicus*, a seminal work in Indian anthropology, Louis Dumont (1970) argued that Hindu Indians are fundamentally different from Western individuals in that they see themselves within the context of the caste system as part of a strict ritual hierarchy. Their sense of individuality is subservient to their identification with their family, caste, and village. Marriot and Inden (1977) modified this to say that an Indian is not an individual as much as a "dividual." A dividual's identity is made up of different transferable "substances" that they give and receive in their interactions with others. These substances then come together in a dynamic, negotiated, interactive manner to achieve a sense of self. Thus personhood is defined entirely in terms of one's relationships to others.

In more recent work, Mines (1994) takes issue with this to argue that Indians have a well-defined sense of individuality but that this individuality is quite different from the Western prototype. Indian individuality, according to Mines, is more exterior or civic than personal and is crucially conditioned by how others estimate and evaluate the person. What kind of person is he? How influential is he? Furthermore, this "civic individuality" is determined within the context to which the individual belongs: his caste, religion, and community. It is also spatially defined by the "size and locality of the constituencies that form a person's social contexts" (22).

Thus one's sense of self is fundamentally influenced by the people whom one knows and interacts with. Mines further argues that it is an individuality of inequality; that is, people of higher status and rank have individualities that are more strongly emphasized—individuality is graded and ranked. Taking all of this into consideration, we see that Indians are strongly driven by status and rank, and the status and rank are not simply a matter of individual or relative wealth but are derived from the size and influence of their familial and social networks and from the public demonstration of access to these networks.[4] The size and quality of one's networks thus have an inherent value, what Appadurai (1990) defines as "the prime value of sociality" (188), and are not only a means to an end.

An Indian, therefore, while not entirely *Homo hierarchicus*, is also quite different from *Homo economicus*. What differentiates Indian individuality from the Western, more than anything else, is Indians' deep anxiety about what others will think of them. And what others think of them is fundamentally shaped by their civic identity: how many important people they know; how closely they are adhering to the behaviors expected from someone in their sociocultural category—that is, are they being good fathers, mothers, sons, headmen, or priests? Thus, unlike the caricature of a rational individual embodied in most economic models, Indians do not live by consumption alone but fundamentally by the perceptions of others.

This perception shapes their identity, their sense of themselves, and their sense of others' sense of them. Their status and role, within the context of their caste and group, therefore drives their behavior. If they do not satisfy the obligations assigned to them by their place within society, they will be penalized with a loss of status or rank and looked upon with less respect, perhaps even with shame. This does not mean that Indians are not rational but merely that their rationality is conditioned by structures and practices derived from their social and cultural context, just as much as it is subject to economic motives and constraints.[5]

Status and rank require constant maintenance (Goffman 1959). In order to participate in social relationships, people have to know if others are good individuals who act in accordance with the their socially delimited roles. Thus the maintenance of rank and stature requires public demonstrations of actions fitting the expected behaviors of one's rank within one's social group. Note that the effort spent in maintaining rank does not preclude individuals from moving up. Wealth, a prestigious job, or the acquisition of a rich husband or son-in-law is desired because they are preconditions to the acquisition of greater public regard and respect. But in order to acquire the higher social rank usually associated with greater assets, these attributes of mobility must not just be acquired but demonstrated by behavior that accords with the class of people who possess such assets. Otherwise, while one may achieve economic mobility, it will not translate into a higher social rank. Non-Indians may also value rank and social status, but Indians face powerful incentives to regularly demonstrate that status, because their behavior is under constant, intimate, and structured scrutiny.

Networks have an inherent value, but in the context of the extremely risky environment of Indian village life, the web of obligations that define the extent of one's networks are also central elements of coping strategies against risk and poverty. The recent development economics literature has focused on empirical investigations of informal insurance, measuring the extent to which families are able to smooth consumption by relying on village networks (for example, Townsend 1994; Udry 1994). It is clear that, in the absence of networks, life would be unimaginably hard. When crops fail or jobs are lost or the main wage-earner dies (all quite routine events in the harsh reality of rural life), one relies on one's friends and relatives to cope. The greater the level of respect and regard one receives from friends and relatives, the easier it is to ask for their help. Networks, however, are useful not only for unanticipated shocks but also for more everyday forms of serious but predictable problems. Households with better connections may be able to get access to better jobs (Collier and Garg 1999) or find ways of getting lower prices for food, or they may be able to get better information on potential marriage partners for their children. Therefore, respect and regard do not merely have direct utility; they are also central elements in poverty alleviation strategies. What others think of a person is not important just for its own sake—it can mean the difference between life and death.

Given this, celebrations, which are a time of intense public scrutiny, become arenas where reputations are managed and enhanced. Life-cycle events become theaters where public reputations are maintained, and stadiums where people compete in games of status competition, going beyond their role as milestones. The rules of the game are determined by kinship systems, ritual calendars, the distribution of wealth and caste, and other structural endowments that are slow to change and therefore can be considered as exogenous constraints in the short term. Because these structures provide rules for what is considered appropriate behavior, they determine the criteria by which people are judged. They are part of the capability set (Sen 1988) available for individuals and families to maximize their preferences. Thus, culturally determined preferences and constraints interact with economic motives to create powerful incentives for expenditures on public celebrations, particularly for individuals seeking social mobility.

The format of the rest of this article is as follows: I present an investigation of wedding celebrations in the next section, followed by an analysis of festivals in section 3. Section 4 concludes the article and presents some policy implications.

ON WEDDING CELEBRATIONS

Wedding celebrations in rural India can seem extremely lavish to an outsider, especially in contrast to the extreme poverty of rural Indian life, with large numbers of people invited for feasts and ceremonies that can go on for several days.[6] Many weddings seem less influenced by norms in the village than by patterns in cities, and celebrations of poor families imitate the more extravagant patterns common in richer families. Take the case of a wedding of the daughter of a small agriculturist with two acres of land that I observed. The teenage daughter was marrying a young man who had finished his B.A. and had a job as a low-level clerk in the city. The groom was dressed in a crisp gray suit, the bride in a silk sari. A large number of guests, including a (minor) local politician, had been invited, and the newlyweds were driven away at the end of the ceremony in a large white Ambassador car. When asked why he had spent so much money on a wedding that was obviously well beyond his means, the father said that his daughter had married into a "good family" (the groom's father was a relatively wealthy landowner from another village), and he wanted to have a "show."

Thus wedding celebrations have a lot to do with social status and prestige. Mobility within a village is often achieved by imitating the behaviors of families of higher social orders (Srinivas 1966). For the parents of a daughter in particular, a marriage is potentially the most important source of mobility since marrying into a good family can greatly enhance how a family is viewed by its peers, and a prestigious match is an occasion for great celebration and status displays. This may explain why some weddings are particularly lavish. When a family marries into a rich family, it is in the interest of the former to demonstrate this to the rest of the village, particularly if the rest of the village does not know the new in-laws. The most effective way of signaling a family's newfound affinity-derived status is to have as lavish a wedding as they can possibly afford. On the flip side, if a family marries into a poor local family—one well known to everyone in the village—this may also be an occasion for celebration, but lavish displays are no longer necessary since not much can be gained by signaling.

To better understand the nature of marriage expenditures in India, it might help to outline the basic nature of Indian marriage markets:[7]

1. Marriage is restricted to endogamous groups; that is, people are permitted to marry only within a well-defined set of families who make up their subcaste.

2. Marriage is patrilocal—brides leave their parents' home to live with their husbands. Marriages are arranged for both grooms and brides by their parents, and the preferences of the parents usually drive all the choices and arrangements.

3. Marriage is considered final and, while there are cases of separation, divorce is not an option.

4. The burden of celebrating a marriage almost always falls on the parents of the bride.

There is a considerable amount of variation between subcastes in terms of marriage and kinship patterns (Karve 1965). While most prohibit marriage outside the subcaste, the size of the group can vary a great deal. Some communities in South India prefer marriage within a circle of close relatives, usually between a man and the daughter of his elder sister or between the children of brothers. Such consanguineous marriages are becoming increasingly rare because suitable grooms are difficult to find. Another characteristic of Indian kinship systems is the variation in their prohibition against marriage between partners who belong to the same village. In the language of kinship studies, such communities whose members marry outside their own village are called "village exogamous." In Karnataka state, where the data for the present article are from, the northern districts show a tendency toward village exogamy, while in the southern districts the majority do not prefer it and may even have prohibitions against it. Such preferences and prohibitions are prescribed by the customs of the community and are exogenous to the choices of households, who may suffer social sanctions by violating them.

Getting one's daughter married, within these constraints, is considered an Indian parent's primary duty; to have an older unmarried daughter is a tremendous misfortune with large social and economic costs. The costs of getting a daughter married, however, have been steadily rising in real terms across the Indian subcontinent. In Karnataka state, dowries have been increasing substantially for several decades (Caldwell, Reddy, and Caldwell 1988), and dowries in the present data average six times the annual income of a family. There are several possible reasons why dowries in India may have increased, but it is beyond the scope of this article to examine them.[8] My focus here is on wedding celebrations, and in particular on the narrow question of whether wedding celebrations are, at least partly, driven by a desire for higher social rank.

Every wedding requires a minimum level of expenditure that depends upon norms in the community. A basic celebration may help maintain one's stature within the village, but a lavish wedding represents something else. Spending more than what is expected provides people in the village with new information that helps them update their perception of one's social status. In particular, if the bride is marrying a prestigious groom—prestigious because he is either rich or well educated—then this marriage alliance has status benefits for the wife's family. However, a lavish wedding without some real change in status may simply give people the impression that the spender is extravagant.

Thus, if families are rational, then this extra money should be spent only when there is new information to communicate. If there is nothing to show off, it would not be rational for a father to spend anything beyond the minimum (maintenance-level) expenditure required to fulfill his social obligations. Furthermore, even if the bride were marrying a rich groom, there would be no new information to communicate to the village if everyone in the village already knew that the groom was rich. The very existence of the marriage alliance provides enough information for the village to update its opinion on the social standing of the bride's family. Therefore, lavish weddings would only make sense when the bride is marrying a prestigious groom *and* when the village has no information about the groom and his family.

The variations in village exogamy provide us with a way to translate this point into a testable hypothesis. When marriage rules prohibit partners from the same village from getting married, then the bride family's home village will not know much about the groom's family. On the other hand, if brides and grooms from the same village customarily marry each other, then the village should have very good information on the groom's family. Thus, if lavish weddings serve as a means of increasing status, it is only when the groom is a high-status "catch" from another village that we should observe particularly lavish weddings.

This hypothesis will be tested by estimating a multivariate regression of wedding celebration expenses on the characteristics of the groom and bride and their families, the number of alternate partners in the marriage market, and whether the subcaste that the family belongs to practices village exogamy.[9] I will interact the village exogamy variable with the education and wealth of the groom. If these interaction terms are positive, we can infer that it is only when grooms are educated and wealthy (that is, prestigious) and also from an outside village—resulting in a lack of information about them in the bride's village—that marriage expenses are significantly higher. This would support the hypothesis that lavish celebrations are a signal of improved social status, communicating new information about mobility via a costly action.

Wealth will be measured by whether the families possess any land, since about 40 percent of the households are landless. To measure the human capital of the husband and wife, I use their years of schooling and their age at marriage. Alternatives in the marriage market are measured by the date of the marriage (to capture exogenous trends) and the ratio of the number of women to the number of men at marriageable ages (defined as women aged 10-19 and men aged 20-29) measured at the year of the marriage for the bride's home district. In addition to these variables, I also include dummies for whether the family is Muslim or belongs to a disadvantaged or scheduled caste.

Data and results

The sample consists of 800 households randomly chosen from five dis-

tricts spread across north and south Karnataka state. Seven villages from each district were randomly chosen, and 20-30 households were then randomly selected from each village. The marriage data that are employed in this article were collected retrospectively from the married women in the sample. About a third of the households in the sample did not have any ever-married women of reproductive age and therefore did not answer the women's questions. Of those that did have eligible women, many did not provide complete answers to the retrospective marriage questions, requiring that they be dropped from the analysis. After eliminating about 10 outliers, we are left with a sample of about 300 women spread across the five districts. There are no significant differences between this subsample and the complete sample for those questions that were answered by all the households.

Table 1 reports summary statistics from the survey data. The average wedding celebration expenses amount to about 3000 rupees, 11 percent as large as the average dowry, which is 26,000 rupees. Average schooling levels are 4.3 years for men and 2.9 years for women. The average age at marriage is about 25 years for men and 17 years for women. The mean marriage took place in 1980, with a standard deviation of 8.4, showing that the marriages span a fairly long time. Over this period, the average marriage squeeze ratio is 1.13, indicating a surplus of women in the marriage market. About 9 percent of the sample is Muslim, and 22 percent belong to scheduled castes. Finally,

TABLE 1
WEDDING CELEBRATION: MEANS AND STANDARD DEVIATIONS

Variable	Mean	Standard Deviation
Net dowry payment (1994 rupees)	26,309	238,069
Wedding celebration expenses (1994 rupees)	2,899	374
Marriage squeeze ratio	1.130	0.146
Year of marriage	80.4	8.4
Wife's schooling (years)	2.94	4.02
Husband's schooling (years)	4.25	4.53
Muslim (dummy)	0.093	0.290
Scheduled caste/tribe (dummy)	0.222	
Husband owned land at marriage (dummy)	0.603	
Wife owned land at marriage (dummy)	0.6	
Husband's age at marriage	24.8	4.3
Wife's age at marriage	17.123	3.464
Village exogamous (dummy)	0.680	
Bidar (dummy)	0.230	
South Kanara (dummy)	0.212	
Kodagu (dummy)	0.201	
Kolar (dummy)	0.114	
Mysore (dummy)	0.241	
Monthly transfers from husband's family	26	292
Emergency transfers from husband's family in the last four years	32	294
N = 297		

68 percent of the households customarily practice village exogamy.

Table 2 reports estimates for the wedding celebration ordinary least squares (OLS) regressions. Looking at the regression with no interactions, we see that grooms with land have celebrations that cost a statistically significant 1394 rupees more than those of landless grooms. Families that belong to subcastes that practice village exogamy have marriage expenses about 1500 rupees higher than those who marry within the village. The results of the interaction effects between village exogamy and the wealth and education of the husband are also consistent with the hypothesis presented above. Note also that village exogamy interacts with whether the groom's family has land such that wedding expenses increase by 2600 rupees, an increase that is significant at the 5 percent level. Similarly, an additional year of groom's schooling in families that practice exogamy increases marriage expenses by about 280 rupees. Thus groom quality significantly matters only for those families practicing village exogamy, where the bride's village has no knowledge of the groom's family.[10] These results are therefore consistent with the notion that wedding celebrations are driven by a desire to provide information about

TABLE 2
WEDDING CELEBRATION EXPENSES:
OLS REGRESSIONS (ROBUST STANDARD ERRORS)

| | Wedding Celebration Expenses | | | |
| | No Interactions | | With Interactions | |
Variable	Coefficient	$\|t\|$	Coefficient	$\|t\|$
Marriage squeeze ratio	−15,596.0	0.87	−15,496.9	0.92
Year of marriage	−140.3	2.52	−154.5	2.57
Wife's schooling (years)	−177.4	0.84	−175.0	0.82
Husband's schooling (years)	267.3	1.10	59.5	0.33
Muslim	840.8	0.48	1,119.5	0.71
Scheduled caste/tribe	−82.2	0.12	131.2	0.15
Wife's land at marriage	80.1	0.09	434.0	0.56
Husband's land at marriage	1,393.6	2.12	−371.5	0.42
Husband's age at marriage	12.3	0.19	−12.2	0.19
Wife's age at marriage	171.7	2.14	199.4	2.25
Village exogamous	1,537.0	2.76	−1,043.4	1.08
Exogamous husband's schooling	—	—	276.1	1.84
Exogamous husband's land	—	—	2,577.3	2.28
Bidar	494.0	0.42	256.7	0.16
South Kanara	2,152.3	0.38	2,244.3	0.22
Kodagu	4,281.0	3.33	4,076.2	3.23
Kolar	−2,279.4	2.73	−2,383.7	2.83
Constant	24,676.8	1.08	27,369.1	1.21
F for joint significance	6.52		5.58	
R-squared	0.21		0.23	

the bride family's enhanced social status.

ON FESTIVALS

Festivals are also centrally important to the lives of Indians (Fuller 1992).[11] Weddings may cost more, but they occur only two or three times in the lifetime of a household head, while festivals take place every few months. Festivals are different from marriages in that they are collective behaviors where everyone celebrates an event simultaneously.

A description of the first time I saw a village festival might be instructive. My team and I had spent several days in a village interviewing poor families from the potter caste. On the sixth day, we were warned that it would be "difficult to find people in their homes [the next day] because they will all be at Mariamma's[12] festival." When we arrived the next morning, the village had been transformed beyond recognition. The women had put on gold and silver jewelry and had jasmine flowers in their hair. There were colorful fragrant garlands strewn on poles around the village and on the pillars of the local temple, along with festive decorations and balloons. Two loudspeakers tied to the temple's roof blared film songs. And then, at about 10 in the morning, the procession began. It was led by a group of traditional musicians. They were followed a brightly painted bullock cart carrying an image of the goddess, swathed in silk, gold, and flowers and tended by two priests. Immediately behind the bullock cart was a group of about 10 important-looking men and women, followed by hordes of dancing children. I asked some people in the crowd who these important-looking people were and was told that they were from the families who had made the largest contributions to the festival and had helped organize the celebrations. The festival was obviously a very expensive event entirely financed by voluntary contributions; and all the contributions, whether small or big, were made public at an auspicious time when the Temple Committee, which organized the event, announced them on loudspeakers.

Sociologists since Durkheim ([1912] 1965) have argued that collective celebrations serve an important function by providing occasions when communities reify their group identity. Turner (1982), for instance, describes festivals as "generally connected with expectable culturally shared events." He suggests that, when a social group celebrates a particular event, it "celebrates itself" by "manifesting in symbolic form what it conceives to be its essential life." Thus festivals may serve to build social cohesion by reinforcing ties within a community. Furthermore, by providing a specific time and place within which families can demonstrate their commitment to being responsible members of the village community and also compete for status with others, festivals provide a

socially sanctioned arena for publicly observable action. By providing a space where everyone can view everyone else's behavior, they also generate "common knowledge"[13] and help solve the coordination problems inherent in collective action (Chwe 1998). In this sense, they help build the capacity for collective action.[14] Thus, at the village level, festivals enhance social cohesion and build trust while providing an arena in which families can maintain and enhance their social status.

The data I have are not adequate to study the relationship between festivals and social cohesion at the village level. Therefore, in the statistical analysis, I focus on a household-level analysis of some of the relationships discussed previously. In particular, I look at the determinants and effects of festival expenditures. Are they driven by private motives, or are they better thought of as altruistic contributions toward a public good? Are households that spend more money on festivals held in higher esteem by their peers? Does festival participation have real economic returns? It is possible that families spend money on festivals for no other reason than pure entertainment, particularly in rural areas with limited access to movie theaters and television sets. But if festivals were pure entertainment, expenditures on them should not generate any other returns.

To test these hypotheses, I regress a household's festival expenditures against various household characteristics, including the household head's age, the number of adults and children in the family, the head's education, the land owned by the household in the past and the present, and the household's income. I also include the number of girls in the family who are of marriageable age. If their presence raises festival expenditures, it is consistent with the notion that they are being put on display in order to find good spouses, thereby indicating that festivals provide an opportunity to communicate information for private gain. Finally, in order to see if festival expenditures are driven by demonstration effects, I include the festival expenditure of the neighboring household as an explanatory variable, as well as a set of village dummy variables.

In addition to analyzing the determinants of festival expenditures, I also examine whether festival expenditures generate social and economic returns. I examine two types of returns: the family's social status and a household-specific index of the unit prices for food faced by the family. The social status variable is constructed by asking each family in the village about its sense of the respect and social standing accorded to other families in the village. This is coded into a measure with four levels, a score of 1 denoting the lowest level of social standing and 4 denoting the highest.[15]

The unit food price index requires some explanation.[16] In the process of doing fieldwork, I noticed that there were large variations in the unit prices charged for food to different members of the village. The primary reason for this was quantity discounts, since many of the families were severely liquidity constrained and were compelled to purchase food

once a week on payday. The fieldwork revealed that households that had good social relationships were able to get around this by forming shopping clubs that would buy food in bulk and then distribute it among the members. Some well-regarded individuals were able to get from the shopkeepers food on credit, which again permitted them to get around liquidity constraints. Thus socially well-connected households seemed to suffer less from high prices. On the other hand, households that did not have good social relationships faced markups of 15-40 percent on their food purchases. To get a summary measure of the variation in unit prices across households, I construct a Laspeyres price index that uses the prices and quantities purchased by the median household as a base to calculate price variations, for a basket of goods, for everyone in the sample. With this method, the median household's index number is 100, and a household with an index of 200 faces prices that are double the sample median.

The social status and price index variables will be regressed against festival expenditures,[17] the household head's age, the number of adults and children in the family, the head's education, the land owned by the household in the past and the present, and the household's income, along with a set of village dummy variables.

Data and statistical analysis

The data used in this article are from a census survey of an endogamous subcaste of potters spread across three villages, Halli,

TABLE 3
FESTIVAL EXPENDITURES: MEANS AND STANDARD DEVIATIONS OF VARIABLES

Variable	Mean	Standard Deviation
Annual festival expenditures (1994 rupees)	1,973	1,305
Annual income	14,471	14,143
Father's land holdings in acres	1.16	3.89
Land in acres	0.59	1.22
Age of household head	45.3	13.1
Maximum years of schooling within the family	4.5	4.1
Number of family members older than 16 years	3.1	1.4
Children aged 10-16 years	0.65	0.82
Girls aged 10-16 years	0.31	0.53
Children less than 10 years	1.09	1.17
Annual F_{-j}	84,334	5,441
Average festival expenditures of neighbors	1,952	902
Number of invitations for meals	1.55	1.51
Price index	100.4	14.3
Beedu	0.25	
Halli	0.44	
Ooru	0.30	
$N = 123$		

Beedu, and Ooru,[18] located within 70 miles of each other, also in the state of Karnataka. Only 20 percent of the adults in these villages actually practice pottery; most are day laborers, with small-scale farming and silk rearing the other major activities. Halli and Ooru are multicaste villages located within commutable distances of large towns. Beedu, a village consisting entirely of potters, is located in a "forward" district with relatively good schools and a long tradition of providing basic social services.

Table 3 provides some summary statistics about the sample. The average annual household income is 14,471 Indian rupees—about $1644 in purchasing power parity (PPP)-adjusted U.S. dollars ($482 at the exchange rate prevalent at the time). The average land holding is very low at 0.59 acres. Education levels are also low, with the average maximum schooling of a person within a family at 4.54 years (the mean number of years of completed schooling among household heads is much lower, 1.6 years). Despite the low levels of education, the villages have recently undergone a fertility transition, with the average household consisting of 3.0 adults and 1.5 children.

Table 4 shows that festival expenditures rise with income, indicating that they are a normal good. They also rise with the maximum level of education in the family, the number of young children, and the number of girls of marriageable age. Thus we can infer that private incentives are important determining factors. The amount spent on festivals by neighbors is not significant, indicating that demonstration effects are not important. The level of expenditures displays a fair amount of variation across two of the three villages, with Beedu having significantly lower levels of festival expenditures than Halli, the omitted category. This is despite the fact that the households in all three villages in this sample belong to the same endogamous subcaste and therefore observe the same religious and ritual calendar. This suggests that the private incentives driving festival expenditures may differ from community to community for reasons other than social custom.

If households derive private benefits from festivals, what are they? To examine this, consider Table 5, which presents results of OLS and instrumental variable (IV) regressions of the price index. Four different sets of regressions are shown. Column (a) shows an OLS regression with festival expenditures included. Column (c) is the same as (a) but includes an interaction term between festival expenditures and income. Columns (b) and (d) follow the same pattern as (a) and (c) but present IV estimates. Since these households are below the Indian poverty line and spend 62 percent of their incomes on food, including income as a regressor should control quantity discount effects. Yet income does not have significant effects on any of the four regressions. This is because it is highly correlated with the number of adults in the family, which in turn is correlated with lower prices because large families are compelled to purchase food in larger quantities. An additional adult in the family reduces the price

TABLE 4
DETERMINANTS OF FESTIVAL EXPENDITURES: OLS WITH HUBER-WHITE STANDARD ERRORS (Itl IN PARENTHESES)

Variable	
Beedu	−0.9679
	(2.6)
Ooru	−0.3659
	(1.1)
Father's land holdings	0.0127
	(0.7)
Annual income/1,000 (1992 rupees)	0.0186
	(2.1)
Land in acres	0.1432
	(1.1)
Number of adults	0.1147
	(1.1)
Number of children 10-16 years	0.0003
	(0.0)
Number of children < 10 years	0.1765
	(1.7)
Maximum years schooling	0.0795
	(2.9)
Age of head	0.0030
	(0.4)
Number of girls 10-16 years	0.6548
	(2.2)
Festival expenditures of next-door neighbors/1,000	−0.0993
	(1.0)
Constant	1.1033
	(2.2)
Adjusted R-squared	0.42

index by more than 2 points in the OLS regressions.

Furthermore, an additional acre in the size of the father's plot of land reduces prices by 0.6 points. However, conditional on the land owned by the father, current land holdings do not affect the price index. Since there has been a rather large net loss of land in this community over the last 20 years, this result suggests that the reputation of the family—indicated by how much land the fam-

TABLE 5
DETERMINANTS OF PRICE INDEX: OLS WITH
HUBER-WHITE STANDARD ERRORS (|t| IN PARENTHESES)

Variable	(a)	(b)	(c)	(d)
Festival expenditures/1,000 (1992 rupees)	−1.8102	—	−2.8529	
	(1.7)		(2.2)	
Festival expenditures × income	—	—	0.0595	
			(1.0)	
Festival expenditures (predicted)	—	−5.5314	—	−7.7058
		(1.8)		(2.2)
Festival expenditures (predicted) × income	—		—	0.1220
				(1.8)
Beedu	5.5849	3.5493	4.4174	1.1021
	(2.1)	(1.0)	(1.5)	(0.3)
Ooru	1.5151	0.0019	1.243	−0.7106
	(0.4)	(0.0)	(0.4)	(0.2)
Annual income/1,000 (1992 rupees)	−0.0591	0.0581	−0.3212	−0.5175
	(0.6)	(0.6)	(1.0)	(1.3)
Father's land holdings	−0.6589	−0.6644	−0.6355	−0.6214
	(4.7)	(4.1)	(4.6)	(3.8)
Land in acres	0.9627	1.9351	0.6652	2.0219
	(0.9)	(1.7)	(0.6)	(1.8)
Number of adults	−2.6409	−2.9491	−2.4313	−2.4876
	(1.8)	(1.8)	(1.6)	(1.5)
Number of children 10-16 years	0.7638	1.9119	1.0651	2.4375
	(0.4)	(0.8)	(0.5)	(1.1)
Number of children < 10 years	0.6116	1.0664	0.7804	1.2709
	(0.6)	(0.8)	(0.7)	(1.0)
Maximum years of schooling	0.0068	0.0383	0.0615	0.1939
	(0.0)	(0.1)	(0.2)	(0.4)
Age of head	0.0262	0.0322	0.0337	0.0319
	(0.3)	(0.3)	(0.4)	(0.3)
Constant	106.2416	112.0663	109.0430	118.7900
	(22.0)	(20.5)	(20.8)	(17.4)
Adjusted R-squared	0.17	0.21	0.18	0.23

ily used to own—is far more important in accessing social networks than current land holdings are.

Most important, higher festival expenditures are negatively correlated with the price index. The effect seems to be stronger for poorer households. Looking at the interaction between income and festival in column (d), a 1000-rupee increase in annual festival expenditures reduces the price index by 6.2 points at the median income. This effect is reduced to 5.7 points at the seventy-fifth percentile income level, and increases to 6.67 points for incomes at the twenty-fifth percentile. This is consistent with the hypothesis that festival expenditures have an effect on prices independent of the other measured household attributes by providing a social return to a family.

TABLE 6

DETERMINANTS OF SOCIAL STATUS: ORDERED PROBIT (|z| IN PARENTHESES)

Variable	(a) OLS, No Interactions	(b) IV, No Interactions	(c) OLS, with Interactions	(d) IV, with Interactions
Festival expenditures/1,000 (1992 rupees)	0.1723	—	0.4289	—
	(1.8)		(3.4)	
Festival expenditures × income	—	—	−0.0165	—
			(3.1)	
Festival expenditures (predicted)	—	0.3094	—	0.5753
		(1.0)		(1.9)
Festival expenditures (predicted) × income	—	—	—	−0.0155
				(3.4)
Beedu	−0.0522	−0.0233	0.3151	0.3216
	(0.2)	(0.1)	(1.0)	(0.9)
Ooru	0.0432	0.0570	0.2172	0.1708
	(0.2)	(0.2)	(0.8)	(0.6)
Annual income/1,000 (1992 rupees)	−0.0122	−0.0157	0.0725	0.0669
	(1.4)	(1.4)	(2.6)	(2.6)
Father's land holdings	0.0084	−0.0037	0.0015	−0.0095
	(0.3)	(0.2)	(0.1)	(0.4)
Land in acres	−0.0560	−0.1304	0.0129	−0.1542
	(0.5)	(1.1)	(0.1)	(0.4)
Number of adults	0.2121	0.2223	0.1083	0.1424
	(2.1)	(2.2)	(1.1)	(1.5)
Number of children 10-16 years	0.0042	0.0438	−0.0764	−0.0371
	(0.0)	(0.3)	(0.6)	(0.2)
Number of children < 10 years	0.0907	0.1241	0.0347	0.0964
	(0.9)	(1.2)	(0.4)	(0.9)
Maximum years of schooling	0.0514	0.0539	0.0348	0.0324
	(1.8)	(1.6)	(1.3)	(1.0)
Age of head	0.0114	0.0926	0.0099	0.0083
	(1.4)	(0.0)	(1.2)	(1.1)
Pseudo R-squared	0.09	0.10	0.13	0.14

NOTE: Coefficients report effect of unit change in x on standard deviation change in y^*.

Thus higher festival expenditures, perhaps achieved by increasing a family's ability to tap into social networks, seem to give a household greater access to lower food prices.

Table 6 presents ordered probit estimates of the determinants of social status. In order to ease interpretation, the results are presented as the effect of a marginal change of an independent variable on the standard deviation of the status variable. Neither current nor past ownership of land has an impact on status. However, controlling for wealth, families with more income have higher social status in the IV specifications. This suggests that a family with greater liquidity and a steady job that produces a high and predictable income is valued, possibly because it is able to provide a buffer against risk. Annual festival expenditures are independently associated with higher social status, and, once again, festival expenditures interacted with income to result in lower status. Looking at the IV estimates in column (d), at the median income a 1000-rupee increase in festival expenditures raises the family's status level by 0.39 standard deviations. Even if one does not believe in the ability of IV estimates to establish causal connections, it is clear that festival expenditures and social status are strongly associated with one another. This is consistent with the notion that festivals serve as arenas where social status is maintained and enhanced.

CONCLUSION

The evidence presented in this article suggests that publicly observable celebrations, such as weddings and festivals, play an important role in the lives of the poor by serving as arenas where reputations are maintained and enhanced. They provide an opportunity for families to communicate information about their mobility, about their willingness to be good members of the village, and about their willingness to participate in webs of obligation. This information takes on a crucial role in the Indian context, where social networks and relationships play a central role in shaping people's identities. They are also extremely important as elements of strategies to cope with risk and poverty. Thus it is perfectly within reason that Indian villagers spend as much as they do on public celebrations.

However, to the extent that these celebrations are status competitions, driven by a need to signal changes in mobility, they may be "wasteful" in the sense that they take resources away from investments in schooling, health, and agriculture. But a judgment of waste should be rendered with care because it may reflect a model of welfare derived from Western notions of individualism. To the extent that celebrations and their expenditures maintain identities, reify social relationships, fulfill obligations, or represent investments in social capital, they are indeed productive expenditures within this cultural context.

This has important implications for development policy. Some sources of economic growth, such as market-driven improvements in urban employment, may reduce a family's dependence upon its traditional networks. This could reduce the incentives to maintain these networks and thus possibly reduce participation in village festivals. This would, in turn, adversely influence the traditional mechanisms of maintaining social cohesion within a village, which may reduce its capacity for collective action and consequently have a negative effect on well-being (Narayan and Pritchett 1999). On the other hand, as individuals become economically better off, their need to demonstrate their mobility to their peers may increase the size of wedding celebrations and other forms of conspicuous consumption. Thus economic development may reduce social cohesion and trust while increasing status displays, moving celebrations away from their role as participatory events and toward an emphasis on their function as competitive games. This could indeed be wasteful.

One possible way to avoid this outcome is to construct development mechanisms that improve well-being in a manner that does not privilege individual over collective action. If an intervention is more participatory, requiring collective decisions and collective management, it would maintain community cohesion and perhaps have more equitable benefits. There are several mechanisms currently in place that are attempting such strategies—micro-finance programs and social funds, for instance—but they have not been adequately studied to determine if they retain and perhaps even build a community's capacity for collective action. Further research will have to be conducted to see whether communities targeted by such interventions move away from conspicuous to what could be called cooperative consumption: celebrations that are less about showing off than they are about maintaining links across families, building bonds, and sustaining webs of obligation.

Notes

1. The data are from two different samples in Karnataka state.

2. For an elaboration on this methodology, see Rao 1997.

3. I use the word "signal" in the technical sense of transmitting information from an informed to an uninformed agent via a costly action (Salanie 1997).

4. This helps explain why Westerners, upon encountering Indians, are often puzzled by their detailed expositions on all the important people they know or are related to.

5. Of course, this is probably true of human beings in all cultures, with the logic of

sosioculturally derived incentives changing according to the context—while the logic of economic incentives stays more or less the same.

6. This section is culled from Bloch, Rao, and Desai 1999.

7. Some of these features have become less restrictive in educated urban circles, but they continue to be a defining aspect of village life.

8. For more on this subject, see Caldwell, Reddy, and Caldwell 1988; Rao 1993; Raheja 1995; Kapadia 1995.

9. Note that the village exogamy variable measures the customary practices prevalent in the community to which the responding household belongs. This can be treated as exogenous to the dowry and wedding celebration decisions since they are unlikely to change in the short term.

10. The village exogamy effect could also occur because husbands from outside the village would increase the size of the wedding party due to the greater number of potential guests who may have to be invited. However, the interaction effects do not necessarily follow from this explanation and are far more consistent with a signaling motive.

11. This section of the article is derived from Rao in press.

12. A local village goddess.

13. A definition of a game where all players know the structure of the game, know that the other players know it, know that others know that they know it, and so on. See Osborne and Rubinstein 1994 for a more precise definition.

14. Or what is now often called social capital (Woolcock and Narayan in press).

15. The social status regressions will be estimated with an ordered probit regression.

16. A detailed analysis of this can be found in Rao 2000.

17. Festival expenditures will be treated as an endogenous variable using instrumental variables (IV), with the number of marriageable daughters and the expenditures of neighbors as excluded variables.

18. The names of the villages have been changed.

References

Appadurai, Arjun. 1990. Technology and the Reproduction of Values in Rural

Western India. In *Dominating Knowledge: Development, Culture, and Resistance*, ed. Frédérique Apffel Marglin and Stephen A. Marglin. Oxford: Clarendon Press.

Bloch, Francis, Vijayendra Rao, and Sonalde Desai. 1999. Wedding Celebrations as Conspicuous Consumption: Signaling Social Status in Rural India. Development Research Group, World Bank. Mimeographed, July.

Caldwell, John C., P. H. Reddy, and Pat Caldwell. 1988. The Causes of Marriage Change. In *The Causes of Demographic Change: Experimental Research in South India*. Madison: University of Wisconsin Press.

Chwe, Michael Suk-Young. 1998. Culture, Circles and Commercials: Publicity, Common Knowledge and Social Coordination. *Rationality and Society* 10:47-75.

Collier, Paul and Ashish Garg. 1999. On Kin Groups and Wages in the Ghanian Labor Market. *Oxford Bulletin of Economics and Statistics* 61(2):133-51.

Dumont, Louis. 1970. *Homo Hierarchicus: The Caste System and Its Implications*. Chicago: University of Chicago Press.

Durkheim, Émile. [1912] 1965. *The Elementary Forms of the Religious Life*. Trans. J. W. Swain. New York: Free Press.

Fruzzetti, Lina. 1990. *The Gift of a Virgin: Women, Marriage and Ritual in a Bengali Society*. New York: Oxford University Press.

Fuller, C. J. 1992. *The Camphor Flame: Popular Hinduism and Society in India*. Princeton, NJ: Princeton University Press.

Goffman, Erving. 1959. *The Presentation of Self in Everyday Life*. New York: Anchor/Doubleday.

Kapadia, Karin. 1995. *Siva and Her Sisters: Gender, Caste and Class in Rural South India*. Boulder, CO: Westview Press.

Karve, Irawati. 1965. *Kinship Organization in India*. 2d rev. ed. Bombay: Asia Publishing House.

Marriot, McKim and Ronald Inden. 1977. Toward an Ethnosociology of South Asian Caste Systems. In *The New Wind: Changing Identities in South Asia*, ed. Ken David. The Hague: Mouton.

Mines, Mattison. 1994. *Public Faces, Private Voices: Community and Individuality in South India*. Berkeley: University of California Press.

Narayan, Deepa and Lant Pritchett. 1999. Cents and Sociability: Household Income and Social Capital in Rural Tanzania. *Economic Development and Cultural Change* 47(4):871-97.

Osborne, Martin J. and Ariel Rubinstein. 1994. *A Course in Game Theory*. Cambridge: MIT Press.

Raheja, Gloria Goodwin. 1995. "Crying When She's Born and Crying When She Goes Away": Marriage and Idiom of the Gift in Pahansu Song Performance. In *From the Margins of Hindu Marriage*, ed. Lindsey Harlan and Paul B. Courtright. New York: Oxford University Press.

Rao, Vijayendra. 1993. The Rising Price of Husbands: A Hedonic Analysis of Dowry Inflation in Rural India. *Journal of Political Economy* Aug.:667-77.

———. 1997. Can Economics Mediate the Link Between Anthropology and Demography? *Population and Development Review* Dec.:833-38.

———. 2000. Price Heterogeneity and "Real" Inequality: A Case-Study of Prices and Poverty in Rural India. *Review of Income and Wealth* 46(2): 201-11.

———. In press. Celebrations as Social Investments: Festival Expenditures, Unit Price Variation and Social Status in Rural India. *Journal of Development Studies*.

Salanie, Bernard. 1997. *The Economics of Contracts*. Cambridge: MIT Press.

Sen, Amartya. 1988. The Standard of Living, Lectures I and II—The Tanner Lectures. In *The Standard of Living*, ed. Geoffrey Hawthorn. New York: Cambridge University Press.

Srinivas. M. N. 1966. *Social Change in Modern India*. Berkeley: University of California Press.

Townsend, Robert M. 1994. Risk and Insurance in Village India. *Econometrica* 62:539-91.

Turner, Victor. 1982. Introduction. In *Celebration: Studies in Festivity and Ritual*, ed. Victor Turner. Washington, DC: Smithsonian Institution Press.

Udry, Christopher. 1994. Risk and Insurance in a Rural Credit Market: An Empirical Investigation in Northern Nigeria. *Review of Economic Studies* 61(3):495-536.

Woolcock, Michael and Deepa Narayan. In press. Social Capital: Implications for Development Theory, Research and Policy. *World Bank Research Observer*.

ANNALS, *AAPSS*, **573**, January 2001

Female Political Participation
and Health in India

By SUZANNE GLEASON

ABSTRACT: This article uses a unique data set to investigate the determinants of political participation in India. In particular, the data from the 1981 census of India are coupled with electoral returns from 1979-80 to examine the factors influencing participation of both genders. Differential impact is explored empirically. Many of the same influences found to be important in developed countries are relevant in India, including income, education, and constituency culture. In addition, labor force participation and familial obligations have an effect, though in the opposite direction from that predicted in the United States. A lack of government-provided resources devoted to health and education also influences participation. A second investigation uses the same census data with 1977-78 election returns to estimate government response to female political participation in India. Regarding the causes of child mortality, no effect of female participation on health outcomes was found. This may result from the aggregation necessary to match census districts and voting constituencies.

Suzanne Gleason is an economist and instructor in the Department of Radiology at Harvard Medical School, where she conducts research into health technology issues as part of the MGH Decision Analysis and Technology Assessment Group. Her research focuses on evaluating the costs and benefits of new medical devices and on health issues affecting children and the aged. Prior to joining Harvard, she was an economist in the Bureau of Economics Antitrust Division at the Federal Trade Commission.

F EMALE political empowerment has been offered as a method to advance economic development and end female disadvantage. Sen (1987) includes political and civic rights among those capabilities necessary to reach a high level of well-being. In the case of India, we find that women exercise their right to vote in large numbers, although participation as candidates and as officeholders is much lower. In fact, as in most of the rest of the world, females are underrepresented in both state and national legislatures. A second aspect of well-being, emphasized by Sen, is good health. How do these two aspects of well-being interact? In particular, what impact does female empowerment actually have? Many papers have examined the influence of female empowerment at the microlevel. Here, I want to step back and examine the issue from a more aggregate view. Do poor health outcomes have an impact on female political participation? Does participating in elections have an impact on health outcomes?

In this article, I investigate the determinants of female political participation in India and the benefits arising from it. In order to meet that goal, I examine the implications of the economic and political science literature for the factors that influence individuals to vote or to seek public office. I combine census and election returns data for this analysis. I find that many of the same influences discussed in the developed country literature are factors in India, though not necessarily in the same direction. Following that investigation, I examine the role of female political

participation in reducing child mortality overall and female child mortality in particular. Although the results are inconclusive, it is clear that this is an area that merits further exploration.

The article is divided into six sections. The first section summarizes the implications of the existing literature regarding the determinants of political participation. Reasons for differential gender participation are explored, and the historical context of female participation in India is described. The second and third sections outline India's electoral arrangements and discuss the Indian female political experience over the 1957-80 time period, respectively. An empirical model of the determinants of Indian female political participation is presented in section 4. The differential effects of these determinants are also examined. Section 5 shows the results of political participation for health outcomes, and the final section offers a conclusion.

POLITICAL PARTICIPATION

To begin, a definition of participation should be established for our context. Crook and Manor (1999, 7) define political participation as "citizens' active engagement with public institutions" including voting, campaigning, and pressuring either individually or through a group. I will focus on two forms only: voting and candidacy. My overview of the literature begins with an exploration of the factors that influence individual participation decisions and then focuses on the explanations for the gender gap in political participation. Finally, I end the section with a discussion of female political participation in the Indian context.

Theories of participation

The first economic model to describe voter participation was proposed by Downs (1957). In his model, perfectly informed voters evaluate the anticipated benefit stream under each alternative government and vote if one party gives higher expected net benefits than the others; if, on the other hand, the individual is indifferent between outcomes, she will not vote. Once the costs of voting and the probability that the individual's vote is decisive are factored in, many individuals will find the difference in benefits between the political parties to be swamped by those costs and therefore will abstain. Thus higher voter turnout is expected when the costs of voting are lower, when the benefits from voting are higher, and when the individual's vote is more likely to matter.

The costs of voting, which include the effort of becoming informed and the time involved in visiting the polls, will be lower for those with higher levels of education and those who place a lower value on time. In fact, there is consensus in the literature that the more highly educated are more likely to participate in politics (Leighley 1995). This relationship holds across the range of participation modes.

The benefits of voting include the returns to having the preferred party in office and psychic benefits. The benefits will be higher the more

issues on the ballot and the more strongly an individual feels about a given issue. For example, redistribution will be more important to the higher-income citizen. Income has a positive influence on turnout, though not as large as education (Leighley 1995). The rich appear to be more efficient at political participation; thus they capture more benefits per unit of participation effort than do the poor (Frey 1971, 1972). This argument implies that the rich face lower costs than would be expected from the value of their time.

Finally, an individual's vote is more likely to matter when the voting constituency is smaller, when the race is closer, and when the individual is voting as a member of a decisive group. Although individuals are aware that their vote has little chance of being decisive, voting as part of a coherent group can change the outcome of an election. A group's circumstances or the belief that a group suffers compared to other groups in society can increase the probability that a group member will vote (Uhlaner 1995). Group leaders, for whom utility increases as candidates approach their ideal position, provide information and incentive to members to vote. The more closely an individual identifies with her group, the more likely she is to participate. We expect to see higher turnout among the affected group, if the group is large enough to be decisive.

Politics is a vocation in which wealth and social status determine eligibility (Fowler 1993). Thus the same factors that influence voting should explain candidacy. In particular, socioeconomic status and the characteristics of the constituency are important.

Theories of differential participation

Although political participation through voting may be roughly even (Leighly and Nagler 1992), it is clear that women are not represented in positions of power in proportion to their presence in the population. Furthermore, women appear to have different attitudes on political and social issues from those of men, and, once in office, they appear to support different types of bills.

As we saw earlier, individual participation is explained by relative costs and benefits and by the likelihood of being decisive. Differential participation thus is explained by gender differences in these variables. If females are perceived to participate less, it will be because women experience higher costs, receive lower benefits, and/or believe they have a lower likelihood of being decisive. In addition, if women are perceived to lack the necessary skills for a political career, their representation will be lower.

Voting. Empirical evidence suggests that females face higher costs of voting than males. For example, traditional gender roles that place the burden of child rearing on females decrease the time available to devote to the political market. In fact, the presence of preschool children does appear to decrease female participation (Pomper 1975; Welch 1977) as does lack of employment outside the home (Verba 1965; Anderson 1975; Welch 1977, 1980). However, the evidence on this point is mixed: in the United Kingdom, married women participate more than single women (Welch 1980). Moreover, Welch (1977) finds that, controlling for marital status, the presence of young children influences male and female participation in the same way. Education has a large influence on participation decisions. Historically, females have had lower educational attainment than males on average. Once educational differences are controlled for, working women appear to vote more often than males, controlling for age (Pomper 1975). Nonpecuniary costs also play a role in explaining differential voting. If women are socialized to believe that politics is a male domain in which they should play a limited role, active participation may generate large psychic costs. Empirical evidence does show that adult gender roles do affect political participation, both in the United States and elsewhere (Anderson 1975; Aviel 1981).

Benefits from voting may differ between genders. If candidate platforms are perceived to be less differentiated on issues important to women, the relative benefits of a particular candidate's winning may be smaller than otherwise. Female support for female candidates arises from a concern that gender issues are overlooked due to the lack of women in office, rather than because they are women. Thus, if female candidates are felt to be less strong on women's issues, they lose votes to their opponents (Paolino 1995).

Finally, women constitute a large group whose members may have common interests and the potential to be decisive. In political theory, groups are collections of individuals who have similar preferences and who benefit from coordinated action (Uhlaner 1995). It is unclear that women constitute such a group. In fact, women belong to many socioeconomic groups, each of which has its own issues that may dominate gender considerations (Paolino 1995).

Candidacy. A primary concern in examining female candidacy is the resources to which females have access when running for office. Women appear to have less money and to have less control over household income than men do; however, men and women were found to have equal amounts of free time (Schlozman, Burns, and Verba 1994). Civic skills, defined as the communication and organizational skills that allow one to use time and money effectively in political life, were higher in men. This male advantage comes from greater educational attainment and more employment experience. Of the three influences, income, time, and civic skills, income was found to be the most important explanatory variable for the gender gap (Schlozman, Burns, and Verba 1994).

Costantini (1990) argues that the lack of political ambition is the cause of lower female political participation. Education, family income, and class of origin do not appear to affect female ambition. Integration into the community, participation in the workforce and church, and civic activity seem to increase political ambition. The feminist movement is an instigating factor for female ambition: women who are active in the feminist movement appear to have more political ambition and, thus, participate more.

District characteristics play a role in female candidature: the smaller the district, the more likely a woman can overcome the lack of resources and, therefore, the greater the representation of women in small districts (Medoff 1986). In addition, male dominance of positions of power and voter reluctance to accept women in those roles is seen as the cause of low female representation (Costantini 1990). Evidence differs as to whether women candidates fare worse than men when running for office (Karnig and Walter 1976; Darcy and Schramm 1977; Welch et al. 1991; Paulino 1995). In general, strong female candidates win votes, while weak ones lose votes. Being a strong, serious candidate is more important than gender (Zipp and Plutzer 1985).

The political culture influences the electoral fortunes of women. If society perceives politics to be a male domain, female political participation is lower (Elazar 1972). Female participation in state government varies considerably across the United States. States with a history of nonegalitarian political culture, such as in the U.S. South, have few women in the legislature (Rule 1981). Hill (1981) found that women candidates in states with a longer history of female participation are more likely to be elected, and he attributes half the variation between states to cultural influences.

Legislative structure has an impact on the representation of women (Rule 1987). In particular, proportional representation gives a higher representation of women than single-member districts (Matland and Studlar 1996). Reasons for this include the incentive to appeal to a wide audience, centralized nomination procedures, and large districts. In Latin America, the nature of the political regime is the most important in explaining female political participation: military regimes include fewer females (Aviel 1981).

Political attitudes and behavior in office. Female participants exhibit a difference in attitude compared to males. Costantini (1990) finds females to be more motivated by issues and to be less centrist then male participants. On the other hand, the voter's socioeconomic status appears to have a larger impact than her gender on the issues with which the voter is concerned (Schlozman et al. 1995). In comparing political opinions, women are found to be more supportive on compassion issues (guaranteed annual income and subsidized health care) and policies such as those concerning seat belt use, speed limits, and drunk driving. Men are more supportive on economic development issues (Shapiro and Mahajan 1986).

These differences carry over to female experience in office. Thomas (1991) found that women propose and support legislation on education and medical issues. Women legislators characterize child and family legislation as a priority, whereas men focus on bills related to business. Women introduce more bills dealing with family issues and are more successful at getting them passed (Thomas and Welch 1991).

In sum, the reasons for the gender gap in political participation appear to be differences in resources—education and income, most importantly—as well as in ambition, culture, and political institutions. I now turn to the existing literature on female political participation in India.

History of female political participation in India

The 1950 Constitution grants universal adult suffrage for all Indian citizens aged 21[1] and older (Butler, Lahiri, and Roy 1992). The British resisted giving females full franchise; Gandhi, who saw political rights as instruments for achieving equality, is credited with this achievement (National Committee on the Status of Women in India [NCSWI] 1975).

Statutory equality, however, has not changed attitudes. Manikyamba (1986) reports that both genders feel that women will be "unsexed" by participation. In addition, the qualities that make for good political participation—leadership, dynamism, initiative, independence, drive, and organizational ability—are not "expected of or appreciated in a woman" (125). Rajalakshmi (1985) lists physiological,[2] cultural, economic, and political constraints as the obstacles to female political participation. Perceived physiological barriers include characteristics that are considered desirable in women: dependence, passivity, empathy, sensitivity, risk avoidance, and yieldingness. Cultural constraints include the traditional household role of females and the low value on female activities outside the home. Economic constraints are even more binding in India than in the United States: Indian women move from their father's house to their husband's and rarely have economic independence. Finally, a political constraint is an increasing reluctance of parties to include women in high-profile roles. In addition, female cultural socialization and family duties stand in the way of female political participation (Swarup et al. 1994). Lack of education and knowledge about party politics has prevented nonelite women from having a very high presence in post-independence politics.

Voting is the most common form of participation in India. Over time, the gender difference in voter turnout in national elections has narrowed from 15.4 percent in 1962 to 11.8 percent in 1971.[3] Female voter turnout is higher in states with high literacy, and the overall regional outlook on women's participation in the wider society appears to be correlated with their political participation (NCSWI 1975). Interestingly, while Muslims and tribal women show lower participation than others, the scheduled castes have higher participation rates. Working women are more

aware of political issues but do not appear to vote in greater numbers, contrary to the evidence we see in the developed countries.

In 1971, 17 percent of the Lok Sabha (national assembly) seats were contested by women, although females account for only 4 percent of the candidates. The largest number of female candidates are found, surprisingly, in states where female voter turnout has been lowest. The majority of female candidates come from families with a long history of political participation or from the wealthy; most are educated. The success of females in seeking office appears to depend on party backing and family background. The exception to this rule is the women candidates from scheduled castes and tribes (Srinivas 1977).

In order to correct the underrepresentation of females in the state and national legislatures, the NCSWI (1975) recommended the formation of panchayats at the village level with their own resources and autonomy from the other village-level governments. Directly electing women to these bodies was thought to give women the opportunity to build experience in policy articulation and to enhance their participation in the regular village offices. Generally, the panchayati raj (local government) is divided into three structures—village level, block level (group of villages), and district level—although adherence to this structure varies by state. Reviewing the performance of women at the panchayat level of government, Manikyamba (1989) finds that states generally hold one to two seats specifically for women at each of the three levels. Although women are elected to these seats, they rarely attend, and, when they do, their participation in discussions is minimal. Manikyamba reports that women feel it is disrespectful to the (male) council leader to voice opposition at the meetings. This experience differs by area; in more advanced villages and at higher levels of panchayati raj, women take active part in the proceedings.

In their analysis of panchayati raj in the state of Karnataka, Crook and Manor (1999) found women members to be unassertive. In the examination of several panchayati raj at various levels within the Warangal and East Godavari districts in Andhra Pradesh, Manikyamba (1989) found that the characteristics of women who participate more successfully are (1) greater education (secondary and more); (2) higher economic position; (3) younger age; (4) previous governmental experience; and (5) a high level of personal interest. Caste and membership in other nonpolitical associations did not have an impact. Manikyama (1986) relates the formation of one all-female panchayati raj in Warangal: in opposition to a scheduled tribe member as head, a woman was accepted as head. However, the men then refused to participate, leading to an all-female committee.

In sum, although women in India have had the right to vote and hold office since independence, they seem to suffer from the same problems witnessed in developed countries—lack of resources, including education, finances, and political skills.

INDIA'S ELECTORAL BACKGROUND AND DATA

In 1980, India comprised 22 states and 9 union territories.[4] The national legislature consists of two houses: the Rajya Sabha (Council of States), filled by a combination of presidential appointment and election by the state legislatures, and the Lok Sabha (House of the People), filled by direct election (Baxter 1987). Each state has a legislature composed of a lower house, the Vidhan Sabha (Legislative Assembly) and, in some cases, an upper house, the Legislative Council. The members of the Vidhan Sabha are directly elected. This analysis will focus on the Vidhan Sabha.[5]

The responsibility for election oversight is placed by the 1950 Constitution on the central government. In India, the responsibility for voter registration rests on the Election Commission, rather than on the individual as in many Western democracies.

Elections are "contests between candidates in single-member constituencies"; victory goes to the contestant with the most votes (Butler, Lahiri, and Roy 1992, 30). A candidate must be a registered voter in some constituency of the legislature to which she is seeking election, but she does not have to contest in her home constituency. The candidate forfeits her election deposit when she receives less than one-sixth of the vote (Palmer 1975).

Candidates contest either with a recognized party or as independents. A party must exist within a state and must have participated in elections and social programs for at least five years in addition to receiving 4 percent of the votes in the previous election to be recognized as a state party (Butler, Lahiri, and Roy 1992). Note that recognized parties differ by state.

India is divided into approximately 3900 legislative assembly constituencies. For national elections, 7 of these constituencies, on average, are grouped together to form 1 parliamentary constituency. Constituencies consisting of more than 50 percent of scheduled tribes or scheduled castes are reserved for a member of the minority.

For this investigation, I combine the Vidhan Sabha election return data with the 1981 Indian census.[6] The Vidhan Sabha data[7] are a compilation of election returns for Indian elections occurring between 1957 and 1980. Variables included are number of registered and actual voters by gender, number of candidates by gender, and indicators for female candidate winner and reserved (scheduled caste or scheduled tribe) seats. The Indian District Data (Release 3) (Vanneman and Barnes 1993) contains demographic data on 366 administrative districts, covering all of India.[8] The data are compiled from the 1981 Indian census, as well as from many secondary sources. To combine these data sets, the constituency-level political participation data must be aggregated to the census district.[9] In general, the census district is divided on a population basis into voting constituencies.

In order to minimize the length of time between election and census, I investigate the 1979-80 elections, which took place in only 14 of the 31 possible states and union territories.[10] Utilizing an earlier election would make the connection between existing socioeconomic conditions represented by the 1981 census and the contextual understanding of the election even more difficult.

FEMALE POLITICAL PARTICIPATION IN INDIA

In general, male voter turnout in Vidhan Sabha elections is greater than the female voter turnout across India and over time. An average of 55 percent of eligible voters in each constituency went to the polls in 1980.[11] In this election, average male turnout was 67 percent, and average female turnout was 43 percent. The average gender gap was 26 percent. Comparing across states and over time, voter turnout is consistently lowest in Orissa and Bihar. This relationship holds for female turnout as well. Other northern states, with the exception of Rajasthan, have higher-than-average turnout for both genders. Paradoxically, these states are traditionally those with the worst performance on women's issues. However, in Kerala, a state noted for its success on women's issues, female turnout is equal to or greater than male turnout in most elections. In the northeast region of India (consisting of the states and union territories east of Bangladesh), turnout is equal across genders and increasing over time. In fact, this region has the highest turnout rates in all of India. Throughout the rest of India, the turnout trend in the Vidhan Sabha elections is mixed. Northern states, as a rule, show a stable or increasing gender gap in electoral turnout. Uttar Pradesh, the exception, is closing its gender gap. In the south, the gender gap remains largely unchanged.

In 1980, 370 (14.6 percent) of 2527 constituencies holding elections had at least one female contesting a seat. In no case did women make up 10 percent or more of the total candidates in the Vidhan Sabha elections. Once they run for office, however, they appear to be more successful than the average male candidate: in those districts where women contested seats in 1980, 106 (28.6 percent) found a woman candidate victorious. Only four state legislatures have reached 10 percent or more female members. Although the number of female candidates has remained relatively stable over time, the number of male candidates has steadily risen, making for an increasing gender gap in candidacy. Female representation appears to be falling over time, though that result is not statistically significant.

On average, 9 percent of state seats are contested by females in any given year. States with an above-average number of females contesting seats are Uttar Pradesh and Bihar. These are the same states that ranked lowest on female voter turnout. At the other extreme are primarily the small states and union territories. The negative correlation between female voter turnout and female candidacy is statistically significant at the 1 percent level. Furthermore, there is a significant negative correlation between female voter turnout and female candidate success. These negative relationships may be due to women in areas with

higher female candidacy and representation feeling their issues are adequately represented, thereby decreasing the benefits to their voting.

Comparing India to its neighbors, Bangladesh and Pakistan, the implications are mixed. Both countries have reserved seats for females in the national legislature. In Bangladesh, female representation has reached 10 percent (Nelson and Chowdhury 1994). However, anecdotal evidence from Bangladesh indicates that these reserved seats have not led to female representation at other levels of government (Cain, Khanam, and Nahar 1979). Little has been published about voter participation in these countries.

DETERMINANTS OF FEMALE
POLITICAL PARTICIPATION

I turn now to the determinants of female political participation and the gender gap in India. Table 1 presents the means and standard deviations of the variables used. The dependent variables measuring female political participation are the female voter turnout rate, defined as the proportion of the female electorate who votes, and the female candidacy rate, defined as the proportion of the female electorate who runs for office. In addition, the male voter turnout and candidacy rates are used as dependent variables. All census variables are for the rural population in the district. The reason for this limitation will become clear below.

The literature on developed countries leads me to expect a positive effect for income and education on

TABLE 1
SUMMARY STATISTICS FOR POLITICAL PARTICIPATION IN RURAL INDIA

Variable	Mean	Standard Deviation
Female voter turnout	0.39	0.13
Male voter turnout	0.65	0.19
Female candidacy rate	0.000004	0.000004
Male candidacy rate	0.00013	0.0001
Agricultural output per person	0.22	0.15
Proportion farm workers landless	0.33	0.18
Gender labor force participation ratio (F/M)	0.42	0.26
Gender literacy ratio (F/M)	0.36	0.18
Dependency ratio	0.53	0.055
Woman winner in the last election	0.23	0.42
Number of constituencies	9.6	5.0
Proportion rural scheduled castes	0.16	0.08
Proportion rural scheduled tribes	0.12	0.20
Proportion rural Muslims	0.07	0.08
Doctors per capita	0.0049	0.0026
Nurses per capita	0.0051	0.0035
Teachers per capita	0.042	0.019

participation. Two indicators of district wealth are used: agricultural output per capita and the proportion of farm workers who are landless. The latter variable gives an indication of the distribution of wealth in the district. Rural female literacy is used to measure the level of female education in the district. In addition, I anticipate female labor force participation to have a positive influence on female political participation. Rural female labor force participation is measured by the proportion of

adult females who are engaged in the labor force as main workers. Similarly, I expect male voter turnout to be influenced by male literacy and male labor force participation. Due to the high correlation between the male and female variables, they enter the regressions as ratios.

Familial obligations prevent women from participating in the political sphere. Here the dependency ratio is used to capture family obligations. The dependency ratio is calculated as the number of children under 10 plus the number of adults over 60, divided by the working age population. Data constraints prohibit adjusting this ratio to take into account the lower life expectancy in developing countries.

History of past female political participation, positively correlated with acceptance of females in political roles, is measured as a binary variable equal to 1 if a woman was elected to any seat in the census district in the last election. In addition, the number of constituencies in each census district is included to control for the electoral climate. Since voting constituencies are based on population, this variable may also capture the effect of urbanization.

Group theory and Indian experience suggest that areas with higher proportions of scheduled castes will have more political participation. I also include the proportion of scheduled tribes and Muslims, both of which are likely to have a group identity. Finally, each regression includes 14 state dummy variables to control for state-level effects caused by differing political party activism within each state and differing panchayati raj arrangements.

Voting can also send a signal regarding voter discontent. I therefore use the proportion of doctors, teachers, and nurses per capita as measures of government provision of resources to the district. In rural areas, health and education services are primarily publicly provided; the same cannot be argued for urban areas.[12] If female voters are responding to a lack of resources devoted to family issues, I expect a negative correlation between the supply of these resources and female participation.

The dependent variables used in this investigation represent proportions of the electorate who vote or run for office. Therefore, I use the grouped data technique to examine the effects of the independent variables on turnout. The observed proportion is an estimate of the probability that any individual participates in the election (Greene 1993). In this case, the error term will be heteroskedastic; I use the White standard correction for this problem. The male and female equations are estimated jointly to account for common district shocks. Differential impact will be investigated empirically.

Table 2 presents the results of the empirical investigation. Model 1 includes the main set of variables, while Model 2 adds the government service variables. The results are presented in the form of elasticities. Therefore, the interpretation is that a 1 percent change in the value of the independent variable implies an x percent change in the dependent variable.

The most robust result across all the equations is the importance of state-specific effects. Comparison of the R-squared with and without these effects indicates that the features of the state political culture common to all districts within the state are important determinants of political participation. In addition, comparing the R-squared across modes of participation, we see that for females the voter turnout models exhibit better fit than the models for candidacy. For males, however, the result is the opposite. This result implies that different modes of political participation are explained by different factors. Furthermore, the determinants of participation differ by gender.

Examining the female voter turnout models, we see that higher female labor force participation relative to males leads to lower voter turnout, suggesting that working women have a higher opportunity cost of time and, therefore, voting. In addition, the dependency ratio is positive and significant, contrary to my prediction. This may indicate that care burdens lead females to be more active in securing the benefits of political participation. The difference from developed countries may be explained by the absence of social programs for care of children and the aged. The number of constituencies has a positive and significant effect. This indicates that the costs of voting are lower in urban areas. In addition, because the smallest states and union territories are treated as single observations, this result may capture the effect of small communities. In smaller communities, the

TABLE 2

**ROBUST NONLINEAR REGRESSION RESULTS FOR POLITICAL
PARTICIPATION—ELASTICITIES (ABSOLUTE t-STATISTIC)**

Variable	Voter Turnout				Candidacy			
	Model 1		Model 2		Model 1		Model 2	
	Female	Male	Female	Male	Female	Male	Female	Male
Agricultural output per person	0.061	0.16	0.017	0.14	−0.32	0.010	−0.48	0.031
	(1.64)	(2.14)	(0.43)	(1.83)	(2.29)	(0.32)	(3.80)	(0.95)
Proportion farm workers landless	0.068	0.10	0.040	0.10	0.045	0.0092	0.13	0.033
	(0.76)	(0.83)	(0.45)	(0.83)	(0.21)	(0.17)	(0.66)	(0.59)
Labor force participation ratio (F/M)	−0.21	0.013	−0.16	0.016	−0.38	−0.062	−0.55	−0.093
	(4.19)	(0.26)	(3.33)	(0.23)	(2.24)	(2.00)	(3.02)	(2.85)
Gender literacy ratio (F/M)	0.22	0.22	0.37	0.17	0.42	−0.12	0.48	−0.23
	(1.92)	(1.42)	(3.42)	(0.92)	(1.02)	(1.34)	(1.06)	(2.28)
Dependency ratio	0.95	0.46	0.87	0.26	1.01	0.068	0.71	0.13
	(2.73)	(0.68)	(2.38)	(0.38)	(0.78)	(0.24)	(0.64)	(0.45)
Woman winner in the last election	−0.0028	−0.021	−0.0055	−0.020	0.16	−0.00053	0.16	0.0011
	(0.30)	(1.40)	(0.60)	(1.26)	(5.32)	(0.08)	(6.01)	(0.17)
Number of constituencies	0.16	−0.046	0.15	−0.065	−0.49	0.033	−0.26	0.042
	(3.70)	(0.72)	(3.33)	(1.01)	(2.50)	(0.90)	(1.42)	(1.17)
Proportion rural scheduled castes	−0.13	0.20	−0.15	0.20	0.34	0.00007	0.34	0.0096
	(1.25)	(1.58)	(1.40)	(1.55)	(1.38)	(0.00)	(1.37)	(0.22)
Proportion rural scheduled tribes	0.023	−0.19	0.012	−0.18	0.23	−0.020	0.19	−0.010
	(1.58)	(5.19)	(0.75)	(4.51)	(4.01)	(1.39)	(3.02)	(0.75)
Proportion rural Muslim	−0.029	0.030	−0.025	0.020	0.034	−0.040	0.044	−0.040
	(0.88)	(0.74)	(0.77)	(0.47)	(0.95)	(2.23)	(0.59)	(2.22)
Teachers per capita			−0.233	0.14			−0.98	0.14
			(2.69)	(1.06)			(2.77)	(1.67)
Doctors per capita			0.0064	0.16			0.035	0.025
			(0.09)	(1.87)			(0.18)	(0.58)
Nurses per capita			0.028	−0.24			0.60	−0.025
			(0.47)	(2.28)			(3.87)	(0.56)
Pseudo-R-squared	0.80	0.66	0.80	0.67	0.53	0.94	0.57	0.94
Pseudo-R-squared omitting state dummies	0.38	0.31	0.43	0.32	0.22	0.62	0.41	0.71
Number of observations = 250								

probability that an individual's vote is decisive increases. The remaining variables are not significant.

The results discussed so far are robust to the inclusion of the government provision variables (doctors, nurses, and teachers). In Model 2, higher female literacy relative to males leads to higher turnout; this result is consistent with my expectations. Regarding the government provision variables, the supply of teachers has a negative and significant effect, indicating a higher turnout where the provision of teachers is low. Thus, if females are using voting as a tool to send a signal to the government, the message is about education.

For male turnout, in Model 1, income, measured as agricultural productivity per capita, is positive and significant, as I expected. This result, however, is not robust to the inclusion of the government provision variables. The proportion of rural scheduled tribes is negative and significant in both models, confirming that this group is less active than the Indian population on average. Among the government provision variables, the supply of nurses is negative and significant. This suggests that men are more interested in health.[13]

The differential impact is calculated by subtracting the female equation from the male equation. A negative sign indicates a smaller gender gap. In Model 1, higher income levels are associated with a larger gender gap in voter turnout ($t = 2.12$). In richer areas, women vote less often than men. This result is consistent

with anecdotal evidence that richer women face more constraints on their behavior—the rich have the luxury of female seclusion. The significance of this variable diminishes when I control for government resources ($t = 1.82$). The proportion of scheduled tribes is negatively correlated with the gender gap ($t = 5.20$). This result is robust to the inclusion of government provision variables. Among these resources, the presence of more nurses is associated with a smaller gender gap ($t = 2.28$). The remaining variables do not have a differential impact.

Turning to the candidacy regressions, we find that income has a negative and significant effect on females, contrary to what we witness in developed countries. This result may indicate higher benefits to female activity in low-income areas or higher costs to female participation in the richer districts. In addition, higher female labor force participation relative to males leads to fewer female candidates, suggesting that women have less time to devote to politics in areas where they have more economic opportunities. A history of female representation in the district has a positive and significant effect, as predicted. Acceptance of females in political roles decreases the psychic costs of candidacy. Finally, the higher the proportion of scheduled tribes, the higher is female candidacy. These results are robust to the inclusion of the government resource variables. The number of constituencies is negative and significant in Model 1, but not once the government variables are added.

For males, the labor force participation ratio has a negative and significant effect. The higher male labor force participation relative to females, the higher the male candidacy rate. Males gain skills from participation in the labor market that translate into lower costs of political participation. The proportion Muslim is also negative and significant. This may indicate that this group has opted out of the mainstream (mainly Hindu) society and participates less. On the other hand, this group may be more cohesively organized behind its candidates, decreasing the probability that other candidates will be successful, leading to a smaller pool of competitors. In Model 2, the literacy ratio is negative and significant, implying a positive relationship between relative male literacy and male candidacy.

Once the government variables are added, the presence of teachers is significant and negative in the female equation, consistent with the earlier result in the voting model. In addition, the number of doctors per capita has a positive effect on female candidacy. This result could indicate a desire by females to redistribute government resources from health to education. An alternative explanation is that female candidates are chosen from the ranks of doctors in the district.

With respect to the candidacy gender gap, in Model 1, the proportion Muslim is the only variable with a significant differential effect ($t = 2.32$). A higher proportion Muslim is associated with a smaller gender gap. This result is robust to the inclusion of the government variables. In

Model 2, both the labor force participation ratio ($t = 2.35$) and the literacy ratio ($t = 2.46$) are correlated with a smaller difference in the number of male and female candidates. In addition, the presence of teachers has a positive and significant ($t = 2.01$) coefficient. Thus the candidacy gender gap is larger where the presence of teachers is higher.

In sum, these regressions confirm the influence of income, acceptance of females in office, and education on Indian female political participation. Although the direction of the influence is different from the U.S. experience, female labor force participation and the responsibilities for the young and old also have an impact. The smaller the number of teachers in the district, the more women are likely to vote. Male participation is affected by many, though not all, of the same influences. The gender gap is affected by education and labor force participation, as well as by the presence of disadvantaged groups.

An interesting question that arises from the consideration of female political participation is, What do they get for their effort? In the next section, we will try to gain some insight into this issue.

THE IMPACT OF PARTICIPATION

One question that has received very little attention in the literature is, What becomes of the efforts of individuals in the political market? Specifically, I am interested in the effect, if any, of political participation on health. In this section, I will examine the impact of female participation on child survival, a very basic measure of health outcomes. I begin by summarizing the limited literature on the topic, and then I use the data set discussed above to investigate the issue.

Dixon-Mueller and Germain (1994) examine the role of feminist political action in the formation of population policy in Brazil, Nigeria, and the Philippines. They find Brazil to illustrate a successful example of the incorporation of feminist ideals into national health policy. While the other two countries are making progress, they have not succeeded to the same degree. Dixon-Mueller and Germain conclude that there is scope for female political participation to influence policy. However, the modes of participation they explore are small activist groups rather than large political movements. In examining the allocation of publicly provided goods in India, Betancourt and Gleason (in press) find that higher voter turnout in a district increases the allocation of nurses to a district. In addition, a higher ratio of female-to-male voter turnout is correlated with an increase in the number of doctors provided to the rural districts of India. Thus there is some evidence that democratic participation affects government allocation of resources and policymaking.

In the only paper directly addressing the role of political participation on health outcomes, LaVeist (1992) examines the role of African American political empowerment and the black postneonatal mortality rate in American cities. Measuring empowerment as the ratio of the proportion of council seats held by blacks to the proportion of blacks in the voting age population, he finds a negative relationship between black representation and black child mortality. That is, areas with higher African American participation have higher levels of child survival. This confirms the hypothesis raised by LaVeist and others (McKnight 1985; Braithwaite and Lythcott 1989) that increasing political participation does have a positive impact on the quality of life. In a later paper, LaVeist (1993) argues that both factors, black representation and improved living status, are the results of characteristics of community organization.

Although a full investigation into the causes of child mortality is beyond the scope of this article, I will examine the role of political participation in child mortality in rural India. Following results found by Murthi, Guio, and Dreze (1995) and Gleason (in press), I assume that the following variables affect child survival: female literacy, female labor force participation, income and its distribution, health inputs, urbanization, and the presence of minority groups (Muslims, scheduled castes, and scheduled tribes). To these explanatory variables, I add three alternative measures of female political participation. First, I use female empowerment, measured as the proportion of a district's constituencies that had a female member of the Legislative Assembly, divided by the proportion of the voting age population that is female. The second variable is the ratio of female to male voters. Finally, the ratio of female to male candidates is used. In order to avoid simultaneity issues (that high child mortality may be leading women to

TABLE 3

SUMMARY STATISTICS FOR HEALTH OUTCOMES IN RURAL INDIA

Variable	Mean	Standard Deviation
Child mortality	0.170	0.049
Female-to-male child mortality ratio	1.067	0.13
Agricultural output per person	0.22	0.15
Proportion farm workers landless	0.33	0.19
Rural female literacy rate	0.28	0.21
Rural female labor force participation	0.41	0.25
Proportion rural Muslim	0.094	0.14
Proportion rural scheduled castes	0.18	0.083
Proportion rural scheduled tribes	0.10	0.18
Doctors per capita	0.005	0.003
Nurses per capita	0.005	0.004
Female empowerment	0.031	0.064
Female-to-male voter turnout ratio	0.75	0.19
Female-to-male candidate ratio	0.025	0.027

Number of observations = 322

participate more), the 1977-78 election data are paired with the 1981 census data. Descriptive data for these variables are presented in Table 3.

The estimation method is as before: child mortality represents the probability that a child dies before age 5, and the regressions are therefore estimated using the grouped data technique described above.

Regression results are presented in Table 4. I find the results from the other articles (Murthi, Guio, and

Dreze 1995; Gleason in press) confirmed. Namely, income, measured by agricultural output per person, has a negative though insignificant impact on child mortality. Moreover, the more unevenly distributed the income in the district, as measured by the proportion of farm workers who are landless, the higher the child mortality. Female literacy and labor force participation have the expected negative signs and are statistically significant. The larger the Muslim population, the higher the child mortality rate. The size of the scheduled tribes and scheduled castes appears to have no impact on child survival, a result consistent with Murthi, Guio, and Dreze (1995). The more doctors in the district, the lower the child mortality, as I would expect. The number of nurses per capita is positively correlated with child mortality, probably indicating a tendency on the part of the government to allocate more resources to bad areas (much like police presence in high-crime neighborhoods).

With regard to the political participation variables, all are positive but insignificant. The lack of significance could be for several reasons. First, the representation of females in the state legislatures is universally low and therefore may be below some threshold necessary to make a difference. Second, the level of my analysis, the district, may be too aggregated, given the low levels of female representation, to see an impact. Note that LaVeist (1992) found his effect at the community level. Census districts are the aggregate of several voting constituencies, as many as 20 in some cases. If having females

TABLE 4

**ROBUST NONLINEAR REGRESSION RESULTS FOR HEALTH
OUTCOMES—ELASTICITIES (ABSOLUTE *t*-STATISTIC)**

Variable	Child Mortality		
	Model 1	Model 2	Model 3
Agricultural output per person	−0.032	−0.035	−0.032
	(1.09)	(1.20)	(1.09)
Proportion farm workers landless	0.12	0.11	0.12
	(3.10)	(2.98)	(3.06)
Rural female literacy rate	−0.20	−0.21	−0.21
	(5.27)	(5.18)	(5.36)
Rural female labor force participation	−0.099	−0.10	−0.10
	(2.79)	(2.90)	(2.83)
Proportion rural Muslim	0.037	0.038	0.038
	(2.37)	(2.50)	(2.42)
Proportion rural scheduled castes	0.050	0.055	0.052
	(1.26)	(1.38)	(1.30)
Proportion rural scheduled tribes	−0.0081	−0.0068	−0.0089
	(0.79)	(0.69)	(0.86)
Doctors per capita	−0.12	−0.12	−0.12
	(2.98)	(3.03)	(2.93)
Nurses per capita	0.16	0.17	0.16
	(3.33)	(3.50)	(3.30)
Female empowerment	0.0054		
	(1.16)		
Female-to-male voter turnout ratio		0.061	
		(0.92)	
Female-to-male candidate ratio			0.012
			(1.26)
Pseudo-*R*-squared	0.58	0.58	0.58
Pseudo-*R*-squared omitting state effects	0.39	0.39	0.39
Number of observations = 322			

in office affects the health in only their constituency, that effect may be swamped by including the other constituencies with male elected officials. Finally, rural India is a stable, slow-moving society (Rosenzweig and Schultz 1982), and I may need to examine a longer trend of female political participation to find an effect. Therefore, the absence of an effect here is not cause to abandon the investigation.

CONCLUSION

I have combined the implications from the existing literature on female participation with a unique data set to examine both the determinants and the benefits of female activity in the political sector. I have found that many of the same influences on political participation identified in developed countries play an important role in India. In particular, literacy and income have the anticipated effects for voting. The latter has a positive association with the voting gender gap. On the other hand, both female labor force participation and household obligations are important, but in the opposite direction from their influence in developed countries. A history of acceptance of women in roles of political power is essential in promoting female candidacy for the state legislature. In addition, the level of government provision of resources also plays some role. Finally, the characteristics of the political and economic atmosphere common to all districts within the state are important determinants of female political participation.

Regarding health outcomes, the results have been disappointing. I find no impact of female participation on child survival. This last set of results should not lead us to conclude that female political participation does not have an effect. Rather, it should indicate the need for further investigation into the issue. In fact, better measures of health are needed at the constituency level, to eliminate the problem of aggregation, and better instruments to control for endogeneity. Clearly, returns to political participation are a fruitful area for future research.

Notes

1. In 1988, the voting age was lowered to 18.

2. Although these traits might be referred to as psychological, the author uses the term "physiological," so I have kept the term.

3. Female turnout has fallen more slowly than male turnout.

4. The current number of states and union territories are 25 and 5, respectively. I concentrate on 1981 here, due to the census data that are available.

5. Difficulties with aggregation of Lok Sabha voting constituencies to census districts prevent using Lok Sabha data in the empirical investigation.

6. The author thanks Reeve Vanneman and Douglas Barnes for making the Indian Development District Database available.

7. The sources and formation of the Political Participation Database are described in detail in Gleason 1996, app. B.

8. This omits eight districts in the state of Assam in which the 1981 census was not conducted due to civil strife.

9. The process is described in detail in Betancourt and Gleason in press.

10. The states included are Arunachal Pradesh, Bihar, Goa, Gujarat, Kerala, Madhya Pradesh, Maharashtra, Mizoram, Orissa, Pondicherry, Punjab, Rajasthan, and Uttar Pradesh. Manipur, which held an election in 1980, is missing the census data necessary to complete the project.

11. A data appendix showing voter turnout and candidates by gender is available upon request from the author.

12. For more detail, see Betancourt and Gleason in press.

13. Note that government service variables exhibit low correlation coefficients with income (agricultural productivity) and population density. Therefore they are unlikely to capture wealth effects or the costs of reaching the polls in sparsely populated areas.

References

Anderson, Kristi. 1975. Working Women and Political Participation, 1952-72. *American Journal of Political Science* 19(Aug.):439-54.

Aviel, JoAnn Fagot. 1981. Political Participation of Women in Latin America. *Western Political Quarterly* 34(1): 156-73.

Baxter, Craig. 1987. *Government and Politics in South Asia*. Boulder, CO: Westview Press.

Betancourt, Roger and Suzanne Gleason. In press. The Allocation of Publicly-Provided Goods to Rural Household in India: On Some Consequences of Caste, Religion and Democracy. *World Development*.

Braithwaite, R. L. and N. Lythcott. 1989. Community Empowerment as a Strategy for Health Promotion for Black and Other Minority Populations. *Journal of the American Medical Association* 261:282-83.

Butler, David, Ashok Lahiri, and Prannoy Roy, eds. 1992. *India Decides: Elections 1952-1991*. New Delhi: UM Books.

Cain, Mead, Syeda Rokeya Khanam, and Shamsun Nahar. 1979. Class, Patriarchy, and Women's Work in Bangladesh. *Population and Development Review* 5(3):405-38.

Costantini, Edmond. 1990. Political Women and Political Ambition: Closing the Gender Gap. *American Journal of Political Science* 34(Aug.):741-70.

Crook, Richard C. and James Manor. 1999. *Democracy and Decentralization in South Asia and West Africa: Participation, Accountability and Performance*. New York: Cambridge University Press.

Darcy, R. and Sarha Slavin Schramm. 1977. When Women Run Against Men. *Public Opinion Quarterly* 41(Spring):1-12.

Dixon-Mueller, Ruth and Adrienne Germain. 1994. Population Policy and Feminist Political Action in Three Developing Countries. *Population and Development Review* 20(supp.): 197-219.

Downs, Anthony. 1957. *An Economic Theory of Democracy*. New York: Harper & Row.

Elazar, Daniel. 1972. *American Federalism: A View from the States*. New York: Thomas Y. Crowell.

Fowler, Linda L. 1993. *Candidates, Congress, and the American Democracy*. Ann Arbor: University of Michigan Press.

Frey, Bruno S. 1971. Why Do High Income People Participate More in Politics? *Public Choice* 11:101-5.

————. 1972. Political Participation and Income Level. *Public Choice* 13:119-22.

Gleason, Suzanne. 1996. Female Well-being and Public Goods: The Case of India. Ph.D. diss., University of Maryland, College Park.

————. In press. Publicly-Provided Goods and Intrafamily Resource Allocation: Female Child Survival in India. *Review of Development Economics*.

Greene, William H. 1993. *Econometric Analysis*. 2d ed. New York: Macmillan.

Hill, David B. 1981. Political Culture and Female Political Representation. *Journal of Politics* 43(Feb.):159-68.

Karnig, Albert K. and B. Oliver Walter. 1976. Election of Women to City Councils. *Social Science Quarterly* 56(Mar.):605-13.

LaVeist, Thomas. 1992. The Political Empowerment and Health Status of African-Americans: Mapping a New Territory. *American Journal of Sociology* 97(4):1080-95.

————. 1993. Segregation, Poverty, and Empowerment: Health Consequences for African Americans. *Milbank Quarterly* 71(1):41-64.

Leighley, Jan E. 1995. Attitudes, Opportunities and Incentives: A Field Essay on Political Participation. *Political Research Quarterly* 48(Mar.):181-209.

Leighley, Jan E. and Jonathan Nagler. 1992. Individual and Systemic Influences on Turnout: Who Votes? 1984. *Journal of Politics* 54(Aug.):718-40.

Manikyamba, P. 1986. The Participatory Predicament: Women in Indian Politics. In *The Changing Division of La-*

bor in South Asia, ed. James Warner Bjorkman. Riverdale, MD: Riverdale.

———. 1989. Women in Panchayati Raj Structures. New Delhi: Gian Publishing House.

Matland, Richard E. and Donley T. Studlar. 1996. The Contagion of Women Candidates in Single-Member District and Proportional Representation Electoral Systems: Canada and Norway. Journal of Politics 58(Aug.): 707-33.

McKnight, J. L. 1985. Health and Empowerment. Canadian Journal of Public Health 76(supp.):37-8.

Medoff, Marshall H. 1986. Determinants of the Political Participation of Women. Public Choice 48:245-53.

Murthi, Mamta, Anne-Catherine Guio, and Jean Dreze. 1995. Mortality, Fertility and Gender Bias in India: A District-Level Analysis. Population and Development Review 21(Dec.):745-82.

National Committee on the Status of Women in India (NCSWI). 1975. Status of Women in India: A Synopsis of the Report of the National Committee on the Status of Women (1971-74). New Delhi: Indian Council on Social Science Research.

Nelson, Barbara J. and Najma Chowdhury, eds. 1994. Women and Politics Worldwide. New Haven, CT: Yale University Press.

Palmer, Norman D. 1975. Elections and Political Development: The South Asian Experience. Durham, NC: Duke University Press.

Paolino, Phillip. 1995. Group-Salient Issues and Group Representation: Support for Women Candidates in the 1992 Senate Elections. American Journal of Political Science 39(May):294-313.

Pomper, Gerald. 1975. Voters' Choice. New York: Dodd Mead.

Rajalakshmi, V. 1985. The Political Behaviour of Women in Tamil Nadu. New Delhi: Inter-India.

Rosenzweig, Mark and T. Paul Schultz. 1982. Market Opportunities, Genetic Endowments, and the Intrafamily Allocation of Resources: Child Survival in Rural India. American Economic Review 72:803-15.

Rule, Wilma. 1981. Why Women Don't Run: The Critical Contextual Factors in Women's Legislative Recruitment. Western Political Quarterly 34(1): 60-77.

———. 1987. Electoral Systems, Contextual Factors and Women's Opportunity for Election to Parliament in Twenty-Three Democracies. Western Political Quarterly 40(3):477-98.

Schlozman, Kay Lehman, Nancy Burns, and Sidney Verba. 1994. Gender and the Pathways to Participation: The Role of Resources. Journal of Politics 56(Nov.):963-90.

Schlozman, Kay Lehman, Nancy Burns, Sidney Verba, and Jesse Donahue. 1995. Gender and Citizen Participation: Is There a Different Voice? American Journal of Political Science 39(May):267-93.

Sen, Amartya. 1987. The Standard of Living. New York: Cambridge University Press.

Shapiro, Robert Y. and Harpreet Mahajan. 1986. Gender Differences in Policy Preferences: A Summary of Trends from the 1960s to the 1980s. Public Opinion Quarterly 50(Spring): 42-61.

Srinivas, M. N. 1977. The Changing Position of Indian Women. Man 12(Aug.):221-38.

Swarup, Hem Lata, Niroj Sinha, Chitra Ghosh, and Pam Rajput. 1994. Women's Political Engagement in India: Some Critical Issues. In Women and Politics Worldwide, ed. Barbara Nelson and Najma Chowdhury. New Haven, CT: Yale University Press.

Thomas, Sue. 1991. The Impact of Women on State Legislative Policies. Journal of Politics 53(4):958-76.

Thomas, Sue and Susan Welch. 1991. The Impact of Gender on Activities and Priorities of State Legislators. *Western Political Quarterly* 44(2):445-55.

Uhlaner, Carole Jean. 1995. What the Downsian Voter Weighs: A Reassessment of the Costs and Benefits of Action. In *Information, Participation, and Choice: An Economic Theory of Democracy in Perspective*, ed. Bernard Grofman. Ann Arbor: University of Michigan Press.

Vanneman, Reeve and Douglas Barnes. 1993. *Indian District Data, 1961-1981: Electronic Data File and Codebook*. College Park, MD: Center on Population Gender and Social Inequality.

Verba, Sidney. 1965. *The Civic Culture*. Boston: Little, Brown.

Welch, Susan. 1977. Women as Political Animals? A Test of Some Explanations for Male-Female Political Participation Differences. *American Journal of Political Science* 21(4):711-30.

———. 1980. Sex Differences in Political Activity in Britain. *Women & Politics* 1(Summer):29-46.

Welch, Susan, Margery M. Ambrosius, Janet Clark, and Robert Darcy. 1991. The Effect of Candidate Gender on Electoral Outcomes in State Legislative Races. *Western Political Quarterly* 44(2):464-73.

Zipp, John F. and Eric Plutzer. 1985. Gender Differences in Voting for Female Candidates: Evidence from the 1982 Election. *Public Opinion Quarterly* 49(Summer):179-97.

ANNALS, *AAPSS*, **573**, January 2001

Cascades of Ethnic Polarization: Lessons from Yugoslavia

By MURAT SOMER

ABSTRACT: By building upon cascades literature, the author offers an explanation for rapid and massive polarization and applies it to the former Yugoslavia. The dominant images of ethnic categories in society change through cascades of individual reactions triggered by traumatic events, ideological shifts, or the activities of ethnic entrepreneurs. Polarization becomes self-propagating if the protagonists of a certain image of ethnic identities, called the divisive image, appear to have reached a critical mass. Downward ethnic preference falsification, people's concealment of their support for the divisive image in public, increases the severity of polarization. The article argues that downward falsification was significant in Yugoslavia before the 1980s due to policies that suppressed the public expression of the divisive image but insufficiently encouraged its elimination in private. In the 1980s, polarization reversed this trend and led to widespread upward ethnic preference falsification, the exaggeration of the support for the divisive image in public.

Murat Somer lectures in the Economics Department of the University of Southern California. He is also the assistant director of the university's Jesse M. Unruh Institute of Politics.

E THNIC polarization, which can be described for the moment, until the definition given below, as the division of a people into mutually exclusive and distrustful ethnic categories, is detrimental to development.[1] Violent ethnic conflict is a likely effect of radical polarization and brings high economic and humanitarian costs to the societies in which it occurs as well as to the international community. However, while its effects have been relatively well researched, a satisfactory explanation of ethnic polarization itself is surprisingly absent.

Often, ethnic polarization is considered exogenous to analysis; at times, ethnolinguistic diversity is used as a proxy, although some level of ethnic heterogeneity can at best be seen as a necessary but insufficient condition for the existence of ethnic polarization. Alternatively, research focuses on those societies that are already ethnically polarized.[2] For all practical purposes, ethnic divisions, especially those that arise after the occurrence of ethnic polarization, are treated as if they were constant and did not require explanation.

Yet, without explaining how ethnic polarization occurs and alters the nature of ethnic identities in society, one cannot understand how and when ethnic identities become inimical to development. Ethnic divisions undermine development only to the extent that people from different ethnic backgrounds distrust each other and exclude each other from their social, political, and economic interactions.

In this article, I present an explanation for rapid and massive ethnic polarization and apply it to the former Yugoslavia.[3] A major premise of the explanation is that the nature of ethnic identities in society is endogenous to changes in public opinion and public discourse. Accordingly, ethnic polarization is defined as a cascade process of individual reactions, whereby a particular image of ethnic identities, what I call the divisive image, is enhanced among the members of a multiethnic society. The divisive image implies a definition of ethnic identities as mutually exclusive and incompatible with belonging to the same nation. If a critical mass of people appears to hold the divisive image, people who secretly held it before, as well as those who now feel obliged to support it, follow suit. Hence, the divisive image becomes the norm, and it becomes inappropriate, even blasphemous, to defend interethnic mixing and brotherhood. Once these circumstances surface, outsiders' image of the society will also tend to change accordingly. Thus, many ex-post analysts will quickly assume that the society in question was always divided by deep-seated ethnic hatreds.

To those analysts, ethnic polarization will appear to be caused by mutually exclusive and antagonistic ethnic groups. In fact, however, ethnic antagonisms, and the perception of ethnic groups as mutually exclusive, are often products of ethnic polarization. The actors and social categories we observe after ethnic polarization are not those that existed before polarization. Subsequent to polarization, we observe ethnic groups with seemingly distinct identities, impervious group boundaries, and historical hatreds. When we dig a bit deeper, however, we unearth a history of mixing and cooperation as well as conflict. Prior to polarization, we discover that different images of ethnic identities coexisted within public opinion and public discourse. Some of these images portrayed ethnic identities as inclusive of each other and compatible, and others as exclusive and incompatible. At some point during polarization, the latter become dominant.

Here, I do not examine the historical, political, and economic roots of the existence of the divisive image among any particular people—these roots can be very diverse, depending on the social and economic history and geography of each country. Instead, I focus on the process that leads to the divisive image's becoming the dominant image in society, at least in public.

ETHNIC POLARIZATION AS A CASCADE

The potentially explosive character of ethnic relations demonstrates that, once ethnic polarization reaches a critical level in a society, interpersonal dependencies, or snowballing or bandwagon effects, can become very influential.[4] Hence the appropriateness of cascade models as a theoretical framework for the examination of ethnic polarization; these models formally incorporate interpersonal behavioral dependencies.

Cascades are self-reinforcing processes that change the behavior of a group of people through interpersonal dependencies. Cascade models explain situations in which the individual's incentives for taking an action, holding a belief, or conforming to a norm depend significantly on the behavior of others.[5] Consider the following example. Suppose you are an ethnic minority member who is contemplating whether to attend a separatist rally. Alone, your personal preferences favoring the cause of the rally are not strong enough to make you attend regardless of what others do. Therefore, in order to decide, you look to others who carry social, political, or economic importance for you. You know that the rally's supporters may ostracize you if you fail to attend but that attending will hurt your standing among opponents. The information you have at that time augurs a low turnout. Hence, you figure that the combined importance for you of the rally's cause and your standing among the rally's expected participants is not sufficient to compensate for the opprobrium that will be attached to participants by those who appear to condemn the rally. Such opprobrium could impair your personal safety and economic, social, and political relationships. Thus you decide to bypass tomorrow's rally.

However, hours before the rally's scheduled start, you see television footage showing a large crowd. This leads you to doubt your earlier expectation of a low turnout. Furthermore, you run into an acquaintance, whom you deem well informed and well connected, on his way to the rally. This makes you wonder whether people whose opinion you value will judge you as a traitor if you fail to attend a successful rally. New information increases the expected number of the rally's supporters and adds to your worries about the social, political, and economic costs of not attending. At some point, you determine that these costs, combined with the personal value of the rally's cause, exceed the expected cost of attending. Hence, you decide to attend. Your behavior may trigger others to follow. If the number of people at the rally reaches a critical mass, this may result in bandwagoning of support for the rally and for its cause among the population. These dynamics are not only in play in ethnic rallies such as those that helped Serbian leader Milošević to come to power; more than a decade later they helped his opponent Kostunica to rally support to bring him down.

By the logic of cascade processes, if the number or social and political significance of the initial advocates of an action, belief, or norm reaches a critical level, the balance of incentives will tip in favor of that action, belief, or norm for a great number of people, who will change their behavior accordingly.[6] Therefore, in the case of ethnic polarization, divisive ethnic entrepreneurs constantly try to tip the balance of incentives in favor of holding the divisive image and undertaking actions that directly or indirectly promote it. They are people who have, for political, economic, intellectual, or psychological reasons, a high level of interest in the diffusion of the divisive image and actively try to promote it. If they succeed, they trigger a chain reaction of individual responses. People who previously were indecisive about or opposed to the behavior

in question jump on the generated bandwagon along with those who had been advocating it all along.

Accordingly, Kuran (1998) rightly argues that the diffusion of ethnic norms can be explained by "reputational cascades," whereby people overstate their genuine attachment to these norms in order to maintain their social status. But he does not emphasize the distinction between divisive and non-divisive norms. The distinction is crucial for determining the social and political effects of the diffusion of ethnic norms. According to the argument here, the enhancement of ethnic norms will lead to ethnic polarization only to the extent that the ethnic norms simultaneously generate divisive changes in people's images of ethnic identities in their society.

DIVISIVE, CLASHING, AND COMPATIBLE ETHNIC IMAGES

What I call here images of ethnic identities refers to the fuzzy ways in which people imagine their ethnic identities relating to the other ethnic identities in their social environment and to their nation.[7] The ways people imagine their ethnic groups and nations are, of course, diverse and complex. Whichever categorization is made, there certainly will be a great variety within each category. At the same time, however, a parsimonious theoretical categorization is crucial for making the unavoidable complexity of the social reality intelligible for analysts. I will attempt such a classification here by defining the divisive, clashing, and compatible images of ethnic identities and by distinguishing between their private and public expressions. Table 1 summarizes the main characteristics of the compatible, divisive, and clashing images. A comprehensive discussion of all the characteristics in Table 1 is beyond the scope of this article. Instead, an example illustrating how the divisive image affects individuals' choices must suffice.

A Catholic Irish man who holds a moderate version of the divisive image may attend political activities or socialize with Protestants but would find it unacceptable to marry a Protestant woman. If a strong version of the divisive image were to take hold in society, the number of spheres of life in which it would become unthinkable for Catholic and Protestant Irish to interact would increase. Not only would the Catholic Irish man find it unimaginable to marry a Protestant woman, but he would also find it unthinkable to hire Protestant employees or vote for the same party as Protestants.

Once a strong version of the divisive image prevails in society, it takes only one more step for the clashing image to emerge. In the clashing image, ethnic identities are seen not only as mutually exclusive and incompatible with the membership of the same nation but as antagonistic. The effect of the divisive image is that people see members of other ethnic groups as "them" or "others." Consequently, the social distance between members of different ethnic groups increases. This leads to the dwindling of the information flow, less competition, and, ultimately, differential economic return rates

TABLE 1

THE CHARACTERISTICS OF THE THREE DIFFERENT COGNITIVE MODELS PORTRAYING ETHNIC IDENTITIES IN A NATION

| | Cognitive Model | | |
	Compatible image	Divisive image	Clashing image
Mutually exclusive ethnic identities	No	Yes	Yes
Unfit to belong to the same nation	No	Yes	Yes
Antagonistic ethnic identities	No	No	Yes

across ethnic groups.[8] Envy and perceived unfairness grow in interethnic group relations: "Successful ethnic groups tend to engender fear and jealousy on the part of outsiders, while members of ethnic groups with low returns tend to become stigmatized" (Wintrobe 1995, 44).[9] Thus, actual social distance between ethnic groups and the development of separate feelings of belonging reinforce each other and lead to the growth of negative and hostile images. Social identity theory demonstrates that negative feelings and attitudes about "others" follow almost automatically the development of perceived separate group membership (Tajfel 1978; Turner 1982; Abrams and Hogg 1990; McAdams 1995).

DOWNWARD AND UPWARD PREFERENCE FALSIFICATION

For my purposes here, the term "public" will denote an activity or preference that is visible or easily knowable by others. The term "private" will indicate either that the associated activity or preference is known only to the person herself or that it is known only to those people the person confides in, such as family members or people living in the same household.[10]

Consider a Mexican American who hangs a Mexican flag on the wall in his living room. Unless seen by strangers, this private activity will not have any consequence beyond cultivating his sense of identity. However, if the same individual puts a sticker of the Mexican flag on his car, possibly next to a sticker in English, it will serve as a badge of his ethnic identity and may affect other people's behavior to the extent that it is publicly visible. It may, for example, encourage others to carry similar symbols, or it may remind Americans of Mexican Americans. It may earn him contacts with other Mexican Americans, which may bring him social or economic benefits. Yet, unless observers perceive it as promoting a divisive image, it will not necessarily cause polarization.

Now imagine a hypothetical Mexican American who is in favor of California's secession from the United States. His activities conducted in the privacy of his home, such as reading ethnopolitical books, will not directly affect other people's behavior. Suppose that this Mexican American carries a Mexican flag at a rally at which no American flags are present and chants secessionist slogans. In this case, his activity will affect others' perceptions and actions. It will increase the salience of the divisive image of the American and Mexican American identities, both among Mexican and non-Mexican Americans. It may contribute to the perception that the divisive image is becoming the norm for three reasons.

First, the more vocal and visible the rally, the more social pressures there will be on Mexican Americans to accentuate their Mexican identity and on non-Mexican Americans to accentuate their own ethnic identity. Second, if the demonstrators are sufficiently numerous, many may decide to ignore their own private information—namely, information indicating that most Mexican Americans hold a compatible image—and decide that most must have been privately holding the divisive image. Third, many will think that it may be economically and politically advantageous to side with the group that seems to be growing in size. All in all, the acts during the rally will induce the observers to take a side in a polarizing environment.

Thus, public ethnic activities and expressions affect the decisions of others, while private activities and expressions do not. The effects I am referring to here are instant or short-run effects. Once we allow sufficient time to pass, all of our choices, whether private or public choices, affect those of others. One's private beliefs and activities, for example, will certainly affect the upbringing of one's children. In that sense, all private choices are interconnected. However, private decisions do not immediately affect those of others because they are not immediately observed.

One consequence of this is that the divisive image can subsist without necessarily affecting public opinion and public discourse insofar as it remains private. Though most people in a society hold the divisive image in their minds, they may prefer to act in public as if they embrace a compatible image. This appears to have been the case for many in the former Yugoslavia and, possibly, in the former Soviet Union. For instance, Roeder (1991, 210) argues that a significant portion of the ethnic elites in Soviet republics had "private primordial agendas," which would be expressed only in private contexts or at "isolated, ineffective, small-scale events."[11]

Another important distinction between private and public expression is that the latter is falsifiable. Believing on the basis of the public acts of others that the value of ethnic attachments is rising, many people may choose to exaggerate their ethnic attachments in public. Kuran (1998) calls this phenomenon "ethnic preference falsification," an extension of the general concept of preference falsification developed in his 1989 dual preference model. Individuals who falsify their ethnic preferences mislead people to deduce that ethnicity is becoming more important, inducing them to exaggerate their ethnic attachments in public. Kuran's model explains how ethnic extremism could gather massive public support in the 1980s even though most Yugoslavs were not ardent ethnonationalists in private.

In addition to ethnic preference falsification's exaggerating private attachments, we should account for ethnic preference falsification's suppressing private attachments. The former kind of ethnic preference falsification, which leads to an ex-

TABLE 2
PRIVATE ATTACHMENT TO, AND PUBLIC EXPRESSION OF, THE DIVISIVE IMAGE AND DOWNWARD AND UPWARD PREFERENCE FALSIFICATION

	Publicly Held Compatible Image	Publicly Held Divisive Image
Privately held compatible image	No preference falsification	Upward preference falsification
Privately held divisive image	Downward preference falsification	No preference falsification

aggeration of ethnic identities, will be called here upward ethnic preference falsification. The reverse is also true: people can publicly underrate the private significance of their ethnic identities or a particular image of their ethnic identities. Ethnic preference falsification that underrates ethnic identities will be called downward ethnic preference falsification. Table 2 summarizes how different types of ethnic preference falsification occur with respect to divisive and compatible images.

As Kuran (1998) demonstrates, due to the possibility of ethnic preference falsification, changes in private and public realms do not necessarily coincide. Therefore, we should define two different types of polarization. Private ethnic polarization can be defined as the process whereby increasingly more people privately hold the divisive image. Similarly, public ethnic polarization is the process whereby more and more people publicly display the divisive image. Public ethnic polarization can occur without private polarization, and vice versa. In cases where private polarization concurs with public polarization, the degree of the latter can exceed or fall short of the former. Similarly, private and public depolarization can take place separately or simultaneously, and in case they concur, they may be of different severity.

The more that downward ethnic preference falsification exists before a cascade of public ethnic polarization occurs, the greater the severity of the change in society resulting from polarization. Public polarization does two things. First, it adds new people to those who already promote the divisive image. Second, it removes the veil from some of those individuals who were previously concealing their private preferences. Hence, public polarization will be more severe the more people had been falsifying their preferences— more people will begin to express a preference they used to conceal. Downward preference falsification may also raise the likelihood that a state is caught off guard by radical polarization, if the government is unaware of the private importance of the divisive image.

After radical polarization, many analysts will conclude that the society was already filled with hatred and that ethnic disintegration was inevitable. This is only partly true. While public polarization leads those who used to downwardly falsify their preferences to reveal their preferences, it also induces many who think that the divisive image is becoming the norm to upwardly falsify their preferences. Moreover, polarization is preventable if those promoting the compatible image can prevent divisive ethnic entrepreneurs from mobilizing a critical mass of people in favor of the divisive image. Ethnic polarization is reversible. If people who hold a compatible image can reverse public opinion before people internalize the divisive image, they can start a cascade of depolarization. In this case, many will cease to undertake upward preference falsification, and others will begin to undertake downward preference falsification.

Individuals are susceptible to changes in public opinion and public discourse to varying degrees. Everything else held constant, those who have a strong preference for the compatible image will be less likely to upwardly falsify their preferences even though public opinion may appear to favor the divisive image. Hence, governments interested in taking long-run measures against the possibility of ethnic polarization should focus on providing incentives for the entrenchment of the compatible image in private. At the same time, they should abstain from creating monopolies of information resources. Informational monopolies can be used by divisive ethnic entrepreneurs to disseminate the impression that the divisive image is becoming the norm as well as by those who want people to believe that everybody favors interethnic solidarity. The failure to take such long-run measures ultimately cost the former Yugoslavia its unity.

ETHNIC POLARIZATION
EXPLOITED: YUGOSLAVIA

We all said publicly that we wanted a mixed Bosnia and that we would defend it, but privately. . . . [12]

Despite all the research done on the subject, Yugoslavia's disintegration remains an unsatisfactorily comprehended phenomenon. Initially, a rich corpus of studies put the blame for Yugoslavia's disintegration on historic animosities peculiar to Balkanites (Connor 1993; Kaplan 1994; and, partly, Mojzes 1994 and Judah 1997). This approach serves more to satisfy the Western onlooker's own self-image by distinguishing between "them" (who are capable of great evil) and "us" (who are immune to conflict caused by ancient hatred) than to explain the real causes of the country's tragedy. Though the deep-seated-hatred argument still pervades popular and journalistic accounts, it has been sufficiently demonstrated that historical evidence indicates the opposite: cooperative and peaceful periods clearly outweigh violent periods in the history of the areas comprising the former Yugoslavia (Gagnon 1994-95; Akhavan 1995; Cigar 1995; Fearon and Laitin 1996; Malcolm 1998).[13]

Alternative views rightly stress the strategic decisions of the country's elites, who exploited ethnic sensitivities to consolidate their own power (Glenny 1993; Denitch 1994; Gagnon 1994-95; Carment and James 1996; Cigar 1995; Maass 1996). Accordingly, Yugoslavia is a case of failed transition from socialism to liberal democracy and market economy. In the power vacuum left by Tito's death in 1980, Yugoslav leaders chose to use ethnonationalism to attain or consolidate power, ultimately leading to their country's destruction. A series of studies has argued convincingly that Serbian leader Milošević rose to power largely by manipulating Serbian nationalism, whereby his strategic exploitation of the sensitive issue of the Serbian minority in Kosovo played a crucial role (Malcolm 1998, 341-43; Mertus 1999). Indeed, divisive ethnic entrepreneurs played a key role in the fall of Yugoslavia.[14]

Even leaders such as Milošević, however, seem to have been surprised by the power of the polarization they helped create, suggesting that the dynamics of rapid and massive polarization were in play. Hence, the theory of ethnic polarization presented in this article can shed light on three aspects of Yugoslavia's dissolution that have been insufficiently explained. The first is the speed at which Yugoslavia disintegrated and the degree of violence and apparent hatred that was created during the process. Interethnic problems in Yugoslavia had been known to exist, yet it was hardly expected that Yugoslavs could turn against each other so fast and so violently.

A second and related issue is the way common people indirectly contributed to the escalation of ethnic tensions. It is true that elites misused the state's control of mass media, especially television, as a propaganda tool to foment interethnic grievances and that wars were launched by armed forces directed from above, not by ordinary civilians (Malcolm 1998, xxvii, 342). Yet, elite strategies of inciting ethnonationalism found a large and responsive audience among common people, which is a factor that needs to be explained not by resorting to ostensible ancient visceral hatreds but by examining ethnic and national self-images in modern Yugoslavia and the policies that cultivated them.

The third task is to explain how the dominant public discourse could take such a sharp turn during the 1990s. How could the once-dominant public discourse emphasizing unity and brotherhood turn into one that emphasizes radical ethnonationalism? Similarly, the paucity of dismal predictions about Yugoslavia before the polarization contrasts with the abundance of ex-post explanations of how inevitable and foreseeable the tragic outcome was.

In response to these questions, here it is argued that in Yugoslavia, policies that nurtured downward ethnic preference falsification and provided insufficient incentives for the development of an overarching Yugoslav identity created a public that was vulnerable to radical ethnic polarization. In general, while Yugoslav policies aimed at eradicating the public expression of the divisive image of ethnic relations in the country, apparently to maintain the regime's safety and Yugoslavia's unity, they insufficiently encouraged the development of the compatible image in private. The result was twofold: downward preference falsification, which understated the private popularity of the divisive image in the public sphere, and insufficient cultivation of the Yugoslav national identity as opposed to ethnic identities. Hence, when elites began to exploit ethnic sensitivities in the 1980s, the public was already susceptible to their discourse. People

indirectly contributed to ethnic disintegration by such acts as voting for ethnonationalist leaders, attending ethnonationalist rallies, or revealing ethnically biased views in reaction to inflammatory events. These activated the interpersonal dependencies that bred public polarization.

The pace and severity of the ensuing polarization exceeded everybody's expectations mainly for two reasons. First, prior downward preference falsification concealed, to most observers, the private importance of the divisive image, which rose to the surface during public polarization. Second, even analysts who had a fair idea about the private significance of the divisive image were surprised by the severity of polarization because interpersonal dependencies triggered by the polarization process led to upward preference falsification.

The argument about downward preference falsification differs in fundamental ways from the argument that the deep-seated hostilities, which resembled a tinderbox, were suppressed before the 1980s and exploded as soon as the Yugoslav state weakened. First, the latter argument implies that the divisive and clashing images dominated private opinion in the former Yugoslavia. According to the argument here, this is not true. Although the private significance of the divisive image was certainly underrepresented by the official discourse, the compatible image was widespread and developing, although insufficiently from the point of view of Yugoslavia's long-term cohesion. Hence, the antagonistic public discourse that became dominant as a result of polarization is as misrepresentative of people's true self-images as the prepolarization official discourse that championed unity and brotherhood. The argument here can be refuted if it can be shown that the divisive and clashing images were indeed dominant among common Yugoslavs before the polarization. Evidence provided here indicates that they were not.

The second way the argument here differs from one based on suppressed antagonisms is in regard to the implication of the latter argument that Yugoslavia's eventual disintegration was inevitable. In contrast, the present article argues that it could have been prevented. This would have happened if those Yugoslavs who held a compatible image could have stopped the social dynamics leading to polarization, reversed the process to one of depolarization, and, in the long run, launched policies that encouraged the cultivation of the compatible image.

It is understandable that today the compatible image of interethnic relations in the former Yugoslavia has little credibility for the average Yugoslav. As a result of ethnic polarization, views and beliefs in support of the compatible image became increasingly unfit to express publicly from the late 1980s onward. As polarization persisted and ethnic conflict ensued, the compatible image also became unthinkable. Today, the compatible image is in the gradual and uncertain process of becoming unthought, both due to the influence of social and political pressures prevalent under authoritarian-nationalistic governments and because of the

vivid memory of ethnic war and the fading memory of the time before.

Most ex-post accounts that paint too gloomy a picture of the ethnic relations in the former Yugoslavia can be seen as a product of ethnic polarization. These accounts generalize the feelings and expressions in a postpolarization environment to a long prepolarization history, which entailed strong unifying forces as well as divisive dynamics.

Was there a Yugoslav nation?

There were myriad reasons for believing that Yugoslavia was a successful salad bowl (if not a melting pot) whose ingredients were integrating. First, as Table 3 demonstrates, about 13 percent of all marriages in the country were mixed marriages, in that they were between people from different ethnic backgrounds.[15] A comparison with the percentage of interracial marriages in the United States may be revealing. As seen in Table 3, only 2.4 percent of all married U.S. couples in 1994 could be identified as interracial; marriages between whites and blacks were only 0.5 percent of all married couples. The percentage of black-white interracial couples was only 0.1 percent in 1970, where all interracial couples made up 0.6 percent of the whole in the same year (Saluter 1996, viii, A-5). Even writers who are skeptical about the significance of the intermarriage ratio in Yugoslavia highlight that there was virtually no marriage barrier between the Croats and Serbs, who were later involved in a brutal war

TABLE 3
INTERMARRIAGE RATES IN THE FORMER YUGOSLAVIA
AND THE UNITED STATES (PERCENTAGE)

	1962-64	1970-72	1980-82	1987-89	1994
United States (interracial)					2.4
United States (black-white interracial)					0.5
Former Yugoslavia	12.7	11.7	13.1	13.0	
Bosnia-Herzegovina	11.4	9.5	12.2	11.9	
Montenegro	17.9	14.6	13.4	13.1	
Croatia	15.8	15.4	17.1	17.4	
Macedonia	13.5	9.9	8.2	7.8	
Slovenia	7.7	7.8	11.0	13.0	
Serbia (total)	12.3	11.9	13.1	12.9	
Serbia proper	8.5	7.8	9.9	10.4	
Vojvodina	22.5	25.3	27.6	28.4	
Kosovo	9.4	7.7	6.1	4.7	

SOURCES: Botev 1994 (469); Saluter 1996. Reprinted by permission of the American Sociological Association.

with each other (Botev and Wagner 1993, 30).

The second factor that was thought to suggest the successful integration of Yugoslav society is the significant number of those who identified themselves as Yugoslavs rather than as members of any ethnonational group. Denitch (1994, 14) notes that these people were more numerous than were Slovenes and Macedonians. As seen in Table 4, in 1981 approximately 8 percent of all people in Bosnia identified themselves as Yugoslavs, by refusing to associate with any ethnonational group.[16] This apparently low percentage is still important because, were they given the option of revealing both an ethnic and a national (Yugoslav) identity, more people could have identified themselves as Yugoslav along with their ethnic identity. For people who hold a compatible image, ethnic and national identities need not be mutually exclusive. However, the Yugoslav national identification was first

introduced in the census in 1961 and then qualified with the explanation "having no identifiable [ethno]-nationality" (Hodson, Sekulić, and Massey 1994, 1542-43).[17]

The interethnic peace, international respectability, and relative economic and political contentment that the former Yugoslavs enjoyed until the late 1980s also contributed to the image of Yugoslavia as a working multiethnic state. Economically, Yugoslavia was more liberal and prosperous than other Communist-led states. According to World Bank data, in terms of gross national product (GNP) per capita, Yugoslavia was the most prosperous country among Communist Balkan states and, among all the Communist states, trailed closely behind Czechoslovakia. The Yugoslav economy grew at a respectable 6.1 percent annual rate between 1965 and 1973 and 6.4 percent between 1973 and 1980. The economic crisis Yugoslavia experienced during the 1980s was severe, as revealed by its negative

TABLE 4
PERCENTAGE OF PEOPLE WHO
SELF-IDENTIFIED AS YUGOSLAVS

	1961	1971	1981	1991
Yugoslavia	1.7	1.3	5.4	3.0
Bosnia-Herzegovina	8.4	1.2	7.9	5.5
Montenegro	0.3	2.1	5.3	4.0
Croatia	0.4	1.9	8.2	2.2
Macedonia	0.1	0.2	0.7	n.a.
Slovenia	0.2	0.4	1.4	0.6
Serbia (excluding Kosovo and Vojvodina)	0.2	1.4	4.8	2.5
Vojvodina	0.2	2.4	8.2	8.4
Kosovo	0.5	0.1	0.1	0.2

SOURCES: Sekulić, Massey, and Hodson 1994 (85); Cohen 1993 (175). Reprinted by permission of the American Sociological Association and Westview Press, a member of Perseus Books, L.L.C. Data in the column for 1991 are from *Broken Bonds: The Disintegration of Yugoslavia* by Leonard J. Cohen. Copyright © 1993 by Westview Press.

average growth rate and hyperinflation, and greatly contributed to a political crisis. However, economic crisis can be only a catalyst for, not a cause of, ethnic conflict. Moreover, all countries in transition sooner or later experience hyperinflation and contraction of output.

More consequential for ethnic relations in Yugoslavia were regional inequalities that gradually became a source of interrepublic tension. In 1988, GNP per capita was $5918 in Slovenia and $3230 in Croatia, while it was $662 in Kosovo, $1499 in Macedonia, and $2238 in Serbia proper (Ding 1991, 2).[18] Prosperous regions, especially Slovenia, pressed for more autonomy, even independence, in order to reduce their contribution to backward regions through central government transfers. Impoverished regions, in return, complained that they were being exploited as a provider of raw materials and wanted more assistance from the federal government. Ethnic entrepreneurs amply exploited these disputes to promote the divisive image and to incite ethnonationalism. The divisive image, of course, reinforced the perception of interregional inequalities as equivalent to interethnic inequalities.

Nevertheless, except for the case of Slovenia, it was not expected that economic inequalities would cause disintegration, as Ding (1991) argued:

Although it is possible that Slovenia, which is economically the most developed and ethnically the most homogeneous, is really demanding independence and will succeed in the end, a total breakup of the rest of Yugoslavia does not seem likely given its history, racial, and territorial intermingling, at least in the foreseeable future. (4)

Despite the lack of liberal democracy, the country also fared better than other socialist countries in terms of social and political freedoms; one foreign observer once admitted that he had "never been in a country with so much freedom and so little democracy" (reported in Crnobrnja 1994, 76). As a leading state of the nonaligned movement—of which Tito became a champion after breaking with Stalin between 1948 and 1951—and as the pioneer of market socialism (self-management) from the 1960s onward, Yugoslavia was highly esteemed abroad, especially in the Third World.

Underneath this surface of harmonious coexistence, however, there were troubling signs. There were tensions between ethnic elites and occasional leakages of demands for more expression of ethnic particularities through the iron facade of Yugoslav nationalism. In addition, it was expected that the weakening of socialism could give rise to some degree of ethnopolitical mobilization because the long-lasting ideological monopoly of the Communists eliminated alternative vehicles of political expression.[19]

What was unimaginable at that time was the speed of ethnic mobilization and the degree of violent hatred that it could later unleash. Prior to the outbreak of war, analysts who were aware of this mixture of tendencies suggested that the weakening of socialism could lead to ethnonationalist crisis, yet they could not imagine, let alone predict, that the Yugoslavs could become polarized to the extent that civil war would result. Accordingly, Glenny (1993), an esteemed observer of the Yugoslav civil war, recounted later, "Though everybody knew the rotten ship of the Yugoslav state was entering troubled seas, nobody in their wildest fantasy would have predicted that within a little more than a year Croat soldiers would massacre innocent Serbs, while Serbs would mutilate innocent Croats" (19).

Similarly, Mojzes (1994) confesses that, although "mounting [ethno]nationalist tensions were evident, [he] did not anticipate that they would lead to the partition of the country" (xvii).[20] In order to counter the claims of the ethnonationalists that the Yugoslav idea never worked, he argues,

At that time "never again" seemed convincing. Surely no one would ever again set these people against each other considering the many intermarriages, a sizable movement of ethnically different people settling in one another's areas, the purchase of properties along Dalmatian coasts by members of all [ethno]nationalities, [and] the successful integration of sports teams that represented the country in myriad international competitions. (3)[21]

Indeed, in 1985, when signs of rising ethnonationalism were evident, a respected scholar, Rusinov, concluded that the tensions would not lead to a grave crisis. He wrote, "Scholars including myself have been unable to justify the contention that the current situation is already analogous [to a period of political crisis and ethnic tensions in 1970-71] and that a similar crisis is likely to ensue" (1985, 32). However, in the years following Rusinov's reassurance, ethnic polarization in Yugoslavia exploded, eventually producing civil war and ethnic cleansing.

Such informed and experienced observers would have duly predicted the pace and severity of the impending polarization if Yugoslavia's disintegration had been inevitable. This would have been the case if the divisive image was preponderant privately or if the compatible image had no support, as ex-post analyses emphasizing ancient antagonisms imply. In fact, the truth lay somewhere in the middle: the compatible image was quite strong and was developing in private, though public opinion overrated its strength.

Institutional incentives and Yugoslavia's vulnerability to ethnic polarization

Economic and political institutions and governmental policies of the former Yugoslavia provided mixed incentives to people for cultivating a compatible image and for reconciling their ethnic identities with Yugoslavness. On the one hand, the particular federal structure encouraged, especially after 1966, the creation of separate ethnonational elites and the regionalization of political interests. It also insufficiently encouraged the development of a Yugoslav national identity. On the other hand, the public expression of ethnonationalist tendencies was harshly repressed. Tito strongly suppressed the public discourse of nationalism except, of course, for that of Yugoslav nationalism. The official ideology and formal education promoted, or at least praised rhetorically, "brotherhood and unity." In addition, the cultivation of a Communist ideology and the creation of a national economy based on the self-management system were supposed to foster the image of national unity by fragmenting ethnic allegiances.

Competition for public offices and for most governmental positions was limited to group members, rendering ethnic identities a political asset and creating vested interests in their preservation. The positions of a vast number of people were closely associated with their ethnonational origin. To quote Denitch (1994, 38), "Rigid use of an affirmative action ethnic 'key' assured a near-equal distribution of cabinet posts, ambassador-

ships, and other important federal appointments between cadres from the republics' provinces. The parliament and other federal institutions made major efforts to be multilingual," although linguistic differences were minor at best. More significantly, competition for constituencies from different regions, and thus from ethnonational groups, was curtailed, reducing the incentives for building interethnic alliances.

Consequently, the articulation and aggregation of interests in Yugoslav politics were regionalized (Burg 1988, 20).[22] Some writers further maintain that the system "rejected the idea of the creation of a new Yugoslav nationality to replace Slovenes, Croats, and Serbs." Tito's emphasis was on "brotherhood," which implied equality and mutual respect between the ethnic groups, not necessarily the intermingling of the groups. Hence people who self-identified as Yugoslavs were "mildy discouraged" from it (Crnobrnja 1994, 69). The definition of the Yugoslav national identity as a residual in national censuses was a reflection of this overall policy.

While certain Yugoslav institutions nurtured ethnonational identities at the expense of Yugoslav identification, others severely limited the public expression of ethnonationalism, especially of the divisive image. These institutions also suppressed the development of ideologies other than socialism. Tito used mutual guilt to underline the history of ethnonational conflicts and neutralize ethnonationalism: "The expression of [ethno]national interests had to take place in a peculiarly circumcribed fashion. While the Croats were haunted by the Ustasha ghost, the Serbs were haunted by the specter of the accusation of Great Serbian Hegemonism" (Judah 1997, 145). Any public expression of ethnic discord and mistrust was stamped as renegade ethnonationalism reminiscent of the atrocities experienced during World War II and was sanctioned.

Hence, people who were not encouraged to abandon their ethnic attachments in favor of Yugoslavness (they were even encouraged to maintain their ethnic attachments) yet were prohibited from publicly expressing ethnonationalism opted for an obvious alternative: they actively conformed to the Yugoslav idea in public, even though they were not enthusiastic about it in private.

The institutional incentives and policies minimized the public expression of the divisive image and constrained any expression of it to the private realm, but they did not eliminate its existence in private. In other words, they generated downward ethnic preference falsification.

As a sign of the existence of significant private polarization, issues that should not have become a problem within a cohesive society became controversial in Yugoslavia. For example, Serbs resented the recognition of Kosovo's status as an autonomous province, while Kosovar Albanians acclaimed it as an insufficient yet proper status (Malcolm 1998; Mertus 1999). As Malcolm (1998) argues, Serbs regarded Kosovo's autonomy as a "punitive truncation of Serbia by the half-Croat, half-Slovene Tito." More significantly for our purposes

here, Malcolm observes that such feelings "would not be expressed in public until Tito's death; but their existence was not a secret in ruling circles." When Dobrica Ćosić, a Serbian novelist and senior Communist, complained in a 1968 meeting of the Serbian Central Committee about policies accommodating Kosovar Albanians, he was dismissed from that body later in the year as a result (329).

The monopolistic structure of information dissemination also reinforced the country's susceptibility to ethnic polarization. Those who controlled the few sources of public information could easily influence public opinion and expectations.[23] State radio and television were widely used by Milošević to disseminate an ethnocentric view of the developments during the 1980s and 1990s.

*Private polarization
  in the 1980s*

In the early 1980s, two changes that the Yugoslav society underwent stand out as likely instigators of initial, private polarization. The first is the consecutive deaths of two prominent figures in Yugoslav history. Kardelj, the Yugoslav Communist party's leading ideologist and Tito's most prominent successor, died in 1979. Then, Tito, whose name and personality were largely identified with Yugoslavness, died in 1980, marking the end of an era.[24] The second probable contributor to private polarization is the gradual yet remarkable descent of communism both worldwide and in Yugoslavia. These two changes, coupled with widespread unemployment, were apt to generate a strengthening of ethnic identities in a Communist country where very few other allegiances were allowed to flourish. When the Yugoslav and Communist self-images were fading away and unemployment impaired the occupational identities of many, some portion of the people turned to their secured and available identities such as their ethnic identities.

According to surveys in which respondents were anonymous and which were thus able to capture changes in people's private preferences, the 1980s weakened the overarching Yugoslav identity. Table 4 illustrates these changes. Between 1981 and 1991, the percentage of Bosnians who declared themselves as Yugoslavs fell from 7.9 percent to 5.5 percent, signifying a 30.3 percent decrease. Considering all the citizens of the former Yugoslavia, the percentage of those who self-identified most with being Yugoslav decreased from 5.4 percent in 1981 to 3.0 percent in 1991, representing a decline of 44.4 percent. The statistics from the other republics of the former Yugoslavia all indicate similar decreases in self-identification with the overarching Yugoslav identity, except for those from Vojvodina, where a slight increase was observed. The most radical decrease, a 73.2 percent fall, was observed in Croatia, where the percentage of the people who embraced the Yugoslav identity more than any ethnic identity diminished from 8.2 percent in 1981 to a mere 2.2 percent in 1991 (Cohen 1993, 175).[25] Cohen (1993) rightly concludes that these changes display a "marked return by many Yugoslavs to their specific ethnic group origins" (176). He does not explain, however, how a small change in private identities could generate the radical, public polarization that occurred.

Public polarization

Public polarization far exceeded private polarization, rapidly dividing the society socially, psychologically, politically, and, finally, militarily. A full account of the public events underlying this period is outside the purview of this article.[26] Fairly detailed accounts of this era are given in various sources published on Yugoslavia's disintegration; a review of these sources is sufficient to demonstrate that the era from 1980 to 1990 was marked by a striking upsurge in the public expression of the divisive image. First, long-suppressed issues resurfaced, almost with a vengeance. Serbian poets described the Croats as "pro-Ustasha" and "there was talk of" the Orthodox ancestry of the Croatian Dalmatian population, while the Croats accused the Serbs of "Stalinist" or "Chetnik" leanings (Ramet 1996a, 22). There was a renewed interest in the past and in ethno-national histories. The media and academia ethnified and, in many cases, began to promote a divisive image. A prominent Slovenian journal, *Nova revija*, published a series of articles, which, inter alia, protested the second-class status of the Slovenian language in Yugoslavia (Ramet 1996a, 24). Notoriously, the

Serbian Academy of Arts and Sciences penned in 1986 the Serbian Memorandum—many writers of which later became key political figures—promoting the idea of a greater, unified Serbia; controversial best-seller authors such as Vuk Draskovic evoked, "in a bending of scholarship," hostile stereotypes about Muslims (Cigar 1995, 22-30).

The divisive ethnic entrepreneurs, whose efforts were concentrated on capturing the Communist party apparatus in order to divide Yugoslavia into ethnonational units, succeeded in creating an atmosphere in which downward preference falsification was replaced by upward falsification. One indirect sign of this was that, in 1989, when public polarization had reached an advanced state, anonymous surveys continued to reveal that interethnic tolerance levels were high by global standards. These levels apparently increased with the degree of diversity in one's region, urban residence, age, and mixed parentage but decreased with unemployment and religiosity (Hodson, Sekulić, and Massey 1994).

Thus, while the public discourse was becoming increasingly more divisive and less tolerant of interethnic differences, private attitudes remained quite tolerant of interethnic differences. Moreover, if all interethnic hostilities expressed during the war had been genuine, one would have expected the most severe hostilities to have occurred in the less tolerant regions. In fact, most atrocities occurred in regions that were found to be more tolerant during the surveys. This suggests

that violence could not be attributed to genuine hatred but to ethnic polarization. In fact, the highest levels of tolerance were found in Bosnia, the site of the most violent crimes.[27]

Desertion and call-up evasion were very common during the civil war when public support for the divisive image was at its peak. This may also attest to the existence of upward preference falsification, although this kind of behavior might also have been caused by economic motives or simply by fear. However, it certainly shows that the division of Yugoslavia did not have sufficient support in private to make young people risk their lives for it. When authorities ordered a mass mobilization of reservists, only 10 percent showed up—others avoided the conscription by sleeping in different places every night (Glenny 1993, 131). Accordingly, Denitch (1994) argues that "widespread refusal to serve in the armed forces in this combination of civil war and war of aggression against Croatia and Bosnia is testimony to its unpopularity. In Belgrade 85 percent of the reservists were refusing the call-ups in the fall of 1991," while many were staying abroad to avoid serving (62-63).

The nationalist revivals in Serbia, Croatia, and Slovenia eventually brought to power nationalist leaders, Milošević, Tudjman, and Kucan, who, in the first free elections of the country in 1990, received electoral majorities. Once in power, Milošević reinforced polarization by, for instance, increasing the amount of Cyryllic in the alphabet, letting the Serbian Orthodox church build new churches and restore old ones, and appointing nationalist and loyal figures to important political and administrative positions. One consequence of public polarization was that interethnic parties were gradually driven out of politics. In Bosnia, for example, the elections resembled a census of the three major ethnonational groups, and "the programmatic parties were completely marginalized" (Denitch 1994, 67).[28] Perhaps more fundamentally, however, the Yugoslavs "lost the ability to understand each other, each others' values, concerns, each others' perceptions" (Ramet 1996a, 29).

Pressures to undertake upward ethnic preference falsification peaked during the war. In provocative accounts of the ethnic cleansing in Bosnia, one renowned journalist reports cases where some soldiers who were "ordered" to rape Muslim women declined to obey the orders but instructed the women to say otherwise in order to avoid appearing on the side of the enemy (Gutman 1993, 69). The point here is that while some Serbian soldiers could willingly commit such terrible crimes, others were either falsifying their preferences or trying to escape from having to commit such inhuman acts. There are numerous reports about the persecution of disloyal Serbs, some of whom even fought alongside Muslims or Croats, by other Serbs.[29] Similarly, tolerant Muslims or Croats faced social pressures and persecution by their own group.

At least partly, the seeds of the radical outcome in Yugoslavia were sown by previous policies that suppressed the public expression of the divisive image but insufficiently encouraged its elimination in private. Hence, the analysis here highlights the significance of social and political institutions in forming individuals' ethnic identities and in encouraging or discouraging downward and upward preference falsification. By analyzing the relationships between institutional incentives, ethnic identities, and preference falsification, one can better understand the dynamics of ethnic disintegration as cascades. The examination of these dynamics serves to remedy a popular misconception that is implicit in many journalistic and political accounts of ethnic conflict in the Balkans, Africa, and the Middle East: the impression that these conflicts are inevitable products of ancient hatreds.[30] In fact, most of the accompanying expressions of interethnic hatred are generated by polarization; similarly, the changing public image of these societies that portrays them as if they had always been ethnically divided should be seen as a product of ethnic polarization.

Notes

1. Theoretical analyses predict that ethnic polarization increases transaction costs, intergroup envy, rent seeking, and political instability (Bates 1974; Landa 1981, 1994; Cornell 1995; Wintrobe 1995; Cornell and Welch 1996). Accordingly, cross-country empirical analyses indicate that ethnic polarization increases corruption and government instability and decreases economic growth, investment, and interpersonal trust (Mauro 1995; Easterly and Levine 1997; Knack and Keefer 1997). Collier and Gunning (1999, 9) argue that eth-

nic and religious diversity bear deleterious effects only under undemocratic governments.

2. An important and valuable strand of research examines institution building for achieving trust and credible commitment between rival ethnic groups in *divided* societies (Fearon and Laitin 1996; Weingast 1998; Fearon 1998; Rotschild and Lake 1998).

3. The theory is explained in full in Somer 1999.

4. Many writers have described ethnic divisions as prone to massive and violent conflict and have attributed this characteristic to the fact that ethnic ties are based on a putative "blood tie." See, for instance, Horowitz 1985, chap. 2; Connor 1993.

5. For a review, see Kuran and Sunstein 1999, 687-91. For early examples of contributions to this literature, see Leibenstein 1950; Schelling 1978; Granovetter 1978. The contributions to this literature have over time become specialized in four types of cascades, each focusing on a different motivational mechanism. The cascades are not mutually exclusive. For informational cascades, see Bikhchandani, Hirshleifer, and Welch 1992, 1998; Banerjee 1993; Anderson and Holt 1997. For reputational cascades, see Akerlof 1976; Kuran 1989, 1995, 1998. For availability cascades, see Kuran and Sunstein 1999. For networking cascades, see Arthur 1994 and, partly, Laitin 1992.

6. Cascade models have been applied to explain, among other things, social movements, residential choices, consumption, fads and rumors, ethnic norms, and language preferences (Schelling 1978; Granovetter and Soong 1986, 1988; Kuran 1989, 1998; Laitin 1992; Banerjee 1993; Hirschleifer 1995; Bikhchandani, Hirshleifer, and Welch 1992, 1998).

7. For nations as imagined communities, see Anderson 1983. Above all, images of ethnic identities are mental models of one's social environment. With respect to their economic consequences, they are comparable to potential "governance structures," which define group boundaries and the "sets of acceptable contracting partners." A governance structure is likely to prevail if it can provide economic rents for insiders (Yarbrough and Yarbrough 2000). To the extent that governance struc-

tures become the norm as a result of cascades, however, there is no guarantee that the more efficacious structure will prevail. Cascades can render the divisive image dominant within a group as an unintended consequence of individual chain reactions, that is, although the divisive image is less advantageous for the average individual than other images.

8. "Weak social relationships" such as those between simple acquaintances can be crucial in determining one's economic and political opportunities. Hence Granovetter's argument (1982) on "the strength of weak ties." See also Landa 1981, 1994.

9. Polarized groups exhibit differential rates of economic return and different patterns of income distribution, which lead to divergent median voter preferences over issues such as taxation, provision of public goods, and government policies including income transfers from rich to poor. Inefficiencies caused by competitive rent seeking, political deadlock, and secessionist demands follow (Alesina and Drazen 1991; Alesina and Rodrik 1994; Easterly and Levine 1997; Bolton and Roland 1997).

10. For related definitions, see Kuran 1998.

11. See also Beissinger 1993; Beissinger highlights the complexity and plasticity of the various images of the Soviet Union that underlay people's private and public identities.

12. Quoted in Judah 1997 (195) from a personal interview with a Bosnian Serb.

13. See also Goodwin 1999.

14. In addition to the elite-based explanation, Posen 1993, Fearon 1998, and Weingast 1998 highlight the security threats that ethnic groups posed to each other and rightly emphasize the lack of institutions that could provide credible commitments between groups in the absence of Tito's iron fist. Other explanations emphasize cultural differences and the dissimilar structures and goals of the Serbian, Croat, and Slovenian nationalist ideologies (Ramet 1996a); increased influence on Serbian politics of the rural population, the "idiocy of rural culture," which accompanied Milošević's coming to power (Ramet 1996b); the opposition generated in reaction to the centralist, unitarist state apparatus (Bose 1995); and the high economic cost caused by economic austerity programs and untimely de-

cisions on the part of the international organizations and Western states (Woodward 1995; Danchev and Halverson 1996).

15. See Botev 1994; Petrović 1991. See also Botev and Wagner 1993, which, in contrast to Petrović, interprets the data differently in that it downplays the integrative consequences of mixed marriages.

16. See the table in Sekulić, Massey, and Hodson 1994, 85. The same statistic was 5.4 percent for the whole of Yugoslavia.

17. The "Muslim" identification was first included in the census in 1971.

18. See also Bookman 1991; Kraft 1992.

19. In the late 1980s, when signs of ethnic tensions were evident and the decline of Soviet socialism was under way, some analysts suggested that the main threat to European security in the 1990s would come from ethnic conflict and political fragmentation in the Balkans (Larrabee 1990-91, 59).

20. Similarly, Denitch (1994) confesses that his optimistic feelings about Yugoslavia's prospects for survival were "an honest mistake, shared with most non-Yugoslav and Yugoslav analysts up to the mid-1980s" (20).

21. Note that, in the Yugoslav context, the term "nationality" is used to denote one of the ethnic groups that constituted the former Yugoslavia.

22. See also Bose 1995, esp. pp. 101-6, for the argument that the republic-based politics of the Yugoslav Communist party prevented the development of political movements that transcend ethnic lines. Denitch (1994) argues that "the system paid far too much attention to the issue of multinationalism and thus kept the fact of [ethno]national identity central in determining career paths of at least two generations of politicians and civil servants" (39).

23. For example, Maass 1996 (227-25).

24. The psychological impact of Tito's death was remarkable because, in Larrabee's (1990-91) words, "his personality [had] kept the system together and [given] it cohesion" (67).

25. The same numbers are given in more detail in Petrović 1992.

26. For a description of the public events of the era, see Ramet 1996a, esp. chaps. 1-5; Cigar 1995; Malcolm 1998.

27. See the table in Hodson, Sekulić, and Massey 1994, 1548.

28. By 1986, the same author argues, "the revived and in some cases invented national questions [had] either [driven] all other issues from the political arena or distorted them" (Denitch 1994, 39).

29. See, for instance, Washington Post, 24 Aug. 1992.

30. For recent accounts of historical cooperation and cultural mixing among the ethnic groups in the Balkans and the Middle East, see Malcolm (1998); Goodwin (1999).

References

Abrams, Dominic and Michael A. Hogg. 1990. An Introduction to the Social Identity Approach. In Social Identity Theory: Constructive and Critical Advances, ed. Dominic Abrams and Michael A. Hogg. New York: Springer-Verlag.

Akerlof, George A. 1976. The Economics of Caste and of the Rat Race and Other Woeful Tales. Quarterly Journal of Economics 90:599-617.

Akhavan, Payam. 1995. Preface. In Yugoslavia, the Former and Future: Reflections by Scholars from the Region, ed. Payam Akhavan and Robert Howse. Washington, DC: Brookings Institution; Geneva: United Nations Research Institute for Social Development.

Alesina, Alberto and Allan Drazen. 1991. Why Are Stabilizations Delayed? American Economic Review 81(Dec.): 1170-88.

Alesina, Alberto and Dani Rodrik. 1994. Distributive Politics and Economic Growth. Quarterly Journal of Economics 59(May):465-90.

Anderson, Benedict. 1983. Imagined Communities: Reflections on the Origin and Spread of Nationalism. London: Verso.

Anderson, Lisa R. and Charles A. Holt. 1997. Information Cascades in the Laboratory. American Economic Review 87(5):847-62.

Arthur, Brian W. 1994. *Increasing Returns and Path Dependence in the Economy.* Ann Arbor: University of Michigan Press.

Banerjee, Abhijit V. 1993. The Economics of Rumours. *Review of Economic Studies* 60(203):309-27.

Bates, Robert H. 1974. Ethnic Competition and Modernization in Contemporary Africa. *Comparative Political Studies* 6(Jan.):457-84.

Beissinger, Mark R. 1993. Demise of an Empire-State: Identity, Legitimacy, and the Deconstruction of Soviet Politics. In *The Rising Tide of Cultural Pluralism: The Nations-State at Bay?* ed. Crawford Young. Madison: University of Wisconsin Press.

Bikhchandani, Sushil, David Hirshleifer, and Ivo Welch. 1992. A Theory of Fads, Fashion, Custom, and Cultural Change as Informational Cascades. *Journal of Political Economy* 100(5):992-1026.

———. 1998. Learning from the Behavior of Others: Conformity, Fads, and Informational Cascades. *Journal of Economic Perspectives* 12(3):151-70.

Bolton, Patrick and Gerard Roland. 1997. The Break-Up of Nations: A Political Economy Analysis. *Quarterly Journal of Economics* 112(Nov.):1057-90.

Bookman, M. Z. 1991. *The Political Economy of Discontinuous Development: Regional Disparities and Interregional Conflict.* New York: Praeger.

Bose, Sumantra. 1995. State Crises and Nationalities Conflict in Sri Lanka and Yugoslavia. *Comparative Political Studies* 28(Apr.):87-116.

Botev, Nikolai. 1994. Where East Meets West: Ethnic Intermarriage in the Former Yugoslavia, 1962 to 1989. *American Sociological Review* 59(June):461-80.

Botev, Nikolai and Richard A. Wagner. 1993. Seeking Past the Barricades: Ethnic Intermarriages in Yugoslavia During the Last Three Decades. *Anthropology of East Europe Review* 11(Fall):27-34.

Burg, Steven L. 1988. Political Structures. In *Yugoslavia: A Fractured Federalism,* ed. Dennison Rusinov. Washington, DC: Wilson Center Press.

Carment, David and Patrick James. 1996. Two-Level Games and Third-Party Intervention: Evidence from Ethnic Conflict in the Balkans and South Asia. *Canadian Journal of Political Science* 29(Sept.):521-54.

Cigar, Norman L. 1995. *Genocide in Bosnia: The Policy of "Ethnic Cleansing."* College Station: Texas A&M University Press.

Cohen, Leonard J. 1993. *Broken Bonds: The Disintegration of Yugoslavia.* Boulder, CO: Westview Press.

Collier, Paul and Jan Willem Gunning. 1999. Why Has Africa Grown Slowly? *Journal of Economic Perspectives* 13(Summer):3-22.

Connor, Walker. 1993. Beyond Reason: The Nature of the Ethnonational Bond. *Ethnic and Racial Studies* 16(July):373-89.

Cornell, Bradford. 1995. A Hypothesis Regarding the Origins of Ethnic Discrimination. *Rationality and Society* 7(Jan.):4-30.

Cornell, Bradford and Ivo Welch. 1996. Culture, Information, and Screening Discrimination. *Journal of Political Economy* 104(June):542-71.

Crnobrnja, Mihailo. 1994. *The Yugoslav Drama.* Montreal and Kingston: McGill-Queen's Press.

Danchev, Alex and Thomas Halverson. 1996. *International Perspectives on the Yugoslav Conflict.* New York: St. Martin's Press.

Denitch, Bogdan. 1994. *Ethnic Nationalism: The Tragic Death of Yugoslavia.* Minneapolis: University of Minnesota Press.

Ding, Wei. 1991. Yugoslavia: Costs and Benefits of Union and Interdependence of Regional Economies. *Comparative Economic Studies* 33(Winter): 1-26.

Easterly, William and Ross Levine. 1997. Africa's Growth Tragedy: Policies and Ethnic Divisions. *Quarterly Journal of Economics* 112(Nov.):1203-50.

Fearon, James D. 1998. Commitment Problems and the Spread of Ethnic Conflict. In *Ethnic Fears and Global Management: The International Spread and Management of Ethnic Conflict*, ed. David A. Lake and Donald Rotschild. Princeton, NJ: Princeton University Press.

Fearon, James D. and David D. Laitin. 1996. Explaining Interethnic Cooperation. *American Political Science Review* 90(Dec.):715-35.

Gagnon, V. P., Jr. 1994-95. Ethnic Nationalism and International Conflict: The Case of Serbia. *International Security* 19(Winter):130-66.

Glenny, Misha. 1993. *The Fall of Yugoslavia: The Third Balkan War*. New York: Penguin Books.

Goodwin, Jason. 1999. *Lords of the Horizons: A History of the Ottoman Empire*. New York: Henry Holt.

Granovetter, Mark. 1978. Threshold Models of Collective Behavior. *American Journal of Sociology* 83:1420-43.

———. 1982. The Strength of Weak Ties: A Network Theory Revisited. In *Social Structure and Network Analysis*, ed. Peter V. Marsden and Nan Lin. Beverly Hills, CA: Sage.

Granovetter, Mark and Roland Soong. 1986. Threshold Models of Interpersonal Effects in Consumer Demand. *Journal of Economic Behavior and Organization* 7(1):83-99.

———. 1988. Threshold Models of Diversity: Chinese Restaurants, Residential Segregation, and the Spiral of Silence. In *Sociological Methodology*, vol. 18, ed. C. C. Clogg. Washington, DC: American Sociological Association.

Gutman, Roy. 1993. *A Witness to Genocide*. New York: Macmillan.

Hirschleifer, David. 1995. The Blind Leading the Blind: Social Influence, Fads, and Informational Cascades. In *The New Economics of Human Behavior*, ed. Mariano Tommasi and Kathryn Ierulli. New York: Cambridge University Press.

Hodson, Randy, Dusko Sekulić, and Garth Massey. 1994. National Tolerance in the Former Yugoslavia. *American Journal of Sociology* 99:1534-58.

Horowitz, Donald L. 1985. *Ethnic Groups in Conflict*. Berkeley: University of California Press.

Judah, Tim. 1997. *The Serbs: History, Myth, and the Destruction of Yugoslavia*. New Haven, CT: Yale University Press.

Kaplan, Robert D. 1994. *Balkan Ghosts: A Journey Through History*. New York: Vintage Books.

Knack, Stephen and Philip Keefer. 1997. Does Social Capital Have an Economic Payoff? A Cross-Country Investigation. *Quarterly Journal of Economics* 112(Nov.):1251-88.

Kraft, Evan. 1992. Evaluating Regional Policy in Yugoslavia, 1966-1990. *Comparative Economic Studies* 34(Fall-Winter):11-33.

Kuran, Timur. 1989. Sparks and Prairie Fires: A Theory of Unanticipated Political Revolution. *Public Choice* 61:41-74.

———. 1995. *Private Truths, Public Lies: The Social Consequences of Preference Falsification*. Cambridge, MA: Harvard University Press.

———. 1998. Ethnic Norms and Their Transformation Through Reputational Cascades. *Journal of Legal Studies* 27(June):623-59.

Kuran, Timur and Cass R. Sunstein. 1999. Availability Cascades and Risk

Regulation. *Stanford Law Review* 51(Apr.):683-768.

Laitin, David D. 1992. Language Normalization in Estonia and Catalonia. *Journal of Baltic Studies* 23(Summer):149-66.

Landa, Janet T. 1981. A Theory of the Ethnically Homogeneous Middleman Group: An Institutional Alternative to Contract Law. *Journal of Legal Studies* 10(June):349-62.

————. 1994. *Trust, Ethnicity, and Identity: Beyond the New Institutional Economics of Ethnic Trading Networks, Contract Law, and Gift-Exchange.* Ann Arbor: University of Michigan Press.

Larrabee, Stephen F. 1990-91. Long Memories and Short Fuses: Change and Instability in the Balkans. *International Security* 15:58-91.

Leibenstein, Harvey. 1950. Bandwagon, Snob, and Veblen Effects in the Theory of Consumers' Demand. *Quarterly Journal of Economics* 64:183-207.

Maass, Peter. 1996. *Love Thy Neighbor: A Story of War.* New York: Vintage Books.

Malcolm, Noel. 1998. *Kosovo: A Short History.* New York: New York University Press.

Mauro, Paolo. 1995. Corruption and Growth. *Quarterly Journal of Economics* 110(Aug.):682-712.

McAdams, Richard H. 1995. Cooperation and Conflict: The Economics of Group Status Production and Race Discrimination. *Harvard Law Review* 108(Mar.):1005-84.

Mertus, Julie A. 1999. *Kosovo: How Myths and Truths Started a War.* Berkeley: University of California Press.

Mojzes, Paul. 1994. *Yugoslavian Inferno: Ethnoreligious Warfare in the Balkans.* New York: Continuum.

Petrović, Ruza. 1991. The Ethnic Identity of Parents and Children. *Yugoslav Survey* 32(2):63-76.

————. 1992. The National Composition of Yugoslavia's Population, 1991. *Yugoslav Survey* 33(1):3-24.

Posen, Barry R. 1993. The Security Dilemma and Ethnic Conflict. *Survival* 35(Spring):27-47.

Ramet, Sabrina P. 1996a. *Balkan Babel: The Disintegration of Yugoslavia from the Death of Tito to Ethnic War.* Boulder, CO: Westview Press.

————. 1996b. Nationalism and the "Idiocy" of the Countryside: The Case of Serbia. *Ethnic and Racial Studies* 19(Jan.):70-87.

Roeder, Philip G. 1991. Soviet Federalism and Ethnic Mobilization. *World Politics* 43(Jan.):196-232.

Rotschild, Donald and David A. Lake. 1998. Containing Fear: The Management of Transnational Ethnic Conflict. In *Ethnic Fear and Its Global Management: The International Spread and Management of Ethnic Conflict,* ed. David A. Lake and Donald Rotschild. Princeton, NJ: Princeton University Press.

Rusinov, Dennison. 1985. Nationalities Policy and the "National Question." In *Yugoslavia in the 1980s,* ed. Pedro Ramet. Boulder, CO: Westview Press.

Saluter, Arlene F. 1996. *Marital Status and Living Arrangements: March 1994.* Current Population Reports, series P20-484. Washington, DC: Government Printing Office.

Schelling, Thomas C. 1978. *Micromotives and Macrobehavior.* New York: Norton.

Sekulić, Dusko, Garth Massey, and Randy Hodson. 1994. Who Were the Yugoslavs? Failed Sources of a Common Identity in the Former Yugoslavia. *American Sociological Review* 59(Feb.):83-97.

Somer, Murat. 1999. Diversity Versus Unity: Causes and Dynamics of Ethnic Polarization. Ph.D. diss., University of Southern California.

Tajfel, Henri. 1978. The Achievement of Group Differentiation. In *Differentia-*

tion Between Social Groups, ed. Henri Tajfel. London: Academic Press, in Cooperation with European Association of Experimental Social Psychology.

Turner, John C. 1982. Towards a Cognitive Redefinition of the Social Group. In *Social Identity and Intergroup Relations*, ed. Henri Tajfel. New York: Cambridge University Press.

Weingast, Barry R. 1998. Constructing Trust: The Political and Economic Roots of Ethnic and Regional Conflict. In *Institutions and Social Order*, ed. Karol Soltan, Eric M. Uslaner, and Virginia Haufler. Ann Arbor: University of Michigan Press.

Wintrobe, Ronald. 1995. Some Economics of Ethnic Capital Formation and Conflict. In *Nationalism and Rationality*, ed. Albert Breton, Gianluigi Galeotti, Pierre Salmon, and Ronald Wintrobe. New York: Cambridge University Press.

Woodward, Susan L. 1995. *Balkan Tragedy: Chaos and Dissolution After the Cold War*. Washington, DC: Brookings Institution.

Yarbrough, Beth V. and Robert M. Yarbrough. 2000. Governance Structures, Insider Status, and Boundary Maintenance. *Journal of Bioeconomics* 1(July):289-310.

ANNALS, *AAPSS*, **573**, January 2001

Culture and Economic Development in South Asia

By JOHN ADAMS

ABSTRACT: The influence of culture on economic development in South Asia has drawn scholarly interest since Max Weber argued that the rise of Protestantism abetted the origination of capitalism. Weber claimed that the spirituality and otherworldliness of Hinduism, along with its associated caste system, were not compatible with this new economic constellation. This sharp dichotomy posited by Weber and others has not been borne out by India's complex post-independence experience. Castes act as interest associations in India's democracy. India's labor force has become increasingly skilled and differentiated. From the Green Revolution onward, India's farmers have consistently raised yields to meet food needs. Large firms governed within joint families have succeeded in the domestic and global realms. South Asian culture and social patternings are best perceived as a multifarious resource out of which the subcontinent's future will be constructed rather than as universally stultifying features.

John Adams served as professor and chair of the Department of Economics at Northeastern University from 1990 to 1998. He was previously professor in the Department of Economics at the University of Maryland, College Park, from 1965 to 1990. He is currently affiliated with the Center for South Asian Studies, University of Virginia, and Harvard University's Center for Middle Eastern Studies. From 1967 to 1968, he was a Senior Fulbright Lecturer at Bangalore University. He has been president of the Eastern Economic Association and the Association for Evolutionary Economics.

Hamlet: *"To die, to sleep; To sleep; per-chance to dream: ay, there's the rub: For in that sleep of death what dreams may come. . . . "* [A rub is "anything that interferes with the ball in the game of bowls." (Rogers 1987, 310)]

Culture, "ay, there's the rub." Culture is the stuff of society: ideas, skills, tools, beliefs, clothing, buildings, language, music, science, values. An economy is part of a society. This almost syllogism should conclude: therefore, culture shapes the economy. The logic is ironclad. Or is it? The logic is not ironclad for modern economists whose discipline claims universality: "Get the prices right, get the policies right, and efficiency and growth are yours for the having." If things are not going well, culture is not the rub. Regardless of the character of religion, the state of knowledge, the habit of dress, or the cast of mind, one society should be able to advance economically as rapidly as any other. Self-interest, the eye for a profit, and the devising of labor-saving advancements are, irrespective of time or place, omnipresent features of the human psyche. Economic gain, economic growth, or economic development is not, and cannot be, held back by the rub of culture. Economic science is no more alien to South Asia, as one example, than is physics or biology. It would be as fatuous to assert that there is a Bangladeshi economics as to claim that there is a Pakistani physics or a Sri Lankan biology.

Salvaging the culture-as-rub syllogism seems daunting in the face of the economists' brashness. There are only two lines of hope. The first is to move into an alternative realm of discourse, such as sociology or anthropology, in which the holism of social life and material livelihood is a foundational premise. The second is to probe around in the field of economics to see whether there are exceptions to the rule of hermeneutical ubiquity. Perhaps the discipline is not quite as equable as its most chauvinistic proponents assert.

South Asia is a perennial candidate to serve as an arena in which to explore the conjunction, if any, between culture and economy. Its societies are profoundly non-European and profoundly poor, and it is easy to draw a connecting line from the first condition to the second. Max Weber was not content merely to argue that there was a strong link between the sprouting of the Protestant denominations in Europe and the rise of capitalist economies, as he did in *The Protestant Ethic and the Spirit of Capitalism* (Weber [1904-5] 1976). He wanted to use the comparative method to explore and to contrast forms of connections between the world's great systems of beliefs and the mundane categories of everyday life. Weber therefore undertook a ponderous study of Hinduism and Buddhism under the title *The Religion of India* (Weber [1921] 1958). Others have explored narrower themes, such as whether dowries and lavish weddings immiserate rural families or whether Indians' affection for their sacred cows imposes debilitating costs on their farm economy. Does tradition utterly bind modernity? For rural economists, a key conundrum is the extent to which South Asian farmers are rational, that is, the extent to which they react to the price and profit signals of the market.

My intent, first, is to aver that it is fallacious for Weber and others to have argued that South Asian culture, and its religious outlook and social expressions in particular, suppress individual and collective economic attainment in a long-term, definitive fashion so that the societies thus afflicted have little chance of applying economic measures that would act efficaciously to start and conduce to economic advancement. Second, I wish to critique and reject the conventional or preponderant view among economists that culture does not matter: that there is no rub in the institutions and cultural features of disparate societies. Third, on a more constructive footing, let us discern a "middle way," to use a pertinent phrase, down which path one proceeds by trying to identify specifically how a culture and its accompanying institutional arrangements affect multifarious aspects of an economy. This amounts to uncoding channels of influence using sound research methods and careful exegesis. It turns out that there are indeed many convincing studies drawn from across the social sciences, including economics, that make plain that cultures do rub economies in ways that matter.

Before moving on to extensive rumination about the validity of the cultural rub hypothesis in South Asia, we must consider some pervasive issues. The temporal and spatial terms of reference need to be specified. As far as time is concerned, South Asian society has roots extending back some 6000 years and for at least the last 2000 years has conspicuously exhibited its characteristic features such as caste, the joint family, and the village community (Basham 1959). The dominance of Hinduism as a syncretic, nonproselytizing religion is coexistent with this social reach. The mostly rural economy features uncertain monsoonal rains, dispersed canal and well irrigation, and heavy use of draft animals for plowing and carting. Depending on ambient conditions, rice, wheat, or a millet serves as the staple in a mixed local agriculture. Fish, game, fruits, fodder, and firewood are harvested from common-property resources. Over time, these social and economic characteristics have changed but not so much that someone could not move a few thousand years backward or forward in time and find conditions familiar enough. Having set maximal temporal parentheses, we must recognize that most of the cultural rub speculation among social scientists has centered on South Asian societies and their capacities for economic progress only after much wider opportunities for interaction with the rest of the world were opened during the age of European exploration and conquest, beginning with Vasco da Gama's disembarkment at Calicut in 1498.

The spatial boundaries of what is today known as South Asia are geologically framed by the Himalayas to the north, hills and jungles to the northeast, deserts to the northwest, and oceans ringing the southerly perimeter. A problematic subtheme in the culture-economy debate revolves around the validity of assuming, overtly or unconsciously, that South Asian society, economy, and religion can be treated as subcontinental wholes. The contrary axiom is that the region's exceptional linguistic, ethnic, ecological, and spiritual diversity renders overarching syntheses specious (Singh 1998). South Asia is as much the fount of Buddhism, Jainism, and Sikhism, and home to Muslims, Christians, Zoroastrians, and Jews, as it is intrinsically Hindu. Hardly monolithic, Hinduism itself lacks a founder, churchly hierarchy, weekly holy day, singular sacred city, prescribed ritual of worship, or irreproachable text; it contains myriad sects, cults, and yogic traditions; it encompasses a panoply of goddesses, gods, and avatars. Today, as earlier, South Asia harbors perennially rivalrous governments with varied prospects for stability. It is a heroic but absolutely necessary gesture to assert that a reified construct named "Hinduism," "Islam," "spirituality," or "otherworldliness" can be connected with a long-running economic stasis enthralling millions of far-flung South Asians across scores of generations, whether one is laying full blame on an abstracted cultural style, type, or geist or depositing responsibility as an offering at the feet of the omnipotently obstructive deities.

Having situated ourselves in South Asian time and place, we must next position our discussion in the context of modern social science. The most direct way to do this is to recall the very large number of posited polarities that make up the bread and butter of the disciplines. Ferdinand Tönnies distinguished "community" and "society" (Tönnies [1887] 1957). In *Ancient Law* (Maine [1861] 1986) and *Village Communities in East and West* (Maine [1871] 1876), Sir Henry Maine used a predominantly jurisprudential interpretation of the history of institutions to argue for a movement from status to contract in Indo-European societies that did not become the fiefs of religions. Other imagined juxtapositions are "spiritual versus material" or "irrational versus rational" or "simplicity versus complexity." Much of twentieth-century sociology sought to discern broad patterns of evolution in the highway from traditional to modern society and in so doing formulated variants of modernization theory. More linear and causally heedful are the sequential stage theories of the economists Karl Marx ([1839] 1967) and Walt W. Rostow ([1965] 1990). As did Weber, these theorists wrestled to a greater or lesser degree with the nature of South Asian society and its place in their schematic formulations. Although the penchant is becoming less fashionable, arguing about how to fit the realities of rural India into Marx's Asiatic Mode of Production and waymarking India's precise degree of advancement on the road to capitalism have long constituted elephantine components of the country's academic enterprise.

Implicitly and explicitly, these polarities or dimensions or ideal types run through all components of the culture-economy controversy. Adding further to the complexity of the analysis are additional perplexities that are best phrased as questions. Is there directionality? That is, do societies move from one early or primitive state of affairs toward a later or more advanced state? Is there determinacy; that is, are inexorable processes at work? What role is there for individual or leadership agency in overcoming the heavy hand of custom or structure and accelerating changes in a social system? How can one be a revolutionary leader or a visionary planner if the course of history is determined by sweeping technological, climatic, class, or demographic forces? What preconditions must obtain for progress to occur? What changes in institutions and values prefigure the spawning of agents of economic alteration such as entrepreneurs or foment the rapid dispersal of technological innovations?

Let us finish brushing aside the cobwebs of sophistry by bringing into unsparing daylight the incubus of cultural hegemonism, sometimes masquerading as Eurocentrism, Orientalism (Said 1979), missionary hubris, or just plain racism, which itself might be based on faulty evolutionary theories, flawed physical anthropometrics, or genetic balderdash. Whenever we follow the nouns "Hindus" or "South Asians" with a verb of action, inaction, or being, we risk veering in this direction. Today's social truth is tomorrow's political incorrectness. Lest the devotees of a universal economics chortle at their seeming insulation from such cross-cultural calumnies, let them be reminded that they recapture these denigrating attitudes in the ill-concealed condescensions of the visiting

policy experts or in their rephrasing of the classic polarities in the recurrent motif, "Our (divinely, theoretically) recommended policies are better than your (silly, indigenous) policies." The specific point I am making is that it is very hard to draw a line between what is good and well-intended diagnostic and prescriptive social science and what is unsavory posturing and specious inanity. If it is difficult for able, dispassionate practitioners to do this, it is correspondingly a challenge for the human victims of their scrutiny and advice to observe with tranquil equanimity the ongoing surgeries and pharmacological experiments being practiced on their social body.

Looking broadly at past and present studies of culture and economic development in South Asia, by no means all of which are products of nonindigenes, one must be struck by the degree to which India and its confreres are deemed ab initio to be failed societies, economies, or polities. This presumptiveness must be predicated on one or more applicable yardsticks. Hindus and their ilk are considered "pagans," meaning "not Christian." Indians have poor personal hygiene and lax standards of public sanitation and thereby bring disease and poverty on themselves: this proposition was a staple of crusading missionaries and do-good social reformers (Mayo 1927). Befuddled Indian farmers are incapable of acting "scientifically." The caste hierarchy and the demands of the joint family block social mobility and thwart the spirit of individual achievement. Gandhi and the Congress leadership are "children who will never be ready for self-rule." Bangladesh is a "basket case." The Indian capital-output ratio is "appallingly high" and indicative of slovenly resource management in the private and public sectors. Of late, of course, the litmus test has been the attainment of high national economic growth rates or, more widely, of rapid economic and social development.

Differentness can be used as an explanation for almost any alleged social, economic, or political failure of individuals or entire societies. This is an issue to which we must inevitably return, but it needs to be placed in the forefront of our consciousness along with the previously adumbrated cautions about setting the appropriate time span, acknowledging the diversities of the South Asian subcontinent, and recognizing the continued reliance of social scientists on simplifying polarities or dualisms. Perhaps it will prove useful to keep in mind two features of the South Asian landscape: first, the six-millennium history of the civilization and, second, its sheer demographic fecundity. On the face of it, neither is consistent with the notion that we are dealing with a society that sagacious onlookers must unanimously judge a transient failure of history; nor does either feature imply that we are witnessing the horrific last hours of an enfeebled people's death throes. The Spanish, Italians, and Japanese will soon disappear from the planet, applying a demographic time scale, but not the Indians, Pakistanis, and Bangladeshis. South Asia's longevity and procreativeness are hardly signals of a steep societal nosedive. As of 2000, explaining how a surviving 1.4 billion people and their forebears have for 6000 contiguous years somehow surmounted irremediable social decay, action-numbing religiosity, economic insufficiency, and political ineptitude is a task this particular pundit would be loath to take up whimsically.

THE HINDU ETHIC AND
THE SPIRIT OF CAPITALISM

To this day a correct Hindu who has dined with a European will disinfect himself . . . by use of cow manure. No correct Hindu will bypass a urinating cow without putting his hand into the stream and wetting forehead, garments, etc. with it as does the Catholic with holy water.
—Weber ([1921] 1958, 28)

These two fascinating sentences could be parsed and deconstructed with endless delight, but here they serve merely to begin our rendezvous with Max Weber. Weber's study of religion in India is much less frequently read or mentioned than his classic treatise connecting the appearance of the Protestant denominations with the early economic advancement of Great Britain, the Low Countries, and the other regions of Europe that led off the Commercial Revolution. The linking variables were a strong work ethic, frugality, and the belief that economic success exhibited that one was in line to be "called" to heaven for doing God's work. Weber thought this conjunction of traits harmonized with an individualistic, rational, cause-and-effect outlook. As translated, *The Religion of India* runs to around 350 pages, only a tiny fraction of which are devoted to explicit comments about the effects of the Hindu conventions of thought on economic behavior. Weber dismissed South Asia's other religious traditions as being offshoots of the Hindu stem or so sufficiently assimilated into the Hindu mode that no distinctions needed to be drawn. A peculiarity is his frequent reference to the "orgiastic" dimension of Hindu worship, epitomized in the Shiva lingam, and he appeared to believe that wild sexual license was a common part of the religion's rituals.

Time has not treated kindly Weber's assessment of Hindu beliefs and practices and their influence on India's material progress. However plausible and methodologically innovative was *The Protestant Ethic*, it is difficult to conceive that informed readers have ever found *The Religion of India* accurate and convincing. If we may assume that the translation accurately renders into English the tone as well as the content of Weber's writing, then his withering disdain for everything he believed he had learned about the life of the peoples of the subcontinent is the volume's most evident feature. The book recapitulates exhaustively India's religious writings and derivative dissections by Western interpreters. Compared to the anthropological literature that emerged after World War II, Weber's depiction of India is a lifeless rendering of putative doctrine, much of it drawn from arid Brahmanic perspectives. Weber is quite blunt that he is drawing conclusions from his textual examination of

economic aims and behavior, not reporting observed conduct. He writes,

We are now in a position to enquire into the effects of the caste system on the economy. These effects were essentially negative and must rather be inferred than inductively assessed. Hence we can but phrase a few generalizations. Our sole point is that this order by its nature is completely traditionalistic and anti-rational in its effects. (Weber [1921] 1958, 111)

In the most derisive contrast Weber draws between the Protestant and Hindu ethics, he writes,

In addition to the ritualistic and traditional inner relation anchored through the caste order to the *samsara* and *karma* teaching . . . , there also appeared the religious anthropolatry of the Hindu laity against the naturally strong, traditionalistic, charismatic clergy of the *gurus*. These hindered the rationalization of life conduct throughout. It is quite evident that no community dominated by inner powers of this sort could out of its own substance arrive at the "spirit of capitalism." (Weber [1921] 1958, 325)

Not content with this sweeping deprecation, Weber proceeds to say that India is incapable of taking over capitalism as an "artifact" as the Japanese did. He adds dismissively that should the "thin conquering strata" of the Europeans vanish, South Asia would relapse into "the old feudal robber romanticism of the Indian Middle Ages" (Weber [1921] 1958, 325).

Weber certainly overstated the rigidities implicit in the impact of the Hindu ethic on labor stratification, as embodied in the caste system and as reinforced by the Brahmanic doctrines of pollution, karma, dharma, and samsara. Further, because of his reliance on scriptures rather than observation and field inquiry, he could not appreciate the many diverse forms of caste, belief, and worship across the whole range of the subcontinent's villages and families. As Harold A. Gould and others have recognized, caste is a multifaceted phenomenon, with sacred, ritualistic, ethnic, and economic dimensions that may vary independently (Gould 1988). The interplay between caste and economic change in the modern world is complex: "Viewed in historical perspective, one sees that the capacity of castes to employ their primordial characteristics for ethnically integrated cooperative action in the modern economy and polity has itself provided the impetus for major modifications in the internal structure" (14-15).

The wide-gauge Weberian critique of South Asian religion and institutions has recent parallel partners. K. William Kapp's *Hindu Culture, Economic Development, and Economic Planning in India* (1963) is representative of post-independence pessimism. Although capital formation and skilled labor were critical variables, Kapp remarks that "it can hardly be doubted" that Hindu culture slowed economic growth, citing "non-secular and pre-technological institutions and values such as the hierarchically organized caste system, the limited or static levels of aspirations, moral aloofness, casteism and factionalism—to name only a few of the major barriers"

(64-65). Kapp's rendering of South Asian institutions and his assertion of their negative impact on development are in retrospect mechanical and deterministic and wholly fail to capture the dynamism set in train by the early years of planning.

Gunnar Myrdal undertook a mammoth survey of South Asia's development prospects in the three-volume *Asian Drama* (1968). Seeking to balance economic and social analysis, Myrdal found religion and social values to be obstructive of developmental gains. *The Asian Drama* is pervaded by Ibsenesque gloom. Perhaps without fully realizing it, Myrdal was thrown off balance by the disorder and squalor of the subcontinent compared to the placidity and tidiness of Scandinavia. His most remembered neologism arose from his disappointment with the Indian version of democratic socialism and with the performances of the other governments of the subcontinent, which spurred him to label the region's polities "soft states." As did Weber and Kapp, Myrdal erred in permitting a stylized depiction of South Asian culture to dominate his assessment of the potential for strong economic performance whether arising from state-managed collective accomplishment or from spontaneous individual achievements.

Myrdal moved down the well-trod path of castigating Hinduism for its mystical, nonrational character. Only a change in values would suffice to permit institutional reform and economic modernization via state planning; inescapably, South Asians would have to absorb the following virtues: efficiency, diligence, orderliness, punctuality, frugality, scrupulous honesty, energetic enterprise, a willingness to take the long view (Myrdal 1968, 1:61-62), although each is "alien to the region" (1:73). Myrdal attacked the plethora of sacred cows (1:89), the South Asian fascination with astrology and horoscopes, and laborers' conformity to the backward-bending supply curve (3:1872). *The Asian Drama* was a strange and dated study when it appeared and is only more so from the contemporary vantage point.

CASTE AND WORK

Weber's pessimism about South Asia's potential for the pursuit of economic advantage rested on twin pillars. The first was the nonrational character of Hindu thought and its antimaterialist spirituality, and the second was the "social expression" of the Hindu ethic, especially in the form of the caste hierarchy. Let us set aside the motivational component for later treatment and examine here several formulations of the caste-as-rub proposition. Weber understood the layers of caste in the bookish terms that defined the four varnas: Brahmans, Kshatriyas, Vaisyas, and Sudras, or Priests, Warriors, Merchants, and Workers, the latter including farmers and craftspeople. A fifth stratum, the Untouchables, was made up of castes, such as the Leatherworkers, whose occupations brought them into contact with polluting materials, and tribals who were not fully assimilated into Hindu society. The broad conjecture that the hierarchical Hindu caste system must stultify social mobility and economic achievement has fueled an important component of the culture-economy squabble. To anticipate the conclusion to the ensuing review of the most interesting features of the caste-mobility discussions, what we will find is that a strict either-or position is not tenable. It turns out that a middle way, based on solid social science investigation, leads to the discovery of which aspects of caste matter in South Asia's economic affairs and where lie the main lines of connection.

From the 1950s on, anthropologists, sociologists, and economists have conducted countless studies of castes in South Asia. Many have looked closely at the economic dimensions of the caste system. The result is a much clearer and sharper focus on culture-economy relationships, and, with allowance for lingering small differences of opinion, there now exists a consensus about the main patterns. On an illustrative basis, we can look at two clusters of well-known studies of the Indian case. The first concerns the relationship between the caste structure and the village economy; the second considers the continuing implications of caste for the modern labor force. The chief conclusion is that caste was and remains a highly influential force in shaping labor relations in India's villages and urban workplaces, although, contrary to Weber or Kapp, the effects of caste do not weigh negatively in any direct way on aggregate measures of economic change and growth.

Although the notion of varna serves as a rough means of defining

India's social strata, the operational unit of the caste system is the *jati*. A *jati* is an endogamous grouping of families, so it follows that an infant is born with an indelible *jati* identity; and, logically, parents and elders must ensure that the boundaries of the *jati* are preserved, making arranged marriages a necessary complement. *Jatis* are known by occupational labels such as Washermen, Barbers, Goldsmiths, Potters, Herdsmen, Distillers, or Priests. In the villages, configurations of these *jatis* constitute the division of labor, along with Peasants or Landowners (for example, Epstein 1962). William Wiser (1936) used the term "*jajmani* system" to summarize the networks of exchange, mostly in labor and kind, that linked the food-producing Peasant families with the artisan and service families. Much detailed work has shown that there has never been a strict one-to-one correspondence of *jati* occupation and village families' actual work (for example, Leaf 1984). Many families may own land or have tenancy rights to small plots, and many families may provide farm labor, although most landless workers are from the lowest caste and Untouchable households. Despite these ambiguities and fluidities, the imprint of caste on the rural division of labor is undeniable and continues forcefully down to the present.

A *jati*'s rank in the social hierarchy of the village derives from three vectors. The first is the degree to which the *jati*'s occupation is ritually demeaning or polluting. Washermen are polluted by their handling of soiled clothing and menstrual cloths.

Leatherworkers are polluted by dealing with dead animals and processing hides. Ironsmiths are not much stigmatized by their work. The second is the wealth in land held by the *jati*'s families and to a lesser extent its holdings of livestock or other assets. The third criterion is the *jati*'s political clout, which derives from its numbers, cohesion, and leadership. As David Mandelbaum (1970) has explained in full detail in his synthesis of the apposite literature, mobility in Indian society is feasible and avidly pursued, but it is a mobility of unified and successful *jatis*, not a mobility of individuals or isolated families. Further, Mandelbaum is explicit about the robust connection between the quest for social advancement and economic gains. He writes, "The drive for collective mobility is of surpassing concern to many villagers because they believe that greater power and material rewards are won by those who gain higher rank" (429).

Does *jati* mobility actually occur in concert with changes in subcastes' relative economic positions, or is this only a theoretical potentiality? F. G. Bailey (1957) wrote one of the first and still one of the best accounts of *jati* mobility growing out of advantages presented by economic change. In an Orissan village, Bisipara, the status of families and *jatis* was revised by the degree to which they successfully responded to opportunities presented by British rule and the spread of commerce. Bailey reports, "The biggest gains went to the Distiller caste-groups, who profited from a monopoly arising out of caste-beliefs and Government support"

(173). Today, Bailey's example can be multiplied manyfold. *Jatis* in India continue to joust for social position, political heft, and economic gain. As important as rising is holding the lower *jatis* down. Not surprisingly, because material benefits are at stake, such conflict often becomes testy and violent. In urban areas, individual accomplishment outside of *jati* membership is now more feasible, but it would be an error of the first order to think that personal achievement had displaced *jati* ascription and collective mobility. The bottom line is that although social mobility takes a different form in India from its form in the United States, material gain is both an instrument and a consequence of the pursuit of status.

Weber ([1921] 1958) remarks that subcastes acting "like quasi-trade unions, facilitate the legitimate defense of both internal and external interests" (33). Others have emphasized the guild-like nature of the occupational quasi-monopolies enjoyed by *jatis*. Thomas Beidelman (1959) criticized Wiser's sentiment that the *jajmani* system involved more or less persistent and agreeable terms of exchange among the landed, craft, and service subcastes, on the grounds that Wiser had underestimated the use of force to maintain a pattern of unequal transfers between the landed families and their retainers. The capacity of the service families to boycott the landed families was rarely converted into a winning hand in disputes over payments, and the latter usually emerged victorious. In fact, this was such a likely outcome that there were many fewer overt breaches of the order of life than one would expect, given the extremes of social and economic inequality that typically prevailed in a village. There can be scant doubt that the doctrines of dharma and karma acclimatized the lower orders to an acceptance of their lot in life, but Hinduism is hardly alone among religions in supporting social stability.

Neither Beidelman nor Wiser argued that the degree of occupational monopoly sustained by the principles of caste and the *jajmani* system exercised a chronic restraint on economic change or growth. To the contrary, as with Bailey's Distillers, they perceived that it was the quickness and effectiveness of *jati* reactions to changing commercial and employment opportunities that injected new dynamisms into the never ending pursuit of relative mobility. Indeed, we may go further and recognize that families and *jatis* in modern India go to great lengths to raise their schooling levels by sending able children upward in the educational system. *Jati* networks are important avenues of job information and search. Regional caste associations have been instrumental in founding many institutions of higher education, much as religious denominations in the United States have sponsored colleges and universities. From the inside, in other words, a *jati* is perceived as an alliance that provides resources and strength for its member families in competing with rivals.

In his comparative study of nations' historical growth trajectories, Mancur Olson (1982) reverted to a position very close to Weber's. Olson used his theory of collective action to argue that village *jatis* acted as multigenerational "distributive coalitions" in seeking to extract the greatest economic gains from their occupational monopolies (157). The struggle between subcastes to maintain or advance their positions and interests meant that fewer collective resources were available for private or public investment, so that India's economic growth wavered for many centuries around zero. Although this précis oversimplifies Olson's logic, his thesis depends crucially on, first, whether *jatis* were the strong labor unions he imagines and, second, whether they would and could successfully compete for pieces of the village economic pie. As has been depicted, the pairing of a *jati*'s occupational label and the types of work its member families actually performed has always been weaker than implied in strictly limned images. Further, most artisan groups in a given village were too small in number or too poorly organized to confront even moderately cohesive Peasant lineages. As intriguing as Olson's postulate is, inter-*jati* economic rivalry was sufficiently limited in scale that it should not be allocated much if any role in India's long-term economic stasis. Moreover, most intra-village conflict takes the form of faction rivalry in which alliances of Peasant households with their client and laborer retainers vie with similar cross-*jati* assemblages.

One of the shibboleths of colonial thought was the conviction that non-European workers were indolent. Put more analytically, their conduct was expected to violate the norm of the upward- and rightward-sloping supply curve of labor. Instead of offering more labor individually or collectively at higher wages, indigenous workers aimed at target incomes and worked less, the resulting function being a backward-bending supply curve of effort. Weber ([1921] 1958) says it nicely: "An increase in wage rate does not mean for them an incentive for more work or for a higher standard of living, but the reverse. They then take longer holidays because they can afford to do so, or their wives decorate themselves with ornaments" (14). From at least the middle of the nineteenth century onward, the expansion of public works, government, banking, the railways, and manufacturing enterprise has generated demands for workers. Obviously, many of the skills and occupations were new to South Asia. The key question is, Have attitudes toward labor effort and reward, or the caste system, blocked or skewed the provision of workers into new occupations in a manner that has retarded economic growth and development?

There is general agreement that the recruitment of an Indian labor force into new tasks as the economy has changed over the past two centuries has not been a sluggish or costly process. One can point to a few cases, such as the early Assam tea estates, where solicitation of labor was difficult except from the poorest areas of Bihar. Even in this instance, the isolation of the plantations, the high mortality rate in transit and in situ, and the onerous terms of contractual bondage are better explanations than any intrinsic unwillingness to move to superior work. The construction of the Indian railways from the 1850s onward drew heavily on local workers, and the rail companies' ever expanding numbers of operations personnel were overwhelmingly composed of Indians and Anglo-Indians. The decennial Indian censuses (from 1871 onward) provide ample evidence of a changing labor force structure marching in step with the evolution of the Indian economy. Morris D. Morris (1965) wrote a benchmark study of the recruitment of labor into the Bombay cotton textile industry, finding little friction in the creation of a committed, productive workforce. Parenthetically, too, we may credit Morris (1967) with an effective rebuttal of Weber's expression of the Hindu ethic's debilitating economic impacts. Morris's insistence on explaining the pace and distribution of economic development by primary reliance on conventional grounds, such as regional advantages, resource abundance, transportation costs, and the allocation of credit, was a salutary remedy for overreaching and speculative theses of social determination.

Representative of modern studies, Marc Holmström's (1984) scrutiny of the formal and informal sectors finds abundant contrivance and agility in reaping rewards from changing employment chances. This is not to say that there are no quirks or anomalies in the Indian labor market. A very common presence is that of the sirdar or mukadum, a labor factor or intermediary. Often a leading figure in a village or jati, this middleman is responsible for recruiting migrant or permanent labor for a particular activity, such as sugarcane cutting or work in a factory or on a construction site in Mumbai or Delhi. The factor is responsible for the mobilization and transport of his recruits and may be involved in small loans against pay. He works through networks in the caste or village and, on the one side, keeps his workers happy and, on the other, relieves the farmer or foreman of many responsibilities for managing workers and dealing with their commonplace human needs.

There is no evidence that Indian workers have been unresponsive to labor market signals, which is scarcely surprising in view of the seasonality of agrarian labor or the very low returns that prevail in many rural occupations. Traditional skills and a modicum of formal education sufficed until accessible modern educational institutions were created after independence. Brahmans cleaved easily to posts in the British colonial regime, and many made the transition into the cadres of the post-independence civil services. The Indian army has absorbed and trained generations of sepoys, often drawing them from the same families and regions. At any point, though, when we align the caste structure of the modern labor force, we see a very strong tendency for replication of the caste hierarchy. Brahmans keep the books, Warrior and farmer castes enter the army, artisans are on the assembly lines, and Sweepers clean the shop floors and toilets.

Differential caste access to education and the absence, surprising in India's liberal democracy, of any constitutional or binding legislative commitment to universal education and literacy have permitted the projection of the traditional caste ladder onto the contemporary workforce. Given the aforementioned delineation of the intensity of *jati* rivalry for social and economic positioning, it should not be astonishing that much of modern Indian politics revolves around populist candidates pledging to widen the access of lower caste groups to reserved school seats and public sector jobs and the countervailing hostility of the high castes to such public favoritism. India's constitution contains lists, or schedules, of tribes and subcastes that are the designated beneficiaries of affirmative action programs. In consequence, there is more competition at the national and state levels to join the public rosters of scheduled castes and scheduled tribes than there is to escape the designation.

In summary, religious values or attitudes have little or no impact on work habits or the work ethic in the Indian scene. The caste system does matter in significant fashion, not by inhibiting labor force availability so much as by imposing discriminatory barriers to jobs and educational openings. The sheer abundance, energy, and skills of India's massive workforce ensure that labor demands are rather easily satisfied for the moment. There is a rub of culture operating in India's labor markets, imposing high current political costs stemming from intrinsic unfairness. The failure to make full and nondiscriminatory use of all the nation's workers' innate industry and intelligence constitutes a potential drag on the economy as it moves closer to full employment, but the play of majoritarian politics and the existing awareness of the political and economic risks of countenancing inequality in perpetuity will not let this happen.

ARE COWS AND FARMERS RATIONAL?

In India, sacred cows graze at the intersection of religion and economy. The painted and belled bull wandering blissfully amid the traffic on an already congested roadway offers an unforgettable image of the conflict of sacred and secular. In the countryside, scrawny beasts wander in the brush, seemingly useless additions to an already overburdened landscape. McDonald's in India eschews beef hamburgers and offers substitutes. Once again, observers encounter differentness and equate it with excessive religiosity and an indifference to economic advantage. Even without technical analysis, one could draw immediate parallels between Hindu feelings about cattle and British feelings about dogs or horses as candidates for the table, or American feelings about their automobiles or guns or abortions. Cattle slaughter in India injects itself into politics, and it is a rare Hindu politician who does not publicly support a ban on the practice. Of course, since Muslims eat beef and most butchers are Muslim, the cow issue is a source of communal friction.

The case of the sacred cow offers an ideal opportunity for the application of good social science analysis, and much has been produced. In the field, anthropologists and agriculturists readily recognize the multiple functions of cattle and buffaloes in rural India. Bullocks are used in matched pairs to plow the fields or pull carts, contributing their traction power hugely to producing and distributing farm products. Cows give milk, which is converted into *ghee* (clarified butter) and curds. Dried manure patties are used for fuel in cooking, and composted dung is applied to the fields. With *gobar* (manure) gas units, farmers can bleed off methane for stoves and then use the residue as fertilizer, effectively doubling the value of the dung. Leatherworkers strip the hides from dead animals and make sandals or leather water buckets for lift irrigation. Somewhere along the way, much of the meat disappears into cooking pots, although India's large and watchful population of vultures takes its portion. Only about 20 percent of Indians are vegetarians (India 2000), but it would be rare for any Hindu openly to admit to a liking for beef, so there is a great discrepancy between social norms and actual conduct.

On the cost side, India's hardy Zebu cattle eat mostly crop waste or wander along munching on roadsides or browsing on village fallow lands. Only when being milked or during plowing season is their diet likely to be supplemented with green fodder. There is very little competition with humans either for harvested foodstuffs, such as grains, or

for land use. Marvin Harris (1989) argues that the taboos on beef eating and culling herds for meat have the effect of ensuring that there will always be an adequate number of head for plowing and milk products, even after a severe drought, and for reproduction. Studies show considerable regional variations in ratios of head to land, buffalo to cattle, females to males, and cattle to tractors. Clearly, local ecological conditions and economic needs make a difference in herd sizes and mixes (Henderson 1998; Lal 1988). Tastes play a role, since buffalo milk is usually preferred to cow milk because of its higher butterfat content and yields. The overall picture that emerges is one of fairly sensible management of valuable resources, with selective care and feeding, controlled breeding, and purchases and sales used to adjust herds as needed.

Economists take tastes as given, but preferences, including dietary profiles, are plainly the product of cultures. Every known people has its dietary enthusiasms and taboos, which greatly circumscribe the human species' naturally wide range of potential foodstuffs, perhaps the most eclectic of any living creature. Here once again is a powerful rub, but minor differentness in the composition of food preferences should not be conflated into an explanation of different rates or levels of economic growth and development.

So, sacred cows are not irrational, but what about South Asian peasants' farming practices? Jawaharlal Nehru and the early leaders of independent India were oriented sharply toward modern industrial and urban development, a bias shared with the national elites throughout the subcontinent. Along with many foreign economists and policy advisers, South Asian leaders held the belief that the great mass of peasant farmers would not be able to play a significant role in development programs until there had been wholesale changes in rural attitudes and institutions. This rural pessimism stemmed from a widely held conviction that illiterate farmers practicing agriculture according to time-honored customs and using primitive methods could not contribute to modernization of technologies and agrarian practices, at least until education, tenure reforms, and community development had sufficient time to create a new context for decision making. This stance was inconsistent with most American agricultural economists' espousal of the principle of universal rationality in the face of price or profit incentives. Theodore Schultz (1964) asserted that the typical Third World peasant was "poor but efficient" and, further, that price and profit signals would elicit the same behaviors everywhere: namely, planting crops on the basis of expected gains in the marketplace and choosing high-payoff technical innovations when the opportunities existed.

During the late 1960s, tracts of Indian and Pakistani Punjab began to experience the Green Revolution. High-yielding seeds, controlled irrigation water, and large doses of chemical fertilizers constituted a package of inputs that drove wheat yields up spectacularly. Schultz's rationality axiom was apparently vindicated, but in fact his salvo only prompted a return cannonade from numerous social scientists who reasserted the importance of an array of cultural, institutional, and attitudinal variables. Among those firing back was Kusum Nair, who emphasized the salience of regional subcultures in her book, *In Defense of the Irrational Peasant* (1979). Nair responded to Schultz by pointing out that the landowners of Bihar were remarkably uninterested in upgrading their farming practices, preferring to live as rentiers. They were "rich but inefficient," while the sons of the soil in Punjab were "born to the profession" and aggressively sought to upgrade their irrigation facilities and farm equipment.

Many empirical studies using data from farmer surveys, or cross-section information on India's districts, have demonstrated that Schultz's proposition was not defensible in its stark formulation (Adams and Neale 1997). Prices and profits do matter, but selectively or conditionally, in shaping efficient resource use and innovation choices. Prodipto Roy et al. (1968) were among the first to use surveys and statistics to sort out relevant parameters. They found that innovating farmers were more likely to have good political knowledge, a secular outlook, and an urban orientation. Bliss and Stern undertook a microeconomics-based study of Palanpur village and found wide differences in farmer responsiveness to opportunities (Bliss and Stern 1982). They concluded, "We are unable to confirm that neoclassical economics is alive and well and residing in Palanpur" (275). The truth is that South Asia's peasants are mightily affected by local subcultural, educational, ecological, and infrastructural conditions that mediate their reactions to the presentation of economic risks and opportunities. They are "demi-rational," and we can understand and predict their responses only when we consider the full range of interplay of culture and economy or, one might say, the rub between institutions and choices (Adams 1982). Again, the moderation of the middle way has much to commend it.

THE HINDU RATE OF GROWTH

Currently, the study of economic growth is broadening well beyond explanations that rely narrowly on expanding inputs in the usual formula entailing land, labor, and capital as the factors of production (Adams and Pigliaru 1999). As this has happened, our understanding of strategic social and political variables and the magnitude of their impacts on comparative rates of economic expansion has been much enhanced. Many economists are now at ease when drawing on related disciplines and fluent in treating measurable cultural and institutional differences in the context of multivariate statistical analysis and formal theory. In a recent example of this genre, Jonathan Temple and Paul A. Johnson (1998) returned to the early pathbreaking study by Irma Adelman and Cynthia Taft Morris (1967) to see whether the latter's measures of social development correlate with nations' long-term growth paths from 1960 through

1985. Their short answer was yes: "We have amassed some interesting evidence that fast growth is partly the outcome of favorable social arrangements," with impacts operating both on factor accumulation and total factor productivity (Temple and Johnson 1998, 965).

The original Adelman-Morris measure of social development included such variables as the extent of urbanization, the importance of the middle class, the extent of literacy, and the extent of mass communications weighted and reduced to a country score by use of factor analysis. Of these, Temple and Johnson find that the mass communications variable stands out robustly in many specifications and may serve as an indicator of the degree of social cooperation or strength of civic communities. Interestingly, if India had enjoyed the same level of social development on the Adelman-Morris scale as Korea in 1960, its income per capita afterward would have risen at over 3.0 percent per year, compared to the actual 1.3 percent (Temple and Johnson 1998, 972). This contrast may offer a rough measure of the rub of India's social conditions on the rate of economic growth through this period, but much care would be needed to sort out the relative roles of education, health, business management, government policies, and international economic conditions, in addition to fine-tuning the subsidiary social features that had an impress.

To illuminate how best to move forward on this broad front, let us center attention on the subject of agencies of change as driving forces in the engines of growth and development. Concretely, let us look at the public sector and its capacities to devise and implement policies and then consider briefly the abundance and role of entrepreneurs. In the mid-1970s, an Indian economist, Raj Krishna, popularized the phrase "the Hindu Rate of Growth," and it has been used frequently right up to the present. It is not widely known that the phrase forever and properly associated with Krishna's name emanated first from a Mr. Vithal, himself a government servant, writing in an unsigned piece in the *Economic and Political Weekly* in the early 1970s (Gupta 2000). Commenting on the prospects of a recently elected nationalist-led coalition government, Jagdish Bhagwati observed delphically, "Ironically it could be a Hindu government that will finally shake off the Hindu rate of growth" (Bhagwati 1998). Although Krishna's phrase seemingly echoes Weber's Hindu ethic thesis, in fact he meant something entirely different. He and many other economists, Indian and foreign, were voicing mounting impatience about India's slow growth rate, which if anything appeared to be slipping rather than accelerating in the 1970s. In effect, the attention was explicitly on policy and the deficiencies in the performance of the public sector as owner and manager of two-thirds of the country's industrial sector and planner and regulator of most of the remainder of the economy (Krishna 1980). Pivotal action points in the economy, such as foreign trade, investment decisions, business initiative, and industrial and scientific research, were bureaucratically enmeshed in what came to be called "permit raj."

Krishna's aphorism and the responsive chord it struck force us to confront the extremely complex problems revolving around policy as an intervening variable in the culture-economy connection. There is the Nehruvian issue of the degree to which policy can be used to drive economic and social change. There is the prior, but rarely asked, question of whether policy can be formulated independently of a cultural setting and of the political ramifications of that setting, such as the aspirations of scheduled castes in India or the wishes of those calling for Islamic banking in Pakistan. We cannot dally to fathom these topics in any depth, but a few remarks are required before sailing on. There cannot be any question that Nehru and the early Congress leadership thought that the introduction of planning and state intervention would jolt the Indian economy forward and relax constraints imposed by such things as landlordism, a weak private industrial sector, and a deficient infrastructure. In this they were correct, and the first 25 years of planning yielded heavy industry, chemicals, fertilizers, airlines, defense firms, irrigation, power stations, telephones, trucks, and ships. At what moment a shift in the direction of less oversight and toward more reliance on private enterprise and markets became desirable and feasible is much debated but not germane here (Adams 1999).

Although the adoption of planning and state direction in India and the other South Asian nations is often attributed to such external sources as Fabian socialism or the Soviet experiment, it could not have been so broadly accepted or so efficacious had it not resonated with deep local cultural predispositions. This proposition has never been fully argued, although analysts have often remarked casually on the low esteem in which private business and money handling were held throughout the region, especially by the Brahmans who dominated the bureaucracy and early governments. One might mention as well the conventional village atmosphere where everyone's affairs are everyone else's affairs and privacy is a little-known commodity, which, translated to the national plateau, is fully consistent with a watchful, meddling bureaucracy. As the Soviet Union and China exhibited, along with India and Pakistan, the large societies of Euro-Asia that came late to development rejected the market model in favor of state direction. In South Asia, one senses as well an amorphous but widely held fear of letting go of economic currents and an extremely dispersed grassroots disposition to expect the raja or patron, now supplanted by formal government, to fix things that go wrong with essentials like food, water, work, or diesel prices. James C. Scott's (1976) delineation of an Asian moral economy of collective village origin is a ground-level variant of this theme. On a different tack, I argued that India's international economic policies have been guided instinctively by a set of values and decision principles transferred from those governing peasant household management, leading to perennial conflicts with proponents of international agency standards over the adequacy of international reserve holdings or the sufficiency of food stocks (Adams 1980-81).

If we can agree that the subcontinent's public agencies have been powerful operants of change and control, with conduct grounded in South Asian cultures and evolving politics, we can next turn to the related question of the vitality of private agents such as entrepreneurs and business managers. This puts us firmly back in the Weberian compass. From at least Roman times, the subcontinent was linked commercially to the Middle East and the Mediterranean basin, traded its goods and spread its religions and culture into Southeast Asia, and in the north was connected to the overland Silk Road trade routes. The arriving Europeans as much insinuated themselves into existing patterns of commerce as created new channels. By the late nineteenth century, the establishment of the jute manufacturing industry in Bengal by British investors was fully matched by Indian ownership of cotton mills on the western littoral (Tomlinson 1993). In brief, there is much evidence that the varied culture of the subcontinent has not been hostile to agents of commerce, business, or finance. Once again, we must move beyond the simplicity of the either-or, East-West dichotomy and focus on substantive research.

Any assessment of industrial entrepreneurship and business management in South Asia must begin and end with treatment of the influence of religion, caste, and the joint family system. Of prime interest is neither the amplitude nor the vigor of industrial leadership but its specific caste origins and its intertwining with the kinship system. Milton Singer (1972, chap. 8) believed that the dharmic injunctions of Hinduism and the opportunities for rebirth into a higher social station implicit in karmic life cycles were not on the face of it much different from the spurs to material gain that Weber claimed characterized the Protestant faiths. He therefore undertook a survey of Hindu industrial leadership in Madras city (now Chennai). Singer's findings are subtle and resist easy summation, but he found little evidence that emerging entrepreneurs were constrained by rigid beliefs; rather, they accommodated tradition and modernity without difficulty. The caste origins of his sample were surprisingly diverse, but others have noted how certain regional caste groups have yielded a great preponderance of India's largest commercial and industrial firms, a classic example being Thomas Timberg's (1978) study of the history of the Marwari diaspora.

All South Asian firms are nestled inside caste, kinship, and family networks. In his history of a merchant-banking caste in South India, David Rudner (1994) says,

Nakarattar banking firms were basically "family firms" which owned and directed the operation of one or more banking offices, plantations, manufacturing companies, or other business ventures outside the South Indian Nakarattar homeland of Chettinad. In general, firms were owned by an undivided joint family (*valavu*) containing several coresident "hearthholds" or "conjugal families" (*pullis*) and extending to three or four generations under the direction of the oldest active male. (109)

Sudipt Dutta (1997) describes how a shared regional language, family meals without outsiders, arranged marriages, and indigenous and even idiosyncratic bookkeeping methods maintain the secrecy and strength of South Asia's family businesses. The range of talent in the extended family permits a highly competent junior family member to hold the reins of authority while senior brothers are relegated to ceremonial posts with lofty titles and ample remuneration. Only recently have newly trained MBAs entered company management alongside family scions. Links to foreign collaborators and a willingness to provide accurate financial statements in order to secure a listing on stock exchanges have begun to erode the closed family-based system of enterprise.

It is perhaps unnecessary to say that, from the inside, the caste, kinship, and family networks provide enormous resources and avenues for success in business and insulation against rivals or predatory governments. The diminution in risk, the gains in trust, the lowering of information costs, and the reduction in principal-agent problems are all advantages of a smoothly operating South Asian business house based on multidimensional social relationships. For a familiar Western counterpart we need not look beyond the operations of the fabled Rothschilds (Ferguson 1998).

When we scan the capacities of public and private agents of change in South Asia, it is hard to discern fundamental shortcomings or blockages. What we do see is differentness in style of governance, in the approaches to state-market relationships, in the unique role of caste collectivities, and in the nigh-ubiquitous conjunction of family and firm. For every conceivable negative valence associated with this institutional congeries, there is a more than offsetting positive charge. None of these ingrained patterns is likely to change speedily in the direction of American or global arrangements, which is not to say that there will not be continuing adaptation to universal standards and practices in such areas as accounting, contract enforcement, information systems, or social accountability.

PRESIDENT CLINTON OVERTURNS MAX WEBER

The foregoing sections have examined many contours of the culture-economy imbroglio on the South Asian stage, but there are major additional topics regrettably left uncovered. These are mentioned for the sake of completeness; the brevity with which they are treated does not mean that they are of lesser consequence. The role of politics, or political economy, as an intervening variable between culture and economy has been most imperfectly conveyed. The caste basis of post-independence politics in India and its impact on national and state politics has been especially shortchanged (Brass 1990). Another lacuna is the failure to report in depth on regional differentiation in ecology, demography, crop pattern, industrial profile, female infanticide, and women's status and workforce participation, all of which have relations to cultural dynamics. In many ways, India's three chief regions—the east, northwest, and south—share more social and economic similarities with the adjacent nations—Bangladesh, Pakistan, and Sri Lanka—than they do with the rest of the country, which after all is only a recent political overlay draped on top of primordial ecological and cultural features (Timberg 1980-81).

Nor has justice been done to the quite convincing analytical history presented in *The Hindu Equilibrium* (1988) by Deepak Lal, in which ecology, demography, institutions, sacred cows, economy, and religion are woven seamlessly together to account for the long-term stability of the subcontinent over its six millennia. I am struck as well by the unfairness of hurling plaudits Japan's way for having an innate cultural proclivity for capitalism, although no one has pointed out that India's receptivity to democracy must at base be attributable to native cultural features. The enthusiasm of Indians for the pleasures of participatory democracy, as revealed in their high voting rates and endless politicking, cannot be ascribed merely to the accidental importation of an alien system. There must be deep, unappreciated resonances that require assiduous unearthing. Neither is it sufficiently realized that, though the societies of the subcontinent are without doubt the world's most hierarchical, the one and a half billion personalities on the contemporary scene are as colorful, heterogeneous, and individualistic as anyone could possibly imagine.

A recapitulation of the case made with respect to culture and economic development in South Asia may be tersely offered in exiting. The continuity and persistence of the ways of life of the subcontinent are a remarkable story of the capacities and plasticities of human civilization. External appraisals of failure stem from facile Western-seated condemnations of "the other" or from the irrefragable fact that in the modern world countries are judged successful according to their economic prowess. This change in the rules of the game caught South Asia on the wrong foot. Signally, it has taken the countries of the region only a half-century to move, tenuously in the case of all but India, toward political stability and economic advance. Bangladesh is currently promising in part because its cultural homogeneity to a degree offsets the depths of its inherited poverty. Sri Lanka is riven with sectarian warfare, and Pakistan, after some promising decades, is poised to tip into a Himalayan abyss, never really having established a viable state. On a longer chronological scale, four or five centuries is not a long time for a massive and weighty culture to regroup and forge on in the face of tectonic shifts in world geopolitics.

Culture rubs in South Asia, but, contrary to Weber and his ofttimes closet allies, it does not foreclose policy initiatives, collective action, nongovernmental associations, corporate initiative, or individual achievement. It shapes the composition of demand; drives political action on the fundaments of *jati*, clan, lineage, faction, sect, and tribe; conduces discrimination against women and less advantaged social groups; sustains unique family management practices; and projects bold entrepreneurship. The cultures of South Asia are an immense resource out of which the future of the subcontinent will be constructed by purposeful public and private agents who have warmed to the new challenges thrust upon them by events of the past four or five centuries. We can conclude in no better fashion than by quoting President William Jefferson Clinton, poised to visit South Asia in March 2000, who perfectly articulated how very radically images of the peoples of the subcontinent have been refashioned in the last few decades:

You're talking about people who are basically immensely talented, have a strong work ethic, a deep devotion to their faith and to their families. There is nothing they couldn't do. And it is heartbreaking to me to see how much they hold each other back by being trapped in yesterday's conflicts. (quoted in Haniffa 2000, 18)

References

Adams, John. 1980-81. India's Foreign Trade and Payments Since 1965: Managing the Nation as Peasant Household. *Pacific Affairs* 53(Winter):632-42.

————. 1982. The Emptiness of Peasant "Rationality": "Demirationality" as an Alternative. *Journal of Economic Issues* 16(Sept.):663-72.

————. 1999. India: Much Achieved, Much to Achieve. In *India and Pakistan: The First Fifty Years*, ed. Selig S. Harrison, Paul H. Kreisberg, and Dennis Kux. Washington, DC: Woodrow Wilson Center Press.

Adams, John and Walter C. Neale. 1997. Institutions, Transactions, and Rationality: Evidence from Indian Village Studies. *South Asia* 20(Dec.):139-56.

Adams, John and Francesco Pigliaru, eds. 1999. *Economic Growth and Change: National and Regional Patterns of Convergence and Divergence*. Cheltenham: Edward Elgar.

Adelman, Irma and Cynthia Taft Morris. 1967. *Society, Politics, and Economic Development*. Baltimore: Johns Hopkins University Press.

Bailey, F. G. 1957. *Caste and the Economic Frontier: A Village in Highland Orissa*. Manchester: Manchester University Press.

Basham, A. L. 1959. *The Wonder That Was India*. New York: Grove Press.

Beidelman, Thomas O. 1959. *A Comparative Analysis of the* Jajmani *System*. Locust Valley, NY: J. J. Augustin for the Association for Asian Studies.

Bhagwati, Jagdish. 1998. A Hindu Government Will Finally Shake off the Hindu Rate of Growth: Bhagwati. Available at http://indiapost.com/bus_news/may98/m22bomb2.htm.

Bliss, C. J. and N. H. Stern. 1982. *Palanpur: The Economy of an Indian Village*. Oxford: Clarendon Press.

Brass, Paul R. 1990. *The Politics of India Since Independence*. IV.1. The New Cambridge History of India. New York: Cambridge University Press.

Dutta, Sudipt. 1997. *Family Business in India*. New Delhi: Response Books.

Epstein, T. Scarlett. 1962. *Economic Development and Social Change in South India*. Manchester: Manchester University Press.

Ferguson, Niall. 1998. *The House of Rothschild, Money's Prophets, 1798-1848*. New York: Penguin Books.

Gould, Harold A. 1988. *The Hindu Caste System*. Vol. 2, *Caste Adaptation in Modernizing Indian Society*. Delhi: Chanakya.

Gupta, Shreekant. 2000. E-mail communication to the author. 15 Feb.

Haniffa, Aziz. 2000. Uncertainty over Islamabad Stopover Persists. *India Abroad*, 25 Feb., 18.

Harris, Marvin. 1989. *Cows, Pigs, Wars, and Witches*. New York: Vintage.

Henderson, Carol. 1998. The Great Cow Explosion in Rajasthan. In *Advances in Historical Ecology*, ed. William L. Ballée. New York: Columbia University Press.

Holmström, Mark. 1984. *Industry and Inequality: The Social Anthropology of Indian Labor*. New York: Cambridge University Press.

India. 2000. *Anthropological Survey of India, 1985-1995*. Reported at http://library.northernlight.com/MG199980922040064602.html. Accessed 17 Feb.

Kapp, K. William. 1963. *Hindu Culture, Economic Development, and Economic Planning in India: A Collection of Essays*. Bombay: Asia Publishing House.

Krishna, Raj. 1980. The Economic Development of India. *Scientific American* Sept.:168-78.

Lal, Deepak. 1988. *Cultural Stability and Economic Stagnation: India, c. 1500 B.C.-A.D. 1980*. Vol. 1, *The Hindu Equilibrium*. New York: Oxford University Press.

Leaf, Murray J. 1984. *Song of Hope: The Green Revolution in a Punjab Village*.

New Brunswick, NJ: Rutgers University Press.

Maine, Sir Henry. [1861] 1986. *Ancient Law*. New York: Dorset Press.

———. [1871] 1876. *Village Communities in East and West*. London: J. Murray.

Mandelbaum, David G. 1970. *Society in India*. Berkeley: University of California Press.

Marx, Karl. [1839] 1967. *Capital*. New York: International.

Mayo, Katherine. 1927. *Mother India*. New York: Harcourt, Brace.

Morris, Morris D. 1965. *The Emergence of an Industrial Labor Force in India: A Study of the Bombay Cotton Mills*. Berkeley: University of California Press.

———. 1967. Values as an Obstacle to Economic Growth in South Asia: An Historical Survey. *Journal of Economic History* 27(Dec.):588-607.

Myrdal, Gunnar. 1968. *The Asian Drama*. New York: Twentieth Century Fund.

Nair, Kusum. 1979. *In Defense of the Irrational Peasant*. Chicago: University of Chicago Press.

Olson, Mancur. 1982. *The Rise and Decline of Nations*. New Haven, CT: Yale University Press.

Rogers, James. 1987. *The Dictionary of Cliches*. New York: Ballantine Books.

Rostow, Walt W. [1965] 1990. *The Stages of Economic Growth*. 3d ed. New York: Cambridge University Press.

Roy, Prodipto, Frederick C. Fliegel, Joseph E. Kivlin, and Lalit K. Sen. 1968. *Agricultural Innovation Among Indian Farmers*. Hyderabad: National Institute of Community Development.

Rudner, David West. 1994. *Caste and Capitalism in Colonial India, the Nattukottai Chettiars*. Berkeley: University of California Press.

Said, Edward W. 1979. *Orientalism*. New York: Random House.

Schultz, Theodore W. 1964. *Transforming Traditional Agriculture*. New Haven, CT: Yale University Press.

Scott, James C. 1976. *The Moral Economy of the Peasant: Rebellion and Subsistence in Southeast Asia*. New Haven, CT: Yale University Press.

Singer, Milton. 1972. *When a Great Tradition Modernizes: An Anthropological Approach to Indian Civilization*. New York: Praeger.

Singh, K. S. 1998. *People of India*. Vols. 4-6, *India's Communities*. Calcutta: Anthropological Survey of India.

Temple, Jonathan and Paul A. Johnson. 1998. Social Capability and Economic Growth. *Quarterly Journal of Economics* 111(Aug.):965-81.

Timberg, Thomas A. 1978. *The Mawaris, from Traders to Industrialists*. New Delhi: Vikas Publishing House.

———. 1980-81. Regions in India's Development. *Pacific Affairs* 53(Winter):643-50.

Tomlinson, B. R. 1993. *The Economy of Modern India, 1860-1970*. The New Cambridge History of India, III.3. New York: Cambridge University Press.

Tönnies, Ferdinand. [1887] 1957. *Community and Society*. East Lansing: Michigan State University Press.

Weber, Max. [1921] 1958. *The Religion of India, the Sociology of Hinduism and Buddhism*. Trans. and ed. Hans H. Gerth and Don Martindale. Glencoe, IL: Free Press.

———. [1904-5] 1976. *The Protestant Ethic and the Spirit of Capitalism*. Trans. Talcott Parsons. New York: Charles Scribner's Sons.

Wiser, William H. 1936. *The Hindu Jajmani System*. Lucknow: Lucknow Publishing House.

Book Department

INTERNATIONAL RELATIONS AND POLITICS

GERGES, FAWAZ A. 1999. *America and Political Islam: Clash of Cultures or Clash of Interests?* Pp. xiii, 282. New York: Cambridge University Press. $59.95. Paperbound, $18.95.

In this timely and important book, Fawaz A. Gerges analyzes developments in the Islamic world that have, in many cases, unnecessarily preoccupied American foreign policymakers since Communism's demise deprived the United States of an ideology against which Americans could put aside their differences and formulate a coherent foreign policy. However, as Gerges points out, not only is the Islamic revival characterized by diversity and complexity, but also American interests vary from one country to another, thereby making it difficult for the United States to use Islamists as a replacement for Communism. Furthermore, divergent interests and views within American society on the threat from Islamist states and movements complicate the formulation of a coherent U.S. policy toward Islam.

Congress is more susceptible to pressure from groups supportive of the Israeli position, which portrays Islamic fundamentalism not only as a danger to Israel but also as a force that is undermining the broader Arab-Israeli peace process and, consequently, American interests in the Middle East. Presidents Carter, Reagan, Bush, and Clinton have generally taken the middle road between the positions of those advocating accommodation with Islamists and those favoring confrontation. In particular, the Clinton administration, extremely sensitive to ethnic group politics, has promoted unity between different ethnic groups in an increasingly multicultural American society. Consequently, Clinton and his senior aides have met regularly with representatives of the growing American Muslim community to counter the view that a clash between Islam and the West is inevitable. Clinton's approach reflects the influence of domestic ethnic groups on U.S. foreign policy and the erosion of the boundary between domestic and foreign affairs.

America and Political Islam is a significant contribution to the small body of scholarly literature on the role that culture plays in foreign policy. Gerges examines the extent to which culture and religion have replaced ideology and national interest as the independent variables in American foreign policy and whether confrontations with Islamists represent a clash of cultures or a clash of interests. But as Gerges's detailed analysis reveals, the search for methodological neatness can often obscure the reality that culture and national interests are usually intertwined. This book shows that cultural values and perceptions help to shape a nation's definition of its interests, perceptions of threats to those interests, and the selection of strategies to safeguard national interests. Although most Americans may have a reservoir of negative stereotypes about the Muslim world, Gerges argues that the United States, unlike Europe, does not have a history of conflict with Muslim societies. In fact, the United States was perceived by many Islamic countries in the first part of the twentieth century as a "progressive island amid European reaction." The United States viewed Muslim states as bulwarks against Communist expansion. Gerges observes that U.S. policy toward Islamist movements not only is driven by cultural differences but also is a response to provocations by Islamists who perceive themselves as challenging the West.

To demonstrate nuanced differences and similarities in America's policy toward Islamic countries and movements, Gerges focuses on Iran, Algeria, Egypt, and Turkey, countries that represent a broad spectrum of Islamism. The author also examines how divergent views within the U.S. foreign policy elite influence America's responses to developments in the Muslim world. Gerges argues that the closer the United States identifies its interests with those of its regional allies—Israel, Turkey, Egypt, and Saudi Arabia—the more it finds itself in conflict with Islamist activists who are seen as the greatest threats to those allies. On the other hand, as shown in the case study of Algeria, the further away a country is from the main U.S. strategic concerns, the more nuanced American foreign policy tends to be. Gerges's detailed and objective analysis of the various countries demonstrates that cultural values and national interests combine to help shape America's foreign policy. In Algeria, where the political landscape is fragmented and where widespread violence is committed by both the state security apparatus and Islamic opposition groups, the United States has maintained a low profile. In sharp contrast to Algeria, Iran is perceived as a serious threat to America's interests. As Gerges

observes, the Iranian revolution and the hostage crisis had the most formative effect on the U.S. policy establishment and the public's views of Islam. Islamists in Iran were perceived by most Americans to be hateful, fanatical, and violent. Apart from humiliating the United States during the hostage crisis, Iran's support of terrorism against Americans, including the bombing of the World Trade Center in New York City in 1993, confirmed Americans' fears of Islamists. Neither Egypt nor Turkey is seen as a threat to U.S. interests. On the contrary, America regards both countries as vital allies. Egypt, the most powerful country in the Arab world, serves as a gate to the Middle East and as an anchor of U.S. policy in the region. Egypt is also an essential player in the Arab-Israeli peace process. Similarly, Turkey, with strong secular traditions and close ties to the West, is a strategically important ally and a model of coexistence between Muslims, Christians, and Jews. The greatest challenges to both Egypt and Turkey come from Islamic groups. In Egypt, in particular, Islamists have attempted to undermine the security of the government and to destroy a country's tourist industry by killing foreigners. Developments within each country as well as cultural factors combine to influence American policy toward Islamists.

America and Political Islam is a significant contribution to the new debate on the role of culture in international relations. The author not only discusses issues that will continue to be central to American foreign policy but also offers workable solutions to conflicts between the United States and Islamists. A constructive suggestion advanced by Gerges is that humanist and democratic voices in Islamic countries should cooperate with their Western counterparts to help avoid a cultural and civilizational war. Although the author seems to exaggerate the threat, he correctly warns against fo-

cusing on cultural differences to manu-
facture a new enemy for the post–Cold
War world. Increasing globalization and
growing interdependence of states challenges American policymakers to focus
less on insignificant differences between
nations and more on the common values
and interests of the global community.

RICHARD J. PAYNE

Illinois State University
Normal

KLOTZ, AUDIE. 1995. *Norms in Interna-
tional Relations: The Struggle Against
Apartheid*. Pp. xi, 183. Ithaca, NY:
Cornell University Press. $39.95.
Paperbound, $16.95.

In the past 10 years, a new approach to
international relations, constructivism,
has been born. Constructivists argue
that world politics is embedded within a
deep structure of norms and values.
These norms alter the identities and
preferences of international actors. This
approach is in contrast to realism (which
argues that the world is anarchic and
states seek to maximize power and security) and liberalism (which argues that
states seek to maximize wealth and use
international regimes to facilitate cooperation). Since the inception of
constructivism, its adherents have faced
two critical hurdles: a need for more case
studies to substantiate their claims, and
an explanation for which norms will affect outcomes when.

Audie Klotz tries to fill these gaps in
Norms in International Relations. She
examines the worldwide effort to politically, economically, and culturally isolate
the apartheid regime of South Africa.
Klotz uses this case to demonstrate the
inadequacies of the realist and liberal
paradigms. The history of apartheid
sanctions shows that the driving force be-

hind them comprised minor and
marginalized actors, such as the Organization of African Unity (OAU) and the
United Nations General Assembly. Eventually, great powers like the United
States and the United Kingdom ignored
security and material interests to join the
sanctions coalition, dragged along by the
growing tide of antiapartheid sentiment.
Norms in International Relations provides a concise but detailed history of the
antiapartheid movement and its ability
to move international regimes and great
powers toward sanctioning South Africa.
Klotz argues that the antiapartheid
norm was effective because it altered the
identities and interests of actors through
discourse and institutions. She supports
this assertion with case studies of key international organizations (the United
Nations, the OAU, and the Commonwealth) and nation-states (the United
States, the United Kingdom, and Zimbabwe) and their adoption of sanctions.

Klotz's case studies are impressive in
fleshing out the history of the
antiapartheid movement and the pressures brought to bear against the relevant governments and international
organizations. However, the histories do
not precisely connect to her larger theoretical points. The U.S. and U.K. cases
mostly reveal the salience of domestic
politics in the decision to sanction; the
transnational norms that Klotz stresses
are either absent or marginal in their effects. The U.N., OAU, and Commonwealth cases are stronger, but Klotz fails
to delineate how the discourse of these organizations altered the preferences of
powerful actors. She also asserts that
South Africa ended apartheid because of
its need for external legitimacy (consistent with constructivism), discounting
the coercive effect of the sanctions (consistent with realism). Given that the
South African government held out
against weak multilateral sanctions for

25 years but started to compromise after the U.S. government imposed sanctions and U.S. corporations withdrew investment, this dismissal seems far too hasty.

Does Klotz advance the constructivist theory? Yes, but not too far. The problem with the South Africa case is that it occurred in a region that was at best peripheral to the larger Cold War struggles of the day. Material and security interests in South Africa were present but not necessarily that important. Norms mattered in this case because little else did. Had norms overridden strategic or material interests in a more pivotal state, such as Saudi Arabia or Thailand, the effect of Klotz's argument would be more powerful. Nevertheless, by highlighting a case involving less powerful actors and regions, this book skillfully demonstrates the limitations of the dominant paradigms.

DANIEL W. DREZNER

University of Chicago
Illinois

MAYER, FREDERICK W. 1998. *Interpreting NAFTA: The Science and Art of Political Analysis*. Pp. xiv, 374. New York: Columbia University Press. $47.50. Paperbound, $17.50.

Frederick W. Mayer deftly employs "the science and art of political analysis" to explain the formulation, negotiation, and approval of the North American Free Trade Agreement (NAFTA), which took effect in the United States, Mexico, and Canada on 1 January 1994. In this ambitious endeavor, he focuses on three levels of analysis (international, domestic/group, and individual) and three modes of politics (rational choice, institutional process, and symbolic response). Even more striking, he applies these constructs to NAFTA's three signatory nations, as well as to the fast-track authority that the U.S. Congress granted to Presidents George Bush and Bill Clinton to expedite the crafting of this international trade accord.

A fellowship from the Council on Foreign Relations enabled Mayer, a Duke University professor, to participate in the NAFTA process as ad hoc whip in the office of Senator Bill Bradley. This vantage point enabled the scholar to enrich his application of relevant social science ideas with firsthand insights into policymaking. At the heart of his study lies the question, Why did so much political conflict surround a tripartite trade accord that apparently offered major benefits and few costs to the signatories? Indeed, why had the three parties not long ago eliminated the barriers attacked in the NAFTA parleys?

Meyer advances a two-level framework to answer these questions. He argues that "national behaviors that are hard to square with notions of rational choice (and, therefore, hard to predict) when viewed solely from an international perspective can be explained as the outcome of bargaining processes among rational actors at the domestic level." He strengthens his thesis by emphasizing the symbolism—as opposed to material payoffs—stressed in the NAFTA debate, especially by trade unions and environmental groups eager to dramatize the pact as a sweetheart deal for job-moving, dolphin-killing corporate giants.

Interpreting NAFTA will enable dedicated readers to deepen their knowledge of both theoretical literature and major events related to the four-year struggle to conceptualize, negotiate, and gain approval for the trilateral accord. Meyer deserves credit for a relative jargon-free, although overly long, *tour d'horizon* of the approaches to multilevel political analysis, which will greatly benefit many graduate students and their professors.

In the final analysis, however, a simpler, more straightforward explanation of the agreement's trajectory may exist apart from the author's impressive theoretical rendering.

First, in contrast to Europe, where post–World War II politicians impelled the cooperation that crystallized in the European Union, the American business community had been spurring U.S.-Mexican integration for almost a half-century. In essence, NAFTA provided a mechanism within which to broaden and regulate a process that would have proceeded, albeit more haphazardly, with or without the imprimatur of government officials.

Second, President Carlos Salinas, by no means the free-trader whom Mayer depicts, looked northward only after the Europeans rebuffed his overtures for closer economic ties with Mexico. The Mexican chief executive believed it imperative to establish linkages with the global economy, lest his nation remain an economic backwater with a rapidly growing population and mounting social unrest.

Third, George Bush's Texas background and big-business ties explain his receptiveness to a continental trade pact, just as Bill Clinton's internationalism and quest for "New Democratic" credentials cast light on his embrace of NAFTA cum side agreements.

Finally, as beguiling as it is to consider a "multilevel, multimode theory" of congressional behavior, the House of Representatives approved NAFTA by a vote of 234 to 200 because in mid-September 1993 the White House—previously distracted by health care legislation and the budget—finally began to court lawmakers and dispense boodle in behalf of the trade accord after Labor Day 1993.

GEORGE W. GRAYSON

College of William and Mary
Williamsburg
Virginia

PRICE, DANIEL E. 1999. *Islamic Political Culture, Democracy, and Human Rights: A Comparative Study.* Pp. xiii, 221. Westport, CT: Praeger. $59.95.

What role does Islam play in fostering or impeding the adoption of democratic institutions and the embrace of international human rights standards? This is one of the most significant questions scholars and policymakers of the developing world face today, and there is a burgeoning literature on the subject. As Price suggests, much of that literature is speculative and anecdotal; the question begs for serious, sustained, and rigorous analysis. Unfortunately, this book does not meet that standard.

Price makes an effort, to be sure. The book is based on a complicated mix of methodologies: a quick tour through Islamic political theory, eight country case studies drawn from the Arab world, and a regression analysis designed to quantify and test the association of Islamic political culture and democratic or human rights practices. Pretty much whatever way Price looks at the question, he finds that Islam has no significant effect on democracy or human rights.

Many readers, including this reviewer, will consider that finding intuitively plausible, although as every first-year social science methods class reminds us, actually proving a negative is no mean feat. Nonetheless, it does seem fair to say that Islam, like every other religious tradition, has proven to be a flexible and accommodating faith that has permitted its followers to meet their religious obligations while living with the varying demands and expectations of social life in many places and many eras over the last 1400 years. There is little in the historical record that would suggest the same could not be true of Islamic approaches to democratic politics or individual rights. That demagogues might choose to use religion for illiberal or undemocratic political purposes certainly does not distinguish Islam from Christianity, Judaism, Hinduism, or any other religious tradition or demonstrate that Islam is particularly prone to demagoguery.

Those who are not predisposed to Price's position, however, are unlikely to be persuaded by his analysis, in spite of all the apparent methodological bells and whistles. This is because Price himself does not really take seriously the demands of the methods he uses. His examination of Islamic political theory is based virtually entirely on English-language secondary sources; indeed, of the 250 or so entries in the bibliography, no more than a dozen are in Arabic or French, and the paragraphs devoted to the four Muslim political theorists he chooses (somewhat arbitrarily) to illustrate Islamic political theory are few and superficial. Similarly, the country case studies reflect little of the fieldwork Price did in Morocco and the visits he made to other Arab countries but are rather routine accounts of modern political history easily obtainable elsewhere. Indeed, even the statistical analysis does not take seriously Price's own, very acute observation about the limits of quantitative approaches; in an early footnote explaining why he did not conduct a survey, he writes, "It is impossible to obtain random samples when nobody is exactly sure how many people there are" (22).

This is certainly true, and the challenge that that presents to social scientific research is a very serious one. Unfortunately, it is not adequately addressed by the creation of variables based on interviews with a few embassy officials, Muslims abroad, and academic experts. Price is to be commended for the candor with which he discusses his methods, but he should take their limitations more seriously.

LISA ANDERSON

Columbia University
New York

AFRICA, ASIA, AND
LATIN AMERICA

BARYLSKI, ROBERT V. 1998. *The Soldier in Russian Politics: Duty, Dictatorship, and Democracy Under Gorbachev and Yeltsin*. Pp. xii, 510. New Brunswick, NJ: Transaction. $59.95.

Robert Barylski has performed yeoman's service in writing this combination of political science, political sociology, and historical narrative. He seeks "to describe what happened [in Russian civil-military relations from approximately 1985 to late 1997] fairly and objectively"—and succeeds in this task. Drawing almost completely from Russian-language sources, *The Soldier in Russian Politics* will especially satisfy those wanting details about the rocky transition from Mikhail Gorbachev to Boris Yeltsin and the uncertain implantation of "civilian control" over Russia's drastically shrunken forces.

Description requires a framework. Barylski draws upon a loose set of ideas he characterizes as "modernization," or a "long-range trend" shown in industrial, democratic countries. He aptly notes that no armed forces can be isolated from partisan considerations: "Military participation influences the political process as a normal part of politics"; "the military is in politics, always has been, and always will be as long as the Russian state maintains armed forces." Basic questions of control remain unresolved, however. Russians still are wrestling with the issue of whether such participation should be regularized or prohibited, an effort complicated by the erratic behavior of President Yeltsin.

The Soviet military became deeply, albeit unwillingly, involved in the struggle between Gorbachev and Yeltsin. To Barylski, disintegration of civilian political institutions is noteworthy; a kind of imperial presidency emerged. He finds a few semi-heroes, as well as many who advanced personal agendas at the expense of effective institutional development. One of the villains is Minister of Defense Dimitry Yazof, who helped launch the abortive August 1991 coup attempt—yet who, in helping to call it off, also acted heroically, precluding possible bloodshed. His successor, Yevgeny Shaposhnikov, clearly merits praise: he presided over the military transition from the USSR to the Commonwealth of Independent States; was "the last Soviet military leader in the best sense of the term"; and "demonstrated that soldiers could be responsible citizens, engage in a dialogue with society about security issues without imposing their views, and provide a stabilizing force during periods of stress without reverting to dictatorship."

Boris Yeltsin emerges from Barylski's scrutiny as a very tarnished individual. A man of courage, foresight, and determination in his endgame with Gorbachev, Yeltsin showed distressing nondemocratic symptoms in consolidating power. While his resistance to the 1991 coup attempt "demonstrates the power individuals have to shape political outcomes," his actions two years later against parliament damaged prospects for democratic development. Yeltsin's leadership style, Barylski concludes, "was ill-suited to the habits of mind and professional discipline valued by top military professionals."

For several decades, professionalism has provided the dominant paradigm for students of civil-military relations, whose models have largely been developed, democratic Western states. Both sides of the equation must be balanced: leaders of the armed forces must be responsive to the government; civilian chiefs must develop responsive political institutions based on the rule of law, not erect bastions of personal power. Barylski makes several relevant comments. "On balance, it appears that the

Soviet military legacy of professionalism was generally well-suited to adapt to Western models. The civilian side of the political equation was the problem." Yeltsin's "hybrid system, a mixture of authoritarian and democratic theory and practice," was not well suited to democratic constitutional control. Too much power resided in the presidency. Yeltsin brought the armed forces "into inappropriate domestic political activity." Russia's main political problem is that of societal control over the presidency, rather than civilian control over the military.

As already suggested, the chief strength of *The Soldier in Russian Politics* lies in its careful recounting of complex events, based on sources inaccessible to most readers. Barylski deserves commendation for this first-rate case study, likely to be consulted for many years to come.

CLAUDE E. WELCH

University at Buffalo
New York

NATHAN, ANDREW J. 1998. *China's Transition*. Pp. xiv, 313. New York: Columbia University Press. Paperbound, $16.50.

The sinological literature of recent decades has portrayed China embarked on a variety of transitions, among them the transition to modernity, the transition to socialism, and, more recently, the transition to capitalism. Andrew Nathan is concerned with the now more fashionable transition to democracy, the latter a bit too easily defined (especially in the case of China) as "authentically competitive elections for national and local offices." It is this concern that gives shape to this book, a somewhat eclectic collection of essays on contemporary Chinese and Taiwanese history and politics.

Save for the introductory essay, the volume's 16 chapters are articles previously published over the past decade, many in *The New Republic*, others in more scholarly periodicals and edited books. Even though some essays have not aged as well as others, the volume as a whole still makes for worthwhile reading. It takes some time and patience to establish this, however. The introductory chapter is a dull and unedifying polemical reply to a petty critique of Professor Nathan that appeared in 1995 in a Chinese-language newspaper published in New York. The critics, mostly Taiwanese Americans sympathetic to the People's Republic, denounced Nathan's somewhat sensationalistic foreword to the rather unremarkable memoir written by Mao Zedong's personal physician, Dr. Li Zhisui. In the foreword reprinted as chapter 3 of the present volume, Nathan sets forth the argument that—as he now summarizes it—"the story of China's modern tragedy has to begin in Mao's mind, his court, and . . . in his bed." From this rather shallow premise follows an obsessive effort to demonstrate that few figures in world history were so evil as was Mao and that "none inflicted such a catastrophe on his nation." So intent is Nathan in pursuing this judgment that he even lets off lightly the demonic secret police chief Kang Sheng, so much the easier then to blame Mao personally for the crimes.

In the early chapters, Nathan has Mao inflicting so many disasters on China that the nonspecialist reader will be puzzled to read in the later chapters that the Maoist revolution and the Mao period created many of the material and cultural preconditions that might facilitate—although hardly guarantee—a democratic transition, as Nathan implicitly acknowledges in several essays. He writes, for example,

Under Mao Zedong, and even more rapidly since the beginning of Den Xiaoping's reform, China made progress in supplying its citizens with economic and social rights. Living standards have increased, compulsory education has been extended to nine years, adult literacy stands at 79 percent according to official figures, and life expectancy at 69 exceeds that of many middle-income countries.

Unfortunately, Nathan does not explain how this apparent progress could have come about under a despotic leader he depicts as a chronic blunderer capable only of producing great catastrophes.

Yet in many essays, particularly in the latter part of the volume, where he is not unduly preoccupied with the late chairman, Nathan writes in well-reasoned and often perceptive fashion. His critique of cultural relativism is particularly valuable, and he is also impressive in dismantling culturalist explanations of contemporary Chinese history and politics, especially the pernicious but widely held view that there are insurmountable cultural barriers to the development of democracy in China. In the process, Nathan makes a strong case for what he terms "evaluative universalism"—the simple but controversial assumption that the values held by the investigator (probably but not necessarily those dominant in one's own society) can validly be applied to any society.

MAURICE MEISNER

University of Wisconsin
Madison

London School of Economics
United Kingdom

EUROPE

BARBOUR, REID. 1998. *English Epicures and Stoics: Ancient Legacies in Early Stuart Culture*. Pp. xii, 312.

Amherst: University of Massachusetts Press. $45.00.

In this carefully researched and clearly written book, Reid Barbour explores the richness of early Stuart response to Hellenistic philosophy. Taking the skeptical turn effectively for granted, Barbour focuses on the two other major Hellenistic creeds, Epicureanism and Stoicism. Barbour recognizes that part of the appeal of those philosophies is that they each represented a distinctive complex of epistemology, ethics, physics, and, in the case of Stoicism, logic. Because they were such complicated animals, Barbour argues, they become for the modern scholar a perfect litmus test for the multiple and often contradictory anxieties characterizing the period between 1603 and 1649. Englishmen in this period had to cope with hitherto unimagined political demands and stresses and with equally vexed religious questions. And because ancient philosophy comprises a series of comprehensive myths about the constitution of the world in its many guises, we witness English writers selecting and testing aspects of those creeds, as a means to render articulate for themselves (as well as, polemically, for others) dimensions of their experience for which there was no ready-made modern vocabulary.

Barbour is most persuasive in two ways. First, he assumes—rather than asserts—that serious political and religious issues are being worked out in and via the medium of what we now call literature. This, in the seventeenth century, was a means of expression that belonged generally to a seamlessly literate and rhetorical culture centrally engaged in working out the constitutional issues with which it was faced. Second, he demonstrates definitively (to my mind) that a given imaginative postulate in, say, Epicureanism, was employed often in contradictory ways. Thus the Epicurean hypothesis about matter could serve as a positive equivalent to the Platonic cult of love associated with the masques, since atoms could be said to combine into gross bodies out of mutual attraction—one reason why Lucretius can propound the atomic hypothesis and indulge in some of the greatest Latin love poetry. On the other hand, the gods' notorious refusal to intervene in human affairs, atomically isolated in their own sphere, served as a means subtly to criticize a Caroline court whom many saw as isolated from the affairs of the country.

What is impressive is that Barbour reengages the standard historiographies concerning both secular and church politics. He negotiates their numerous complexities with alacrity, providing the reader with some sense of the general state of affairs in the historical discipline. In addition, he brings his own commentary to bear by showing how ancient culture pervaded the polemical atmosphere. Barbour divides his book up cleverly: the first half is given to Epicureanism, in secular, then religious, affairs; a chapter on Ford and Stoic resolve (a revision of one of the best essays on that author) leads the reader to the portion on Stoicism, first at court, then in church matters; and a final chapter addresses the collapse of the fragile imaginative economy to which Barbour has sensitized us, in the wake of the Interregnum and Restoration.

Given how much Barbour does achieve in a relatively short space, it seems almost churlish to ask for some more exploration of the formal, literary consequences of the attitudes he describes. The final chapter throws out a number of tantalizing but not entirely developed possibilities for a range of authors, including Lucy Hutchinson and John Milton. For example, we find that authors who had developed earlier in the century had after 1660 to revise their commitments to Epicurus or the Stoa. However, this book is still an impressive achievement.

RICHARD KROLL

University of California
Irvine

COCKERHAM, WILLIAM C. 1999. *Health and Social Change in Russia and Eastern Europe*. Pp. xii, 284. New York: Routledge. $75.00. Paperbound, $22.99.

The changing health status of the people of the former Soviet Union and other countries of Eastern Europe is the major subject of this book. It explains how the Russian Revolution of 1917 led to social changes that brought a steady increase of life expectancy for a period of some 50 years. Then in the mid-1960s, conditions changed, and the mortality of infants and adults began to rise.

The 50 years of progress may be attributed to economic improvements in the health care resources (physicians and other personnel, health centers, polyclinics, hospitals, pharmaceuticals, and so forth) as well as to reasonably good lifestyles. Unfortunately, the book gives only perfunctory attention to this period of great progress. Its overwhelming emphasis is on the later decline in health status of populations in Russia and other countries of Eastern Europe, associated with the lifestyles of these people.

The major components of these lifestyles are behavioral responses to social stress. Of greatest importance are excessive tobacco smoking, high alcohol consumption, high-fat diets, and little exercise. These personal habits have become embedded in the socialist culture, particularly for middle-aged males.

Other writers (particularly Mark Field) have shown how the great change in the health status of the Soviet people, occurring around 1970, was associated with the Cold War and the enormous military expenditures that it engendered. In order to match the massive American military output, the Soviet Union had to increase its military investments greatly. This led to the substantial reduction in expenditures for health care and other social programs. These went down to barely 3 percent of national wealth (gross national product), when most European countries were spending 8 or 9 percent and the United States more than 14 percent.

Despite these shortcomings, Cockerham's book makes a substantial contribution to understanding the importance of lifestyle in analysis of health conditions in the former Soviet Union and other Eastern European countries. It also explains briefly recent policies that emphasize the use of health insurance financing as a strategy for change. It is noteworthy that the book concludes with a call for "extensive public education programs to help people realize the necessity of living healthier lifestyles."

MILTON I. ROEMER

University of California
Los Angeles

EDWARDS, JILL. 1999. *Anglo-American Relations and the Franco Question 1945-1955*. Pp. xviii, 291. Oxford: Clarendon Press. $78.00.

This is Jill Edwards's second book on Spain, and in many ways it is better than her first, *The British Government and the Spanish Civil War* (1980). From a research point of view, Anglo-American discussions about the Franco regime of 1945-53 (listing 1955 in the title was a poor decision by Clarendon) make for a good project, since the author is familiar with the leading characters and sources in the three countries.

At the end of World War II, Spain posed religious and ideological problems to three democratic powers: the United States, Great Britain, and France. Although this book very much presents the view from London, it is unlikely that many new documents will turn up on this theme in either the Public Record Office or the National Archives.

Edwards has woven the British and U.S. archival material into a comprehensive account dealing with Anglo-American relations toward General Francisco Franco's Spain on four levels: the political, the religious-ideological, the military, and the economic. Moreover, the general diplomatic historian with little interest in Spain can learn much about American policy toward specific issues like the American cotton industry, France, NATO, naval strategy, Anglo-American war games, nuclear policy, and the Soviet Union from 1944 to 1953. Edwards's research for that time period is very thorough.

The State Department and the Foreign Office in those years considered Spain's strategic position important for their growing anti-Soviet stance. Just how important, and how much the United States should have paid for Spanish air and naval bases able to deliver nuclear bombs to the USSR, was subjected to long debate. Washington and London found an essentially weak Spain hard to influence because of the prickly heritage of Franco's victory in the civil war and his early collaboration with Hitler and Mussolini, from 1936 to 1945. Many Protestant and Jewish democrats in both countries found Franco as a dictator hard to forgive.

Pressure to accommodate Franco for the sake of anti-Communist foreign policy came from the U.S. Senate, the Defense Department, the cotton industry, the National Security Council, and eventually the State Department. Britain and other democratic members of NATO were more hostile to Franco. President Harry Truman, Mrs. Franklin Roosevelt, and, surprisingly, John Foster Dulles (p. 141) favored continuing the Potsdam boycott of Franco until 1949-50.

Today's reader might find unusual the influence of Freemasonry on Truman's opposition to granting loans and subsidies to Spain. American anti-Communist historians are fond of citing Truman's anti-Stalinist remarks made in 1945. Edwards brings out a forgotten Truman. The U.S. president had a personal hostility to Franco (pp. 40-42, 60-62). He blocked many suggestions from Congress and the Pentagon to lend Franco money. However, in August 1950, Truman finally gave in to the anti-Communist ideologues because of the Korean War and the news that the Soviet Union had successfully tested a nuclear bomb (p. 169).

Franco himself did not beg for foreign aid or make concessions on the Masonic or the Gibraltar questions to get American subsidies. Still, the few Spanish memoirs available on this topic are the weakest part of the author's sources.

The base agreement, eventually concluded in September 1953 under the Eisenhower administration, had obtained Truman's reluctant blessing in June 1951 (pp. 226, 257). The next month, Dean Acheson and George Marshall were pressing Truman to authorize Admiral Forrest Sherman to discuss a bilateral U.S.-Spanish base agreement with the Franco regime. This decision was made over the objections of democratic Britain and France. Actually, when the naval and air force bases became operational in 1959-60, at the cost of more than $500 million, they already had become mostly obsolete for deterring Nikita Khrushchev's Soviet air force and army (p. 256).

This book will inevitably be compared to Boris Liedtke's *Embracing a Dictatorship: US Relations with Spain, 1945-53*, reviewed in the *International History Re-*

view (September 1999). However, Edwards's archival documentation is far superior from both the American and British sources. Edwards qualifies Liedtke's view that George Kennan was, as of 1947, an advocate of accommodation with Franco's Spain. Specifically, Kennan on 6 January 1948 advised the Pentagon that the Soviets had no intention of "walking straight through the Iberian Peninsula" (p. 222).

ROBERT H. WHEALEY

Ohio University
Athens

FRANCE, JOHN. 1999. *Western Warfare in the Age of the Crusades, 1000-1300.* Pp. xv, 327. Ithaca, NY: Cornell University Press. $49.95. Paperbound, $19.95.

Professor John France is an eminent medievalist whose earlier work includes *Victory in the East*, a military history of the First Crusade. With *Western Warfare*, France extends his astute investigations to broader questions of medieval European military history.

Rather than presenting a narrative history, this book is thematic in its approach, including chapters on feudal nobility, weapons, technology, warfare and society, authority, cavalry, infantry, castles, sieges, armies, techniques of command, campaigns, battles, ideologies of warfare, and crusading warfare. France's extensive notes and current bibliography provide an invaluable resource for further study. His work is written for specialists in medieval history and assumes a solid background in medieval studies. As such, it may not be suitable as a textbook for undergraduate classes unless supplemented by additional readings.

France's overall theme is summarized as follows: "Warfare was shaped by four main factors: (a) the dominance of land as

a form of wealth; (b) the limited competence of government; (c) the state of technology which, broadly, favoured the defence over attack; (d) the geography and climate of the west." France also rightly sets out to debunk the "myth of the [dominance] of the mounted knight," providing a useful reevaluation of the relative strengths and weaknesses of cavalry and infantry in medieval battles. He also rejects technological determinism in medieval warfare. For France, "social and political forces interacting with the technology of the age" caused changes in warfare to be slow and erratic, and "not always sustained."

Although France focuses on his four themes and the broader patterns of warfare, he nonetheless provides numerous detailed studies of specific battles and sieges ranging from Scotland to Egypt. These include Coutrai, Legnano, Acre, Muret, Las Navas de Tolosa, Bovines, Bannockburn, Hattin, and Tagliacozzo, among many others. Broader campaigns are also studied—such as those of Charles of Anjou—with a major emphasis on the campaigns of the Crusades in chapter 15. This broad perspective, while necessary to his thematic approach, may obscure important regional differences in the theory and practice of warfare.

Of course, some of France's interpretations are open to debate. For example, given the dramatic developments in castle-building techniques and trebuchet technology in this period, he may be overstating his position on technological continuity. Although France does use Muslim sources, they are generally in translation. Future studies on warfare during the age of the Crusades might also benefit from an interdisciplinary approach. With Western European armies ranging throughout Eastern Europe, the Byzantine domain, North Africa, and the Near East, their military activities are recorded in a wide range of non-Western sources. A team of specialists carefully scrutinizing these sources in their original languages could reveal important new information on Western European military techniques, serving as a useful counterbalance to the sometimes tendentious descriptions provided by European sources.

Nevertheless, even when one differs with France, one remains impressed with his sound approach and careful analysis, which is always based solidly in the sources. In summary, despite these quibbles, France's book represents a very valuable study of warfare during the age of the Crusades and is highly recommended.

WILLIAM JAMES HAMBLIN

Brigham Young University
Provo
Utah

UNITED STATES

ATKINSON, DAVID N. 1999. *Leaving the Bench: Supreme Court Justices at the End*. Pp. xiii, 248. Lawrence: University Press of Kansas. $29.95.

Building on several of his articles and extensive research, political scientist David N. Atkinson has produced a definitive work on Supreme Court justices at the end of their service: it details the reasons why and the conditions under which they left the high bench, along with the circumstances of their lives after leaving and surrounding their deaths. In constructing descriptive narratives on each justice from John Jay to Harry A. Blackmun, Atkinson draws on a range of sources, including "newspapers, biographies, memoirs, diaries, historical studies, private letters, and interviews."

Chapter 1 deals generally with the matter of why justices leave or stay on the bench. Notably, the most significant historical factors bearing on the justices'

decisions to step down was the enactment in 1937 of a generous retirement system, the increased use of peer pressure among the justices to induce retirements, and the mass media's increasing scrutiny of the justices and their health.

The next five chapters focus chronologically on the Antebellum Court, 1789-1864; the late nineteenth century, 1865-99; the Court from 1900 to 1936; the Roosevelt Court to the Warren Court, 1937-68; and, finally, the period from 1968 to 1998. Each chapter contains a brief overview and a statistical analysis of the age of the justices' retirements and deaths, followed by a narrative on each justice, ranging from a few paragraphs to several pages. Chapter 7 concludes with the question of "when should justices leave?"

Besides a selected bibliography, there are three appendices. The first addresses whether Justice Stephen J. Field acted alone or with his colleagues in doing the "dirty work" of persuading the ailing Justice Robert C. Grier to resign in 1869. The second contains a table on the average age and tenure of the bench for each term. The third lists the justices' grave sites.

When considering when justices should leave and how to induce those who are unwilling to leave to do so, Atkinson reaches some provocative conclusions. On the one hand, he does not favor establishing a mandatory retirement age because, unlike the nineteenth century, "there have been no recent instances of justices clinging to their seats for years after falling into decrepitude, despite relatively short-term disabilities." Still, he believes that some justices' refusal to leave when their capacities decline may damage the Court as an institution and that reforms are needed, for, as he says, "unless some changes are made, I am pessimistic about the Court's future."

The problem with the contemporary Court, in Atkinson's view, is that the justices delegate too much work to their law clerks and, thus, are too insulated and isolated from each other. Weak justices, therefore, may carry on with their clerks doing their work and are removed from the peer pressures once wielded by other justices to force retirements. Hence, Atkinson proposes that the justices no longer hire their own clerks but instead have them work collectively for the Court. Yet such a reform is unlikely given the working relationships of justices and their clerks, as well as the process for opinion assignments and the historical trend toward more individual concurring, dissenting, and separate opinions. In addition, it would reinforce the already bureaucratic handling of the Court's business. His other recommendations, such as expanding the size of the Court, fare no better.

In sum, *Leaving the Bench* is a useful reference and makes an important contribution, even if Atkinson's pessimism seems unsupported and his proposed reforms unpersuasive.

DAVID M. O'BRIEN

University of Virginia
Charlottesville

DAVIS, RICHARD. 1999. *The Web of Politics: The Internet's Impact on the American Political System*. Pp. xi, 225. New York: Oxford University Press. $39.95. Paperbound, $18.95.

Not since the entrance of broadcast television into American political campaigns have claims been made for a new communication technology that are as extravagant as those being made for the Internet. It has been said, for example, that the Internet will revolutionize political participation, that it will free citizens from media filters, and that it will replace political parties (not with new groups but with nothing) and thereby completely upset political power in the United States.

Such hyperbole is not unlike that heard in the initial stages in the development of other tools of mass communication in that its use is filled with bizarre and paranoid claims from the political Left and Right about centralized information resources that will lead to a technologically driven perfect world. The reality, according to Richard Davis in *The Web of Politics*, is that the Net, although sophisticated, is simply an alternate way to transport messages. In fact, in provocative, detailed, and well-documented analysis, Davis pretty much demolishes the assertion that the Internet, as a single communication tool, will transform American political life. Instead, he argues that those individuals and communication organizations with established credibility will continue to be dominant simply by adapting to the Web and adding it to their communication arsenals. Thus his thesis, that the Web will not turn passive Americans into political activists who seize all Internet information, seems on target and consistent with adaptation to earlier technologies.

The book is organized into an introduction and seven chapters on the impact of the Internet on the current players in American politics, including news media organizations, lobbying groups, campaigns, government, and the public. The final chapter, "The Internet as Participatory Forum," summarizes Davis's argument that the Net will not achieve the revolutionary status some have predicted for it. It will not, Davis argues, upset existing power structures because the media, interest groups, candidates, and policymakers have already adapted to the Internet to retain their preeminence.

One of the most important chapters, in part because of the advent of the 2000 campaign, is "The Virtual Campaign." In it, Davis provides a useful chronology of the ways in which candidates, political parties (at national, state, and local levels), newspapers, and education groups used the Internet during the 1996 campaign to advance their causes. As he makes clear, however, the most significant change was the proliferation of candidate Web sites. In 1996, candidates running for all manner of offices found it necessary to have at least some exposure on the Net, although for most, exposure was not synonymous with interactivity. Using a sample of 100 candidate sites, Davis found that the Internet was primarily used as a personal-image advertising tool, providing the candidate's biography, a solicitation for help from potential activists, and the perception of interaction with the candidate. Given the even more heightened use of candidate Web sites for campaign 2000, the thoughtful questions posed by Davis regarding real or perceived Internet interactivity should allow us an even more in-depth understanding of the way in which this newest campaign communication tool is or is not ultimately revolutionary.

JUDITH S. TRENT

University of Cincinnati
Ohio

FEINBERG, WALTER, 1998. *Common Schools and Uncommon Identities: National Unity and Cultural Differences.* Pp. x, 264. New Haven, CT: Yale University Press. $28.50.

The argument of this excellent book by Walter Feinberg can be viewed as a dialogue between two positions, which Feinberg terms pluralism and multiculturalism. Pluralists hold that cultural diversity belongs in the sphere of the home, congregation, or community. The role of the public school is to create a unified American identity. Multiculturalists, in contrast, want schools to actively recognize and reinforce diverse identities. Feinberg seeks a middle ground: the school must indeed develop an inclusive national identity, but he also holds that there are special cases in which groups are entitled to public support to maintain a subcultural identity. Feinberg, however, rejects sweeping demands for an education that emphasizes the reinforcement of particularistic identities. The great strength of this book is the careful and dispassionate assessment of arguments in the search for a principled and balanced position.

Feinberg argues his case from what he calls a liberal position. His liberalism gives significant weight to three principles: equal opportunity, free association, and individual growth.

A second, less visible dialogue in the book is between Feinberg's rather Dewian view of liberalism and procedural liberalism, a view he identifies with Rawls. The tension here is between "democracy as a way of life" and a view of liberalism that seeks neutrality between different conceptions of the good. This dialogue is, I think, more important to Feinberg's view than the amount of space given to it suggests. It is of particular importance in considering the standing of "traditionalist" groups, who may be pacific and law abiding but who are illiberal so far as the education of their children is concerned. This dialogue comes off less well, however. Feinberg's discussion suggests that procedural liberalism seeks to be culturally neutral, a reading of Rawls that I find doubtful. Nor does it recognize the significance of Rawls's distinction between ethical liberalism and political liberalism for political socialization. The real issue is not whether liberalism has cultural implications. It is how "thick" a liberal democratic culture should be and when it can be made obligatory for the political socialization of the children of those who resist it.

There are two more discussions I would have liked to have seen in this book. First, it needed a more robust justification of constructing the issues as issues of identity and an assessment of the consequences of this choice. What are the alternatives? Many who discuss these matters view them as issues of belief. Rawls, for example, defends a pluralism of comprehensive doctrines. These different formulations are not neutral to the issues. For example, Feinberg treats religious issues as matters of religious identity. However, for the Amish and the parents who brought *Mozert* v. *Hawkins*, the issues are likely to be conceptualized as concerning the truth of their fundamental convictions and, accordingly, as one of freedom of conscience. Identity talk shades the issues differently from the way belief talk does. It makes questions of truth and falsity less central, and it diminishes the standing of freedom of conscience. It enhances the importance of the integrity of the self. It makes convictions important because they are mine or those of my culture rather than because they are either fundamental or reasonable. My beard may be a part of my identity, but it is not connected to my fundamental convictions. If I am compelled to shave, I may be aggrieved, but I cannot say, "I must obey God rather than man." (There is also an odd passage [p. 111] where the issue for Socrates in the *Crito* is said to be his moral identity.) I find the relationship between identity and belief in this book unclear. Hence I am not entirely clear what it is that one has when one has a national identity, and I am suspicious of the adequacy of identity talk when the issues concern religious toleration. The principles underlying pluralism and multiculturalism are in part those of the First Amendment. What would change if it began, "Congress shall make no law effecting the establishment of an identity or prohibiting the free expression thereof"?

The second discussion I would have wanted concerns an appraisal of the current practice of public schools. I think it is at least possible to wonder whether public schools are not currently dominated by an education that is largely instrumental in character and promotes a consumerist culture that serves neither the formation of a national identity nor uncommon identities.

Notwithstanding these concerns, the treatment of multiculturalism in this book is superb. It is required reading on the topic.

KENNETH A. STRIKE

Cornell University
Ithaca
New York

FENSTER, MARK. 1999. *Conspiracy Theories: Secrecy and Power in American Culture*. Pp. vii, 282. Minneapolis: University of Minnesota Press. $24.95.

In this intelligent book, Mark Fenster stages a debate about the significance of conspiracy theories in contemporary American politics. On one side is the proposition, developed by political scientists such as Richard Hofstadter in the 1950s and 1960s, that conspiracy theories are the mark of an unfortunate "paranoid style" in American politics. On the other side of the debate is the proposition, drawing on contemporary cultural studies, that conspiracy theories are a form of populist resistance against hegemonic power. Fenster hopes the debate will illuminate the strengths and weaknesses of each position. His framework also promises an intriguing engagement between social scientific and humanist analyses of political culture.

Fenster's critical instincts are sharp. He argues persuasively that paranoid-style analysis wrongly dismisses conspiracy theories, along with all serious challenges to the actually existing American political order, as merely pathological. As he puts it, "Just because overarching conspiracy theories are wrong does not mean that they are not on to something," and the something they are on to is "a withering civil society and the concentration of the ownership of the means of production, which together leave the political subject without the ability to be recognized or to signify in the public realm." Rather than simply dismissing conspiracy theories as the product of maladjusted minds, then, Fenster argues that we must take them seriously. This project, in turn, requires us to look at the cultural and social significance of conspiracy theorizing itself—rather than simply debunking, one more time, *The Protocols of the Elders of Zion*.

Examining a wide variety of conspiracy texts—from the movie *JFK* to the many fantasies of the right-wing Clinton-conspiracy crowd to the television show *The X-Files* to racist and fundamentalist Christian novels—Fenster finds some common characteristics. Conspiracy theories demonstrate high "narrative velocity"; they make individual agency central to their narratives yet question its very possibility; they fetishize and defer the revealing of ultimate Truth; and they provide the participant-observer with an emotional rush that inspires some people to consume and construct conspiracy theories as a form of play. At the end of the day, however, Fenster rejects the romantic notion that conspiracy theories are an authentic voice of counterhegemonic cultural resistance that should be celebrated; in his view, conspiracy theorizing hinders rather than facilitates the collective action necessary for meaningful political change.

Fenster's analysis is sharp and sensible and his observations acute. Why then was I disappointed by this book? First, Fenster never quite succeeds in getting his inner cultural analyst to engage productively with his inner political scientist. One dutifully plods through the difference between premillennialist and postmillennialist fundamentalist Christians, for example, without much sense of their significance on the American political scene or the role that conspiracy theorizing has recently played in national politics. Second, though the conspiracy theories that Fenster examines are bizarre, funny, scary, absorbing, and deeply troubling by turns, Fenster's analysis nearly makes them boring. Save for a few welcome flashes of humor, his exploration of the far outposts of American political critique is curiously devoid of the vertiginous pleasures for which conspiracy junkies live. What emotional hook drew Fenster to his subject? Affection? Curiosity? Contempt? Outrage? Without any sense of why it matters to him, *Conspiracy Theories* is edifying but not very much fun.

ANGELA P. HARRIS

University of California
Berkeley

JEFFREYS-JONES, RHODRI. 1999. *Peace Now! American Society and the Ending of the Vietnam War.* Pp. ix, 308. New Haven, CT: Yale University Press. $25.00.

Within the past decade, several scholars have examined the impact of the Vietnam war on American society. Prominent among their works are *An American Ordeal: The Antiwar Movement of the Vietnam Era* (1990), by Charles DeBenedetti, with Charles Chatfield; *Johnson, Nixon, and the Doves* (1988) and *Covering Dissent: The Media and the Anti-Vietnam War Movement* (1994), by Melvin Small; *The War Within: America's Battle over Vietnam* (1994), by Tom Wells; *The Movement and the Sixties: Protest in America from Greensboro to Wounded Knee* (1995), by Terry H. Anderson; *The Debate over Vietnam* (2d ed., 1995), by David W. Levy; and *Telltale Hearts: The Origins and Impact of the Antiwar War* (1995), by Adam Garfinkle. An underlying problem confronting each of these scholars was the complexity of the amorphous war protest movement, with its shifting constituencies, organizations, publications, strategies, and activities. In *Peace Now!*, Rhodri Jeffreys-Jones focuses on the ways that four important groups—students, African Americans, women, and labor—responded to the war, and, in the process, he adds to an understanding of the origins, development, and influence of antiwar sentiment.

The strength of this book is the thorough and subtle analysis of each of the groups in the context of its economic interests, involvement in local politics (particularly in California and New York), connections with the Democratic coalition, and "minority mentality." All of these groups instinctively identified with the U.S. war effort in its early stages not only because they accepted the prevalent Cold War consensus but also because, as "outsiders," they represented "breakthrough syndrome" aspirations. In each group (except labor), however, large numbers came to feel "separated in a significant way from the white, old, rich, or male [and] that feeling of difference gave them their political importance." Students, who were not restrained by the imperatives of breakthrough, gave the war protest movement its initial impetus, with prominence shifting later to the African Americans and finally to the women. The cumulative effect "sapped the resistance power of the policy makers . . . [and] was among the more significant causes of American withdrawal from the Vietnam War."

Some aspects of *Peace Now!*, however, are puzzling. Jeffreys-Jones contends that Vietnam was "one of America's most popular wars"; besides citing irrelevant opinion data pertaining to World Wars I and II, he writes that "85 percent supported Johnson's interventionist policy in 1964, and 65 percent backed Nixon's Vietnam policy at the end of 1969." This implies continuous popular support, which was not the case, as polls revealed a steady decline. Moreover, the 1964 and 1969 polls need to be seen in context: Johnson's support was over his response to the emotional Gulf of Tonkin incident, which was not generally seen as a prelude to the massive intervention that came a year later; Nixon's resulted from the popularity of his Vietnamization policy and early U.S. troop withdrawals. Jeffreys-Jones also strains to get the students off center stage, seeing a "second phase of student protest, 1966-1968 . . . [as] a time of diminishing momentum and power." This interpretation is important to his argument that African Americans and women became more prominent. Yet his ensuing discussion of student activism between 1966 and 1968 makes any distinction from earlier protest seem arbitrary. Most important, Jeffrey-Jones's discourse on labor is less illustrative than that on the other groups. He provides relatively little insight into internal dynamics and instead deals mostly with the ways that national and state leaders tried to manipulate labor's general pro-war stance to their advantage. Moreover, that very hawkish sentiment gives this chapter little salience in fulfilling the purpose stated in the book's subtitle.

On balance, *Peace Now!* is an important contribution, clearly written and thoroughly documented, to the understanding of American society during the Vietnam era.

GARY R. HESS

Bowling Green State University
Ohio

NYE, DAVID E. 1999. *Consuming Power: A Social History of American Energies.* Pp. xii, 331. Cambridge: MIT Press. Paperbound, $15.00.

Anyone familiar with American history knows that the application of new technological systems and high-energy intensive use underpinned the remarkable productivity of the country's modernizing economy. David E. Nye's thoughtful and lucidly presented book, while reminding us of this, offers a deeply probing investigation of how Americans came to consume energy so much more profligately than any other people. Nye's story and analysis, beginning during the colonial period and concluding in the final years of the twentieth century, at which time the United States consumed 25 percent of global energy and two times more per capita than the European Union, reveals a historical record of choices made, systems applied, and consequences both applauded and deplored.

Two key themes provide the warp and the weft: one accentuates choices, and particularly personal choices in contrast to somewhat more collective energy choices made, say, in Western Europe; the second suggests that the energy choices of bygone days, then seemingly logical, evolved into systems resistant, even impervious, to change. Today, Americans find themselves ensnared by a fossil fuel and nuclear mix that defies transformation. All of this began back in the colonial period, when settlers improved upon the medieval plough and old-fashioned furnaces, the objective being to substitute equipment for muscle power and reduce costs. Always, Nye rejects all forms of determinism.

The book proceeds chronologically, each chapter molded around energy transitions from muscle and wind to water power, steam power, and electrification. By the 1900s, a mature industrial society had committed to fossil fuel–based energy systems, manifest most dramatically in electricity, automobiles, the city, and mass-production factories. Each of these reflected the choice of particular technologies that appeared to make life easier. Electrification and the car, we are told, transformed American popular culture and nurtured the emergence of the famous, or infamous, consumer society, alive and well as the bizarre twentieth century ends. Chapter 7, for instance, whisks the reader back to the New York World's Fair of 1967 to demonstrate how the federal government, big business, and Walt Disney urged Americans to journey to a fabulous future "wrapped in a technological cocoon of conveniences."

As Nye's story of ostentatious consumption unfolds, the theme of ensnarement becomes blurred. Can a society be considered entrapped by the fulfillment of its preferences, in this case, cheap, abundant, and accessible energy? Perhaps, but only if alternatives are unavailable. Have alternatives to the dominant energy systems been lacking? Amory Lovins, among others, has for decades advocated greater energy efficiency and conservation as viable ways to transform the system and reduce environmental degradation. True, governments at all levels ignored, except for a brief moment during the Carter administration, such feasible suggestions. Admitting this alters the architecture of entrapment. Are we captives to rigid energy systems because of accumulated personal energy choices, or have we been manipulated, as we were after World War I, when General Motors and others managed the dismantlement of efficient electric trolley lines?

Absent from this engaging study is the integration of evolving political configurations and culture. It is not satisfactory for Nye to simply assert that Americans must choose between high- and low-energy-efficiency technologies and support at the polls recycling and nonsprawl zoning. A tight web of vested interests obstructs the way. Who can deny the huge political power of the fossil fuel and electric generation industries and their allies? What energy choices are possible in a nation of sunshine democrats? Did Americans elect to deregulate industry, privatize, and countenance enormous mergers? What is the future of democracy and personal choice in a nation in which 2.6 million people earn as much as the poorest 100 million?

JOHN G. CLARK

University of Kansas
Lawrence

PRENDERGAST, WILLIAM B. 1999. *The Catholic Voter in American Politics: The Passing of the Democratic Monolith.* Pp. xiv, 260. Washington, DC: Georgetown University Press. $35.00.

The main argument of William Prendergast's *Catholic Voter in American Politics* is that Catholic voters, once a mainstay of the Democratic Party, have become much less predictable in their voting patterns in recent decades. Through a rather careful examination of recent election campaigns, particularly since 1976, Prendergast argues that there has been a "political homogenization of American Catholics," that Catholics are now much less distinct in political terms from other voters of similar socioeconomic circumstances than they once were.

Admirably, Prendergast does not oversell his case. He does not argue, for example, that Catholics have in some predictable way moved over to the Republican side, nor that they are likely to expand the ranks of the Christian Right in the foreseeable future. Instead, he follows the data where they lead, to the pretty inescapable conclusion that the percentage of the Catholic vote that a Re-

publican candidate can expect to get in, say, the 2000 presidential election is considerably higher than it would have been 30 or 50 years ago.

This conclusion, in truth, will not be much of a surprise for close observers of the Catholic Church in America. The movement of Catholic voters toward Reagan and Bush in the 1980s was widely reported and well documented at the time. What in Prendergast's book should be of interest to all readers, however, is the way in which he places these more recent results firmly within the much broader historical context of the role of Catholicism in the United States, the development of the American party system, and, most crucially, the relationship between those two. Despite his subtitle, for example, Prendergast's book shows that the Catholic vote may not have been such a Democratic monolith in the first place. In fact, he illustrates that there have been three distinct periods during which the Catholic vote drifted away from the Democratic Party: once early in this century, just before Al Smith's historic campaign in 1928; once at mid-century, just before Kennedy's more successful run for the White House; and once in the 1980s, during the Reagan-Bush era. Prendergast does a persuasive, and interesting, job of analyzing these drifts, and their reversals, in terms of both the socioeconomic advancement of American Catholics and the changing shape of the national political debate.

For my taste, Prendergast does not pay quite enough attention to accounting for what one might argue was the surprising Catholic support for Clinton in 1992 and 1996 and for Democratic congressional candidates in 1998. But he does raise a very important question for the future through his emphasis on the growing role that Hispanics are coming to play within the Catholic electorate.

William Prendergast is identified on the book jacket as an official of the Republican National Committee and as "an author of Republican national platforms." Given his affiliations, he might have done better to avoid some of the gratuitous swipes at liberal targets like the *New York Times* editorial page and Catholics for a Free Choice that pop up here and there throughout the book. But, at the same time, he is to be commended for a data analysis that is, on the whole, careful, judicious, and persuasive. In *The Catholic Voter in American Politics*, Prendergast has produced a readable, clear-eyed treatment of a very important slice of the American electorate.

TIMOTHY A. BYRNES

Colgate University
Hamilton
New York

SANDER, ALFRED D. 1999. *Eisenhower's Executive Office*. Pp. 212. Westport, CT: Greenwood Press. $59.95.

Eisenhower's Executive Office offers a useful history of President Eisenhower's actions to shape and modernize executive office agencies in ways that would ensure their utility for decades to come. John Burke, John Hart, Stephen Hess, and Bradley Patterson are among those who have provided excellent studies on the broad outlines of the executive office and the modern White House, but Sander's study is valuable for its in-depth profiles of agencies and directors during the administration of arguably the most skilled chief executive of the twentieth century, Dwight D. Eisenhower.

Although the material in Sander's four chapters on the National Security Council and Operations Coordinating Board is somewhat redundant with earlier studies, there are, nonetheless, new insights into these organs as well as informative discussion on agencies of Eisenhower's presidency that have received less study, such as the Council of Economic Advisers, the Council on Foreign Economic Policy, and the Bureau of the Budget. Sander suggests that Senator Henry M. Jackson's Subcommittee on National Policy Machinery aided Democratic Party efforts to soil Eisenhower's reputation as an effective manager by attacking the processes of the National Security Council and Operations Coordinating Board, which had become the cornerstone of the president's advisory apparatus. "The critics did such a good job of condemning the system," Sander writes, "that its reputation was blackened for twenty years until documents in the Eisenhower Library showed how wrong they were."

Sander's work is bolstered by his diligent use of primary sources from the Eisenhower Library, including the relatively untapped records of the Council on Foreign Economic Policy and a thorough mining of several key oral history interviews. Sander provides deft profiles of top agency personnel and gives the reader a sense of appreciation for the unparalleled professionalism that distinguished Eisenhower's top aides from many of their successors. The administration was brimming with young talents like Arthur Burns, a Columbia University Ph.D. in economics, who was given the task of reorganizing the Council of Economic Advisers, which he ultimately headed. Burns was "an analyst of economic phenomena without peer" and so impressed Eisenhower in his presentations and "skillful use of statistical data" that he was called upon to brief the cabinet on a regular basis. Another shining star, Andrew Goodpaster, served as Eisenhower's second appointee in the newly created position of staff secretary and is depicted by Sander as a "thoughtful, provocative, one hundred percent loyal" assistant, who had "more capacity to see over the horizon than almost anybody else . . . and a greater capacity than others to synthesize as opposed to compromise on issues."

Some would take exception to Sander's contention that "it was probably inevitable that Eisenhower should base his White House organization on the army prototype" and that Eisenhower's staff, "like a military staff," was "more compartmentalized." Although Eisenhower did appoint several top-flight military officers to his administration, he also sought to distance himself from a military model, as former staff secretary Goodpaster and assistant secretary for the cabinet Bradley Patterson have noted elsewhere.

Sander concludes his book with a particularly interesting discussion of Eisenhower's fascination with his brother Milton's idea for the creation of a "super secretary of state" who would hold special status in the cabinet and would have subordinates with rank equal to that of a traditional department secretary. The idea of a "first secretary" was the object of serious study in the administration, and readers will undoubtedly be reminded of the parallels between this proposal and the brief negotiations between Ronald Reagan and former president Gerald Ford during the 1980 Republican Convention concerning the prospective role of a vice president with "first secretary" status. Such discussions make Sander's book a readable and worthwhile addition to the list of books on the organization and management of the presidency and on Eisenhower's important legacy in this area.

PHILLIP G. HENDERSON

Catholic University of America
Washington, D.C.

SCHRECKER, ELLEN. 1998. *Many Are the Crimes: McCarthyism in America.* Pp. xx, 550. Princeton, NJ: Princeton University Press. Paperbound, $17.95.

Ellen Schrecker is one of the foremost historians of the McCarthy era in U.S. history. Her book *No Ivory Tower: McCarthyism and the Universities* broke new ground in the understanding of the effects of the 1950s Red Scare on the world of academia. Her small volume *The Age of McCarthyism: A Brief History with Documents* has helped to open up to college students that era of political repression. So, too, will this paperback edition, with a new preface, of *Many Are the Crimes: McCarthyism in America.*

The volume under review is an examination of the anti-Communist movement of the 1950s. By placing the movement under the rubric of a "mainstream movement," Schrecker reveals its effects upon the nation's public and private institutions, causing those in power to infringe upon people's civil liberties. Schrecker breaks down McCarthyism into several categories, including the ultraconservatives, exemplified by patriotic and right-wing activists; the liberals, who supported policies that prevented Communists from enjoying free speech; the anti-Stalinist left wingers; and the partisanship of such ambitious politicians as Richard Nixon. All added up to the longest period of political repression in this country's history.

To illustrate her points, the body of the text examines various individual cases, such as that of the U.S. Communist Party, dating from the 1920s to the 1950s; the response of the Federal Bureau of Investigation (FBI) to the party and its development of a red-baiting agenda; and the ever present House Un-American Activities Committee (HUAC) and its growth during the Roosevelt years. Of particular interest are some of the case studies that Schrecker weaves into her narrative. That of Clinton Jencks, for example, traces the FBI's hounding of this organizer with the International Union of Mine, Mill, and Smelter Workers in southern New Mexico, whose life was turned upside-down because of his connections to labor organizing, communism, and the making of the classic film *Salt of the Earth*. While relating how Jencks's union experience brought the film to life, Schrecker also reveals the intricate connections between Hollywood and McCarthyism, giving it new depth and insights.

Schrecker takes the same approach in effectively and movingly linking the personal and political sides of McCarthyism throughout the book, concluding it with an examination of the effects of fear of government repression on people's lives. She relates how some "red diaper babies" attending a conference in the early 1980s refused to allow their last names to be published in an account of their discussions, reflecting the same fear their parents had had during their own lives. There were 1950s survivors whom, Schrecker relates, later committed suicide, suffered heart attacks, were beaten or received hate mail, lost jobs and professions—never to find an equivalent—and many who for years suffered from psychological stress and a paranoia not unfounded. Personal lives as well as a leftist political movement were destroyed in the 1950s, only weakly resurfacing in the civil rights and peace movements of the 1960s and 1970s.

Many Are the Crimes is a fascinating book, one that can be appropriately used as a college text or for personal consumption. It is another of Ellen Schrecker's clear, moving accounts of the nation's continuing struggle with its anti-Communist nature.

HARRIET HYMAN ALONSO

City College of New York
New York City

SOCIOLOGY

CURRIE, ELLIOTT. 1998. *Crime and Punishment in America*. Pp. 230. New York: Metropolitan Books. $23.00.

Crime and Punishment in America is a thought-provoking, intelligent, and balanced analysis of U.S. crime-control polices. Throughout the book, Currie's recommendations for changes in the nation's responses to the crime problem are supported by cogent arguments, hard data, and detailed examples of programs that effectively ameliorate the social and economic conditions that foster crime. Currie contends that America's heavy reliance, during the past 25 years, on incarceration and other harsh penalties has been a disastrous "experiment" that has largely ignored "what we know about the roots of crime and the uses and limits of punishment."

Currie's view is that crime and violence stem more from social and economic deprivation than from moral decay or individual depravity. He deftly and convincingly refutes each of the arguments that have been advanced in support of prison, which he calls the "social agency of first resort." Under Currie's powerful scrutiny, imprisonment falls short of attaining its principal objectives (deterrence, incapacitation, and rehabilitation) and instead leaves us with an "army of ex-offenders" who are unable or unwilling to reintegrate successfully into the community and to join the ranks of the legitimately employed.

According to Currie, proponents of the "prison works" philosophy of crime control have greatly inflated the costs of crime and have exaggerated the benefits of incarceration, especially for nonviolent and older offenders. Prison proponents have also neglected to weigh the effectiveness and costs of imprisonment against those of community-based sanctions and of crime prevention efforts. In a sobering reminder of the trade-offs involved, Currie notes that the expense of building and operating prisons has taken money away from mental health care, drug treatment, school programs, employment training, and other interventions that, in his opinion, have tremendous potential to alleviate the nation's crime problem.

Currie presents persuasive evidence of the effectiveness of crime-control strategies that focus on improving the living conditions of at-risk families and children and on reforming the criminal justice system. He is a strong advocate of living-wage and federal job creation initiatives, maintaining that a poor labor market intensifies the "poverty, social isolation, and community fragmentation that breeds violent crime."

Currie's recommendations for criminal justice reforms include the following three elements. First, we need greater investment in rehabilitation and educational programs that address offenders' "criminogenic needs" and help them to develop the skills and experience required to change their lives in positive and productive ways. Second, we must use prisons more selectively, keeping out persons who could benefit from community-based correctional options and keeping in persons who pose a violent threat to public safety. Finally, Currie promotes innovative policing strategies that attempt to prevent crime and to minimize its pernicious consequences for individuals, families, and communities.

Crime and Punishment in America is an excellent and highly readable book for any person who wants to learn about the causes of crime in America and about solutions that are based on solid research and clear thinking. The volume is a short, but impressive, treatise on our country's (mostly) failed attempts to address one of the most important problems affecting it currently.

ARTHUR J. LURIGIO

Loyola University
Chicago

HOBSON, FRED. 1999. *But Now I See: The White Southern Racial Conversion Narrative.* Pp. xiv, 159. Baton Rouge: Louisiana State University Press. $30.00. Paperbound, $14.95.

Given first as the 1998 Walter Lynwood Fleming Lectures in Southern History at Louisiana State University, Fred Hobson's four-chapter essay *But Now I See* is a literary and cultural history treatment of how selected gifted and sensitive white twentieth-century U.S. Southern writers told their stories of change from submission to their cultural environment of racism to rejection of racism and racist practices. Hobson's thesis is that the change is uniformly reported by the writers as instantaneous and equivalent to a religious experience, indeed, connected to features of their forms of Southern Protestantism. Thus he calls the books he discusses "conversion narratives," drawing his model from conversion narratives in American religious literature written by seventeenth- and eighteenth-century Puritan divines in New England.

Beginning in the 1940s, Hobson claims, these Southern social conversion narratives appear as new autobiographies and autobiographical essays or fiction by white Southerners who embrace liberal positions on race. Invariably, Hobson points out, these white Southerners use the language and description of cultural formation of pietistic Protestantism—"sin," "guilt," "salvation," "repentance," "damnation," and change by "conversion" for "redemption"—to express their personal transformation from willing participant in segregated and racist society to passionate opponent of racist social structure and customary behavior. Moreover, they follow the outline of the Christian conversion narrative in which the penitent takes a spiritual journey from the "darkness" of ignorance or shameful behavior to the "light" of new understanding in a momentary realization in which the past is shed and the future is enlightened. This conversion experience is followed by a changed life.

The first of Hobson's four chapters is entitled "The Sins of the Fathers" and treats primarily the works of Lillian Smith (*Killers of the Dream* [1949]) and Katharine Du Pre Lumpkin (*The Making of a Southerner* [1947]). While acknowledging the antecedent and contemporaneous work of W. J. Cash, Ralph McGill, and Hodding Carter in questioning the rightness of segregation, Hobson presents Smith and Lumpkin as providing depth of emotion and power of conscience in their works. These women, he suggests, wrote out of an agony of conscience, in opposition to their parents, and couched their arguments on behalf of their families and their region, as well as themselves. He notes that Smith says that Southern women have "never been as loyal to the ideology of race and segregation as have southern men."

The second chapter, "God's Determination," covers writings of James McBride Dabbs, Sarah Patton Boyle, and Will Campbell from the 1950s and early 1960s. "Freedom" is the third chapter, and the writers covered are Willie Morris, Larry L. King, and Pat Watters, who published in the 1960s and 1970s, during the civil rights movement. The final chapter, "Curious Intersections: Race and Class at Century's End," addresses works published in the 1980s and 1990s and also raises the question largely left out of the earlier Southern writings, the issue of class. Through the works of all these writers, Hobson shows a persistent pattern of a conversion narrative, the writer of each work testifying to a life-changing personal experience that drew her or him out of the "sin" of youthful participation in the racially segregated and race-hating "Southern way of life" to a new life of advocacy of desegregation and racial justice.

Hobson effectively argues his thesis and supports it well with information from the texts he chose.

GAYLE GRAHAM YATES

University of Minnesota
Minneapolis

ROBILLARD, ALBERT B. 1999. *Meaning of a Disability: The Lived Experience of Paralysis.* Pp. xv, 191. Philadelphia: Temple University Press. $59.50. Paperbound, $19.95.

How do most "temporarily able-bodied" folks learn what a long-term physical disability feels like? If they dare to take a wheelchair-user's perspective, they can experience the frustrations of the built environment (when the chair flips over on them or their destination is inaccessible) and the embarrassments of civic life (when they acquire nonperson status in social spaces). Such firsthand adventures expose able-bodied people's privileges and the unseen work that people with disabilities carry out in public. But simulations cannot fully capture this reality; the best information comes from living with a disability and telling others about it, as Robillard does in this book. *Meaning of a Disability* fits in the disability studies genre exemplified by Irving Zola's *Missing Pieces* (1982), Nancy Mairs's *Waist-High in the World: A Life Among the Nondisabled* (1997), and Robert Murphy's *Body Silent* (1987).

By exploiting his ethnomethodological roots (in 1974, he earned his doctorate under ethnomethodologist Harold Garfinkel), Robillard makes sense of living with a motor neuron disease (amyotrophic lateral sclerosis, or ALS). He demonstrates convincingly how smooth social interactions depend not only on shared beliefs but also on basic "bodily accomplishments." This became clear to Robillard as he lost the ability to walk; to will his limbs, hands, and feet to move; to turn his head; and to speak. Robillard charts the maddening, dismaying, and even life-threatening consequences of being unable to engage others' attention and sustain contact with them through bodily cues (a wave, a nod, a head tilt, voice contact, eye contact, facial expressions, and so forth). He describes experiencing sudden but complete isolation and situations where others rudely made social and physical decisions for him without his consent.

Due to the loss of facial muscular control vital for mouthing words, Robillard, in collaboration with his wife, Divina, developed a system of "lip-signing" letters of the alphabet. Other family members and his student research assistants (at the University of Hawaii) then learned the system (some better than others). Robillard produced the entire manuscript of *Meaning of a Disability* by lip-signing to his student research assistants. He analyzes how lip-signing every letter of every word—his only reliable communication technique—prohibits "real-time" interaction. When trying to converse with others, he and his facilitators must exercise great patience, but often the timing, the next topic, or the listener's impatience disrupts the interaction.

Perhaps most people facing these conditions would become defeatist and depressed. Robillard, however, turned living with his motor neuron disease into an object of study. Isolation granted him the opportunity to think and work more intensely and productively than before the disease developed. He deflects other people's attempts to cast him as a hero consumed by the "tragedy" of his disease, as a lost cause who should give up and die, as "lucky" that his wife "stuck" with him, or as an imbecile who cannot think. He turns these reactions around and analyzes their meanings without demanding our sympathy or taking a self-righteous stance.

The book's most serious limitation hits readers immediately: for more than 30 pages in the first chapter, Robillard relates his life story from the onset of his motor neuron disease until the book's publication. The sheer volume and specificity of this narrative may bewilder readers at first. Even though the introduction contains useful information, it cries out for a thorough editing of the minutiae: visits to specialists, family arrangements, household shifts, career changes, visits from friends, favorite television shows, and more. Even the acknowledgments contain a welter of information. Stronger editing could have preserved the full appreciation of the conditions and people with whom Robillard worked to pull off the publication of this book. We are much the richer for his perspective on disability and society. This book is recommended for general readers, students, and disability researchers.

MARTHA COPP

East Tennessee State University
Johnson City

ROGERS, NAOMI. 1998. *An Alternative Path: The Making and Remaking of Hahnemann Medical College and Hospital of Philadelphia.* Pp. xi, 348. New Brunswick, NJ: Rutgers University Press. $50.00.

The history of homeopathy in America remains to be written. Homeopathy was, in the nineteenth century, a major medical modality, unlike medical sects whose history was short-lived and controversial (for example, Thomsonianism, eclecticism, phrenopathy, and hydropathy). From its introduction in America in the 1820s by a Swedenborgian homeopath, Hans Burch Gram (1786-1840), homeopathy flourished for over a hundred years.

In 1905, William Harvey King, dean of the faculty at the New York Homoeopathic Medical College, triumphantly called attention to the singular achievements of homeopathy in the United States. By the turn of the century, the homeopaths had established their own network of some 112 hospitals, 59 dispensaries, 143 homeopathic medical societies, and scores of medical journals; homeopathic practitioners numbered some 15,000, many of whom were women, all served by some two-score homeopathic medical colleges (William Harvey King, ed., *History of Homoeopathy and Its Institutions in America*, 1905).

In the immensity of this homeopathic medical world, no institution became more important than the Homoeopathic Medical College of Philadelphia, founded in 1848. It epitomizes the success of homeopathy in its own history, and after many vicissitudes it became the Hahnemann Medical College of Philadelphia in 1866. It survives today as the Hahnemann University of the Medical Sciences. It is the history of Hahnemann and its hospital that Naomi Rogers tells in this welcome and important book.

Rogers acknowledges first that she undertook to write "not a coffee table book but a serious historical work with proper documentation, a work that would place Hahnemann's history into a larger social and political context." And this she has done. The work is conveniently divided into three sections: "The First Fifty Years, 1848-1898: Creating a School and a Distinctive Identity"; "The Second Fifty Years: An Alternative Path from Medical Orthodoxy"; and "The Final Fifty Years: Recreating a School and an Identity." Each of these sections is a self-contained entity, and each explores the evolution of the medical arts and practice in America during the designated time span, with Hahnemann as a central point of reference.

Rogers provides a short and illuminating prologue in which she describes the medical world of America before 1850. Here she includes short but incisive accounts of the medical system of Samuel Thomson (1769-1843), a system based on indigenous botanic medicine that had a tremendous following in the 1820s through the 1840s. She also describes the emergence of the eclectics, who considered themselves successors to Thomson, with some notice of Russell Thatcher Trall (1812-1877), the enigmatic founder of hydropathy. It is into this variegated medical landscape that homeopathy makes its appearance in America in the late 1820s, introduced by German immigrants.

Homeopathy originated in the work of the German physician Samuel Hahnemann (1755-1843), who developed a system of therapeutics whose first principle was *similia similibus curantur* ("like cures like"). Hahnemann maintained that disease was "an alteration in the inner working of the human organism," a morbid change in the vital principle (*Organon of the Rational Art of Healing*, 1810).

Although homeopathy was subject to continuing attacks by the medical orthodoxy, it flourished, largely due to the fact that homeopathic therapeutics were preferred to the debilitating administrations of orthodox physicians.

Rogers's history of the Hahnemann Medical College has special significance. The college survived the disappearance of the homeopathic world of which it was so vital a part, and the question may be asked, Why? In 1910, Abraham Flexner examined 15 homeopathic medical schools; in 1922, only New York Homoeopathic Medical College (later renamed New York Medical College) and

Hahnemann survived. Rogers's answer is straightforward: "In struggling to integrate homeopathic tradition with the new scientific medicine, Hahnemann reconstructed itself as a pragmatic facility and achieved a stable place in Philadelphia medical training and health care." The reasons for the decline of homeopathy in America are at best very complex. There are certain commanding factors that explain the decline. Factors include the doctrinal split in homeopathic therapeutics (highs versus lows) and the continuing attacks by the American Medical Association against the network of homeopathic medical schools. Gradually, the homeopathic schools went out of business; with the decline of the schools, the number of homeopathic practitioners also fell. Despite the achievements of homeopathy and the increasing indications that the orthodox physicians and the American Medical Association were coming to accept a modus vivendi with the homeopaths and their doctrines, the homeopathic universe was irretrievably in decline.

The history of homeopathy in America will be written as histories of individual institutions, not unlike Naomi Rogers's *Alternative Path*, appear.

FRANCESCO CORDASCO

Montclair State University
Upper Montclair
New Jersey

SHARPLESS, REBECCA. 1999. *Fertile Ground, Narrow Choices: Women on Texas Cotton Farms, 1900-1940*. Pp. xxiii, 352. Chapel Hill: University of North Carolina Press. $59.95. Paperbound, $19.95.

Rebecca Sharpless's book about the rural women of Central Texas combines oral history and written memoirs with Bettina Aptheker's concept of women's dailiness to produce a moving and detailed history of a marginalized people. Examining the specificities of everyday life for these German, Czech, African American, Mexican, and Anglo-American farm women, Sharpless skillfully weaves the tapestry of life in the cotton fields under a relentless Texas sun with the continuum of household and child-rearing tasks.

Sharpless chose for the book's cover a striking brown-toned photograph of a young African American mother in men's clothes wearing a tired Stetson hat. She stands against a farm wagon with her two children, one at her breast and the other at her knee. The expression on the woman's face lets us know she is formidable—someone to be reckoned with both as a worker in the cotton field, which we can see in the background behind the wagon, and, at the same time, as a competent mother. The image is one of strength and fortitude. What bothers me about this photograph is that this African American woman's breast is exposed; apparently she has just nursed her youngest child, whom, along with an older child, she has brought to the field with her. Some readers may feel that this powerful image is exploited since the book is mostly about white women. For some readers, it may even recall the photographs of barebreasted African tribal women so popular in *National Geographic*, which were hidden in the hall closets and served as soft porn in the 1950s. On the other hand, the photograph portrays the simultaneous roles of southern rural women as mothers and as fieldworkers, which is what this book is about.

The book includes a close examination of the private sphere of women in the Blacklands Prairie in rural Texas in the first half of the century, including gender and family relationships, housekeeping and clothing, food production and preparation, and of the public sphere, in chapters that concentrate on women's labor in the fields, women in their communities, and urbanization and depopulation of the rural Blackland Prairie. Although Sharpless makes good use of the oral histories of the southern farm women in her analysis of their lives (the chapter on food made me crave my grandmother's cooking and made me just generally homesick for the South), I would liked to have heard more from the women themselves. Among those interviewed were women who faced isolated lives of unremitting hard work. The survival of their families depended on their ability to provide a home for their many children in the run-down Blackland Prairie farmhouses provided by landowners from whom they rented or sharecropped. It depended also on their resolve to maintain gardens, chickens, and hogs to feed their families and then to can everything that would fit into a jar. They made all their family's clothes and even the soap that was used to wash them out by hand. In addition, they worked alongside their men in the fields. Fourteen- to 16-hour workdays were routine. By the 1930s and 1940s, the New Deal and World War II brought to a close this 300-year-old rural tradition. According to Sharpless, most women did not miss the farm—the shacks, the near starvation, the rags that passed for clothes, the toting of water and chopping of wood. Farm women's daughters for the most part moved to the Texas cities like nearby Waco, where they were able to keep house full-time without working in the fields, or they sought employment in the sewing factory and learned to rely on consumerism to feed their families.

This book is essential reading for women's studies scholars and scholars of the South, providing an intimate look at the material conditions of early-twentieth-century rural life and women's role in it.

VICTORIA BYERLY

San Jose State University
California

VOLCANSEK, MARY R. with ELISABETTA DE FRANCISIS and JACQUELINE LUCIENNE LAFON. 1996. *Judicial Misconduct: A Cross-National Comparison*. Pp. ix, 163. Gainesville: University Press of Florida. $39.95.

Mary Volcansek is professor of political science at Florida International University. She accomplishes in *Judical Misconduct* what scholars have, to date, rarely attempted: to produce a genuinely comparative, multination analysis of judicial institutions and processes. To assist her in this effort, she calls upon the talents of two European colleagues, Elisabetta De Francisis and Jacqueline Lucienne Lafon, to write the book's case study chapters on Italy and France, respectively. Volcansek personally tackles the case study chapters on England and the United States. But more important, she introduces the book with a very clear and thoughtful chapter, "Judges and Democracy," and concludes it nicely with a chapter entitled "Judging the Judges."

Judicial Misconduct delivers on the promise of its title. Its four case study chapters provide thorough synopses of the history of judicial misconduct and the rules and procedures designed to regulate it in France, Italy, England, and the United States. But in fact, the book is about more than judicial misconduct, important as that topic may be to the health of legal and judicial systems. Its most vital theoretical concern is with the perennial problem of the relationship between judges and democracy.

Judicial misconduct is intimately intertwined with judicial independence and the requirements of democratic accountability. Judges are rarely elected, so "there is no direct way for citizens to control judges or to hold them accountable" once they have been selected. Perhaps this would not matter very much if judges did not exercise important roles in democratic government, if they were merely, as continental tradition asserts they should be, *la bouche de la loi*. But it would still matter, since the idealized judicial role requires that judges demonstrate competence, integrity, impartiality, and independence in order to serve effectively as "the mouth of the law." Given these expectations, judicial misconduct—ineptness, venality, bias, toadyism—and its regulation would still be serious concerns, at least for the administration of democratic governments.

Volcansek convincingly reminds us, however, of what most students of the judiciary now acknowledge: that the judicial role requires as a matter of function that judges must, in fact, be more than merely the mouth of the law, no matter what they or those selecting them believe. She also emphasizes for her readers the growing evidence that there has been a nearly global increase in the political importance and policymaking significance of courts and judges that highlights, rather than dims, the problem of the accountability of judges in democracy.

A central problem in preventing judicial misconduct and maintaining accountability is that regulations and mechanisms that attempt to do so may directly or indirectly diminish judicial independence and impartiality. Volcansek considers this problem carefully and describes the balance that she believes will guide one through the horns of this apparent dilemma, at least in principle. She closes her excellent beginning chapter by explaining the comparative research design that guides her study and by laying out a heuristic model of judicial accountability. The model links the exogenous variables "judicial status" and "legal culture" to the intervening variable "monitoring mechanisms," and it links the exogenous variables "political environment" and "judicial authority" to the intervening variable "ethical norms" before linking the intervening variables to the ultimate dependent variable "judicial accountability."

Volcansek uses the heuristic model to guide the analyses and to construct her own final chapter, which ties up many of the themes of the book and offers appropriate conclusions about the regulation of judicial conduct in democracies. She carefully ties the findings of the book to her initial concerns about the role of judges and the status of judicial accountability in democracy.

Volcansek writes clearly and well. The book has an excellent bibliography, is competently indexed, and is well footnoted, although the footnotes are, irritatingly, placed at the end of the text, rather than at the bottom of the page, where they would be most useful.

C. NEAL TATE

University of North Texas
Denton

ECONOMICS

DOREMUS, PAUL N., WILLIAM H. KELLER, LOUIS W. PAULY, and SIMON REICH. 1998. *The Myth of the Global Corporation*. Pp. xiii, 193. Princeton, NJ: Princeton University Press. $29.95. Paperbound, $16.95.

This book makes an overwhelming case that it is a myth that global corporations are eclipsing nation-states. It does not, however, argue that globalization is a myth. The authors question whether multinational firms are losing their national moorings. They attack the idea that convergence will sweep away national differences, heralding a new global corporate economy. The authors of this plucky volume compare the activities of multinational firms in technology and capital-intensive sectors based in the United States, Germany, and Japan. They conclude that where a firm comes from still matters.

The argument is that corporate leaders and their firms grow up in unique national institutional and cultural environments and are shaped by them. Corporate governance, financing systems, approaches to innovation, and attitudes toward inward foreign direct investment all differ profoundly in the United States, Germany, and Japan. American, German, and Japanese multinationals "continue to differ in the relative priorities they assign to the maximization of share-holder value, the satisfaction of customer needs, and the stabilization of employer-employee relations." In short, markets are more open and production processes more global, but firms are still more national than global.

In addition, the authors contend that except when non-U.S. research and development (R&D) is flowing into the United States or R&D facilities are acquired through merger or acquisition, "R&D moves overseas much more slowly than production, sourcing, and other business activities." Their analysis of U.S. technology trade data suggests that most cross-border exchange of technology flows from parents to their affiliates and that companies based in different countries acquire technology in different ways. Further, they indicate that U.S. firms, especially in information technology industries, are more likely than their German or Japanese counterparts to initiate technology alliances designed to reduce R&D costs, spread product development risks, and maintain access to a broad portfolio of technologies and

market opportunities beyond their core competencies. Finally, American and British "firms tend to be more integrated with foreign economies in which they operate, while German and especially Japanese [multinational corporations] tend to retain large shares of their innovation and trading operation within their own networks."

This volume should put to rest the simplistic notion that, as one reviewer put it, "globalization is homogenizing corporate structures and debilitating the state." The authors are quite correct to warn that "efficient global markets with a modicum of stability will not likely evolve through the unhindered competition of globe-spanning firms." Governments and international institutions still are needed to ensure equity and fairness.

An easy but ultimately unfair criticism of this book would be that the differences do not matter that much because of the triumph of the open, Silicon Valley-Seattle-Hollywood-driven U.S. economy in the 1990s. Cyberspace may be global, but it is dominated by U.S. firms. Japanese and particularly German firms simply do not matter that much to the fundamental issues driving the world information economy. Still, it is important to be clear that evidence of the enduring nature of corporate cultures and differences is not a refutation of the globalization of the world economy. Global and regional production, markets, and networks are emerging. For example, Thomas Friedman's much-cited view of globalization in *The Lexus and the Olive Tree* rests on three shifting, interrelated balances, none of which directly involves global corporations (balances between nation-states, between nation-states and global markets, and between nation-states and individuals). In short, the volume reviewed here constitutes an important effort to understand the dynamics of corporate-government interactions in a globalizing economy that is evolving at Internet speed.

JONATHAN D. ARONSON

University of Southern California
Los Angeles

GRAETZ, MICHAEL J. and JERRY L. MASHAW. 1999. *True Security: Rethinking American Social Insurance.* Pp. x, 369. New Haven, CT: Yale University Press. $40.00. Paperbound, $16.95.

This book, by two distinguished Yale Law School professors, differs from the usual survey of American social insurance programs in at least two ways. Unlike many of their fellow policy wonks, Graetz and Mashaw cover not only Social Security—the 2000-pound gorilla of social welfare programs—but also such relatively obscure programs as unemployment compensation and workers' compensation. Unlike many liberal social commentators, they do not defend existing social insurance programs down the line as, in effect, the best that we can do in a conservative age. Instead, they propose many bold changes in the programs in order to achieve, as they put it, "true security." They would even supplement Social Security, the object of considerable liberal efforts to defend the status quo, with something like personal savings accounts that beneficiaries could draw upon to supplement their retirement income or cover a spell of unemployment.

Indeed, the linkage between the problems of unemployment and old-age security is typical of the authors' strategy. Instead of looking at the programs in isolation from one another, they encourage us to take a life cycle perspective on social

insurance. Such a perspective reveals the fact that, for example, risks associated with childhood are not well provided for under today's social arrangements. Graetz and Mashaw propose to remedy the problems by using the government to subsidize the costs of housing, medical care, and child care. Further along the life course, problems associated with disability become more prevalent, and here the authors would make what might be described as radical incremental changes, such as limiting workers' compensation to the payment of "damages" for workers' sustaining impairments and in effect mandating that state temporary disability programs become national in scope.

The book has a refreshingly iconoclastic quality. Graetz and Mashaw, for example, are not much taken with the contemporary notion of increasing the responsibilities of the states, regarding state administration of workers' compensation and unemployment compensation as administrative and policy disasters. Nor do they believe that tax subsidies lie at the heart of the solution to contemporary problems. They also do not reflexively oppose such things as means tests or privilege payroll taxes, as called for in the social insurance orthodoxy.

The book is not without limitations. For a monograph concerned with the definition of social insurance and its proper place in social policy, it pays surprisingly little attention to what Douglas Brown once described as the American philosophy of social insurance. For a book that highlights the importance of ideas, it is also difficult to take away many overarching ideas on the order of "Make work pay" from this book crammed with so many ideas. Graetz and Mashaw do not apologize for the complexity of their policy suggestions. Throughout, the authors urge us to get the ideas right before we engage in the sort of political realism that pervades Washington. Yet they do not provide many hints on how to get from here to there, although they assure us that their suggestions are incremental, in line with American economic traditions, and not more costly than the present system. Finally, the lack of attention to American particulars—in particular to the problem of race—may cause some to dismiss the book as an academic exercise.

It is that, but it is also a very thoughtful and ambitious look into the very heart of our social policy. Among many other contributions, this book breaks down the barriers that have caused us to focus on the financing issue in Social Security as *the* social insurance issue when the problems go so much beyond that.

EDWARD D. BERKOWITZ

George Washington University
Washington, D.C.

LIEBOWITZ, STAN J. and STEPHEN E. MARGOLIS. 1999. *Winners, Losers and Microsoft*. Pp. xiv, 288. Oakland, CA: Independent Institute. $29.95.

Winners, Losers and Microsoft is the skeptic's guide to the economics of networks and path dependence. When the value of a good to any user increases with the number of users, the good is subject to network effects. The more people who have telephones, for example, the greater the value each user derives. The theory of path dependence postulates that standards are initially chosen for little reason, even as the result of historical accident, but then become locked in, largely because network effects discourage switching. The first typewriter keyboard is arranged in the familiar QWERTY pattern for a reason that loses force as technology improves, but changing to a different layout is nearly impossible: people will not learn a new layout because they cannot buy typewriters with other layouts, and manufacturers will not make machines with alternative layouts because too few people, having learned QWERTY, would buy them. Many proponents of these theories assert that network effects and path dependence often result in market failure. They may cause the predictable deadweight loss produced when a monopolist raises price. But more important, the wrong products prevail. Thus QWERTY is inferior to other layouts. This is pernicious lock-in.

Liebowitz and Margolis are the leading critics of these theories. Those unfamiliar with the subject will find their book's critical exposition of the theories illuminating. The authors argue that the theories rely on peculiar assumptions. For example, some models of path dependence assume that actors are passive, so that early adopters choose an inferior technology because no market mechanism exists to induce them to choose the standard that will generate the most value in the long run. But in fact, technologies frequently can be owned, and the owner of the better technology is likely to prevail in a competitive struggle.

Liebowitz and Margolis are careful, however, not to claim that pernicious lock-in is theoretically impossible. Indeed, they argue that network effects are real and can result in monopoly, and they identify the conditions necessary for inferior products to win the market. But they predict that the monopoly technology will usually be the best one available, given limited information. The markets will exhibit serial monopoly, with the best product emerging victorious for a short period until it is replaced by a better product.

For those versed in the theories, the authors' most important contribution is powerful empirical analysis of real-world markets to determine whether the monopolies result from pernicious lock-in or healthy competition. In their classic paper on the QWERTY keyboard, included almost verbatim as chapter 2, they demonstrated that the layout is not inferior, and they summarize studies that have discredited other claims of market failure, such as the VHS video recording standard. In this book, they examine for the first time several major software markets. Consistent with their theory, they find that, while many markets are dominated at a given time by a single product, the better products win out. Moreover, the rate at which products are replaced in the market and the prices charged are inconsistent with lock-in.

Their analysis implies a limited role for government, in part because pernicious lock-in is rare. In particular, antitrust intervention is usually misplaced because anticompetitive conduct cannot be distinguished from legitimate tactics in markets subject to serial monopoly. Accordingly, Liebowitz and Margolis argue in an appendix that the government was mistaken in its antitrust case against Microsoft.

The book incorporates several papers the authors previously published, which produces a degree of distracting repetition. Otherwise, the presentation is excellent. The prose is clear and lively, even entertaining—for instance, the concept of equilibrium is explained by analogy to stickball—without sacrificing professional credibility.

JOHN E. LOPATKA

University of South Carolina
Columbia

OTHER BOOKS

ACS, ZOLTAN J., ed. 2000. *Regional Innovation, Knowledge and Global Change*. Pp. vi, 275. New York: Pinter. Paperbound, no price.

BECKER, TED and CHRISTA DARYL SLATON. 2000. *The Future of Teledemocracy*. Pp. xii, 230. Westport, CT: Praeger. $65.00. Paperbound, $24.95.

BUENO DE MESQUITA, BRUCE and HILTON L. ROOT, eds. 2000. *Governing for Prosperity*. Pp. vi, 266. New Haven, CT: Yale University Press. $35.00. Paperbound, $18.00.

CABLE, VINCENT. 2000. *Globalization and Global Governance*. Pp. xvi, 139. Lexington, NY: Continuum. $74.95. Paperbound, $24.95.

DONALDSON, TERENCE L., ed. 2000. *Religious Rivalries and the Struggle for Success in Caesarea Maritima*. Pp. xiv, 398. Waterloo, Ontario: Wilfrid Laurier University Press. Paperbound, $29.95.

DUNN, TIMOTHY J. 1996. *The Militarization of the United States–Mexico Border, 1978-1992*. Pp. xii, 307. Austin: University of Texas Press. $35.00. Paperbound, $14.95.

ECKES, ALFRED E., JR. 1999. *Opening America's Market: United States Foreign Trade Policy Since 1776*. Pp. xxi, 402. Chapel Hill: University of North Carolina Press. Paperbound, $19.95.

EDIN, KATHRYN and LAURA LEIN. 1998. *Making Ends Meet: How Single Mothers Survive Welfare and Low-Wage Work*. Pp. xxxi, 305. New York: Russell Sage Foundation. $34.95.

EDWARDS, GEOFFREY and GEORG WIESSALA, eds. 1999. *The European Union*. Pp. vi, 254. Malden, MA: Blackwell. Paperbound, $32.95.

EISENDRATH, CRAIG, ed. 2000. *National Insecurity: United States Intelligence After the Cold War*. Pp. viii, 241. Philadelphia: Temple University Press. $34.50.

EKSTEROWICZ, ANTHONY J. and GLENN P. HASTEDT. 1999. *The Post–Cold War Presidency*. Pp. xii, 192. Lanham, MD: Rowman & Littlefield. $49.00. Paperbound, $16.95.

ELIASOPH, NINA. 1998. *Avoiding Politics: How Americans Produce Apathy in Everyday Life*. Pp. x, 330. New York: Cambridge University Press. $64.95. Paperbound, $22.95.

ELLIS, RICHARD J. 1998. *The Dark Side of the Left: Illiberal Egalitarianism in America*. Pp. xiii, 426. Lawrence: University Press of Kansas. No price.

EMMERSON, DONALD K., ed. 1999. *Indonesia Beyond Suharto: Polity, Economy, Society, Transition*. Pp. xxviii, 395. Armonk, NY: M. E. Sharpe. $69.95. Paperbound, $26.95.

GHOSH, B. N., ed. 2000. *Privatisation: The ASEAN Connection*. Pp. viii, 285. Huntington, NY: Nova Science. No price.

GIDDENS, ANTHONY and CHRISTOPHER PIERSON. 1998. *Conversations with Anthony Giddens: Making Sense of Modernity*. Pp. ix, 233. Stanford, CA: Stanford University Press. $45.00. Paperbound, $16.95.

GIERZYNSKI, ANTHONY. 2000. *Money Rules: Financing Elections in America*. Pp. xv, 141. Boulder, CO: Westview Press. $59.00. Paperbound, $17.00.

GLANTZ, STANTON A., JOHN SLADE, LISA A. BERO, PETER HANAUER, and DEBORAH E. BARNES. 1996. *The Cigarette Papers*. Pp. xix, 539. Berkeley: University of California Press. $29.95.

GLASBERG, DAVITA SILFEN and DAN SKIDMORE. 1997. *Corporate Welfare Policy and the Welfare State:*

Bank Deregulation and the Savings and Loan Bailout. Pp. vii, 172. New York: Aldine de Gruyter. $42.95. Paperbound, $20.95.

GLASER, JAMES M. 1996. *Race, Campaign Politics, and the Realignment in the South.* Pp. xv, 229. New Haven, CT: Yale University Press. Paperbound, no price.

GLASSICK, CHARLES E., MARY TAYLOR HUBER, and GENE I. MAEROFF. 1997. *Scholarship Assessed: Evaluation of the Professoriate.* Pp. xiii, 130. San Francisco: Jossey-Bass. Paperbound, no price.

GLICKMAN, CARL D. 1998. *Revolutionizing America's Schools.* Pp. xiii, 207. San Francisco: Jossey-Bass. $28.95.

GLYNN, CARROLL J., SUSAN HERBST, GARRETT J. O'KEEFE, and ROBERT Y. SHAPIRO. 1999. *Public Opinion.* Pp. xvi, 471. Boulder, CO: Westview Press. $69.00. Paperbound, $25.00.

GOLDFARB, JEFFREY C. 1998. *Civility and Subversion: The Intellectual in Democratic Society.* Pp. ix, 253. New York: Cambridge University Press. $59.95. Paperbound, $22.95.

GREENE, JOHN ROBERT. 2000. *The Presidency of George Bush.* Pp. xiii, 245. Lawrence: University Press of Kansas. $35.00.

HARRIS, IAN, ed. 2000. *Buddhism and Politics in Twentieth- Century Asia.* Pp. xii, 300. New York: Continuum. $75.00.

HAZLETT, JOHN DOWNTON. 1998. *My Generation: Collective Autobiography and Identity Politics.* Pp. xii, 263. Madison: University of Wisconsin Press. $45.00. Paperbound, $19.95.

HEATH, ANTHONY, RICHARD BREEN, and CHRISTOPHER T. WHELAN, eds. 1999. *Ireland North and South: Perspectives from Social Science.* Pp. xii, 535. New York: Oxford University Press. $52.00.

HELLMANN, JOHN. 1997. *The Kennedy Obsession: The American Myth of JFK.* Pp. xvi, 206. New York: Columbia University Press. Paperbound, $16.95.

HELMS, MARY W. 1998. *Access to Origins: Affines, Ancestors and Aristocrats.* Pp. xiii, 258. Austin: University Press of Texas. No price.

HENDERSON, PHILLIP G., ed. 1999. *The Presidency Then and Now.* Pp. xx, 300. Lanham, MD: Rowman & Littlefield. $70.00. Paperbound, $24.95.

HERSEY, GEORGE L. 1998. *The Evolution of Allure: Sexual Selection from the Medici Venus to the Incredible Hulk.* Pp. xvi, 219. Cambridge: MIT Press. Paperbound, $17.50.

HERZENBERG, STEPHEN A., JOHN A. ALIC, and HOWARD WIAL. 1998. *New Rules for a New Economy: Employment and Opportunity in Postindustrial America.* Pp. xiii, 216. Ithaca, NY: Cornell University Press. $26.50.

HETHERINGTON, KEVIN. 2000. *New Age Travellers: Vanloads of Uproarious Humanity.* Pp. x, 191. New York: Continuum. $74.95. Paperbound, $26.95.

HOFFMAN, JOHN. 1999. *Sovereignty.* Pp. ix, 129. Minneapolis: University of Minnesota Press. $37.95. Paperbound, $14.95.

HOGANSON, KRISTIN L. 1998. *Fighting for American Manhood: How Gender Politics Provoked the Spanish-American and Philippine-American Wars.* Pp. xii, 305. New Haven, CT: Yale University Press. $30.00.

IRWIN, RAYMOND D. 2000. *Books on Early American History and Culture, 1991-1995: An Annotated Bibliography.* Pp. viii, 301. Westport, CT: Greenwood Press. $79.50.

JENKINS, PHILIP. 1998. *Moral Panic: Changing Concepts of the Child Molester in Modern America.* Pp. xii, 302. New Haven, CT: Yale University Press. $30.00.

JEREMY, DAVID J. 1998. *Artisans, Entrepreneurs and Machines.* Pp. viii, 216. Brookfield, VT: Ashgate. $99.95.

JING, JUN. 2000. *Feeding China's Little Emperors: Food, Children, and Social Change.* Pp. xiii, 279. Stanford, CA: Stanford University Press. $49.50. Paperbound, $17.95.

JOHNSON, MICHELLE N. and FRANK COLUMBUS, eds. 2000. *America in the 21st Century: Political and Economic Issues.* Vol. 1. Pp. vi, 243. Huntington, NY: Nova Science. $59.00.

JOHNSON, R. W. and DAVID WELSH, eds. 1999. *Ironic Victory: Liberalism in Post-Liberation South Africa.* Pp. x, 420. New York: Oxford University Press. Paperbound, $29.95.

JOHNSTON, ALASTAIR IAIN. 1995. *Cultural Realism: Strategic Culture and Grand Strategy in Chinese History.* Pp. xiii, 307. Princeton, NJ: Princeton University Press. Paperbound, $18.95.

JONES, NANCY BAKER and RUTHE WINEGARTEN. 2000. *Capitol Women: Texas Female Legislators, 1923-1999.* Pp. xiv, 328. Austin: University of Texas Press. $45.00. Paperbound, $22.95.

JOPPKE, CHRISTIAN and STEVEN LUKES, eds. 1999. *Multicultural Questions.* Pp. viii, 267. New York: Oxford University Press. $52.00.

JOYNER, CHRISTOPHER C. 1998. *Governing the Frozen Commons: The Antarctic Regime and Environmental Protection.* Pp. xvii, 363. Columbia: University of South Carolina Press. $49.95. Paperbound, $24.95.

JUDAH, TIM. 1998. *The Serbs: History, Myth and the Destruction of Yugoslavia.* Pp. xvii, 350. New Haven, CT: Yale University Press. $35.00. Paperbound, $16.00.

————. 2000. *Kosovo: War and Revenge.* Pp. xx, 348. New Haven, CT: Yale University Press. $37.50. Paperbound, $17.95.

KIRK, TIM and ANTHONY McELLIGOTT, eds. 1999. *Opposing Fascism: Community, Authority and Resistance in Europe.* Pp. ix, 246. New York: Cambridge University Press. No price.

KNIGHT, G. ROGER. 2000. *Narratives of Colonialism: Sugar, Java and the Dutch.* Pp. xx, 191. Huntington, NY: Nova Science. $69.00.

KNOEPFLMACHER, U. C. 1998. *Ventures into Childland: Victorians, Fairy Tales, and Femininity.* Pp. xxi, 444. Chicago: University of Chicago Press. $35.00.

KOITHARA, VERGHESE. 1999. *Society, State and Security: The Indian Experience.* Pp. 414. New Delhi: Sage. $59.95.

KOLLMAN, KEN. 1998. *Outside Lobbying: Public Opinion and Interest Group Strategies.* Pp. xiv, 215. Princeton, NJ: Princeton University Press. $55.00. Paperbound, $18.95.

KOLP, JOHN GILMAN. 1998. *Gentlemen and Freeholders: Electoral Politics in Colonial Virginia.* Pp. xi, 249. Baltimore, MD: Johns Hopkins University Press. No price.

KRAMER, HILTON and ROGER KIMBALL, eds. 1999. *The Betrayal of Liberalism: How the Disciples of Freedom and Equality Helped Foster the Illiberal Politics of Coercion and Control.* Pp. 248. Chicago: Ivan R. Dee. $28.95. Paperbound, $14.95.

KREHBIEL, KEITH. 1998. *Pivotal Politics: A Theory of United States Lawmaking.* Pp. xvi, 258. Chicago: University of Chicago Press. $50.00. Paperbound, $17.00.

KRISTOL, IRVING. 1995. *Neoconversatism: The Autobiography of an Idea.* Pp. xi, 493. Chicago: Ivan R. Dee. Paperbound, no price.

KUIC, VUKAN. 1999. *Yves R. Simon: Real Democracy.* Pp. vi, 167. Lanham, MD: Rowman & Littlefield. $60.00. Paperbound, $22.95.

KYMLICKA, WILL. 1998. *Finding Our Way: Rethinking Ethnocultural Relations in Canada.* Pp. viii, 220. New York: Oxford University Press. Paperbound, $24.95.

LAHAM, NICHOLAS. 2000. *Ronald Reagan and the Politics of Immigration Reform.* Pp. xvi, 247. Westport, CT: Praeger. $65.00.

LEE KAM HING and TAN CHEE-BENG, eds. 2000. *The Chinese in Malaysia.* Pp. xxix, 418. New York: Oxford University Press. $45.00.

LUKACS, JOHN. 2000. *A Student's Guide to the Study of History.* Pp. 49. Wilmington, DE: ISI Books. Paperbound, $5.95.

MAHAJAN, SUCHETA. 2000. *Independence and Partition: The Erosion of Colonial Power in India.* Pp. 425. New Delhi: Sage. $49.95.

MAIONI, ANTONIA. 1998. *Parting at the Crossroads: The Emergence of Health Insurance in the United States and Canada.* Pp. xiv, 205. Princeton, NJ: Princeton University Press. $37.50.

MANDERY, EVAN J. 1999. *The Campaign: Rudy Giuliani, Ruth Messinger, Al Sharpton, and the Race to be Mayor of New York City.* Pp. viii, 400. Boulder, CO: Westview Press. $27.00.

MANUEL, PAUL CHRISTOPHER and ANNE MARIE CAMMISA. 1998. *Checks and Balances? How a Parliamentary System Could Change American Politics.* Pp. xiv, 226. Boulder, CO: Westview Press. $49.00. Paperbound, $15.00.

MARCUSE, PETER and RONALD VAN KEMPEN, eds. 2000. *Globalizing Cities: A New Spatial Order?* Pp. xviii, 318. Malden, MA: Blackwell. Paperbound, $24.95.

MARDIN, SERIF. 2000. *The Genesis of Young Ottoman Thought: A Study in the Modernization of Turkish Political Ideas.* Pp. xii, 456. Syracuse, NY: Syracuse University Press. Paperbound, $26.95.

MARKS, SUSAN COLLIN. 2000. *Watching the Wind: Conflict Resolution During South Africa's Transition to Democracy.* Pp. xviii, 225. Washington, DC: United States Institute of Peace Press. Paperbound, $14.95.

MARMOR, THEODORE R. 2000. *The Politics of Medicare.* 2d ed. Pp. xxv, 228. New York: Aldine De Gruyter. $35.95. Paperbound, $16.95.

MARTEL, FREDERIC. 2000. *The Pink and the Black: Homosexuals in France Since 1968.* Pp. xx, 442. Stanford, CA: Stanford University Press. $60.00. Paperbound, $19.95.

MARTIN, CALVIN LUTHER. 2000. *The Way of the Human Being.* Pp. xii, 235. New Haven, CT: Yale University Press. $30.00. Paperbound, $14.95.

MARTIN, MART. 2000. *The Almanac of Women and Minorities in World Politics.* Pp. xxxiii, 466. Boulder, CO: Westview Press. $49.00.

MARX, ANTHONY W. 1998. *Making Race and Nation: A Comparison of the United States, South Africa, and Brazil.* Pp. xviii, 390. New York: Cambridge University Press. $29.95.

MASON, MARY ANN. 1999. *The Custody Wars: Why Children Are Losing the Legal Battle and What We Can Do About It.* Pp. x, 278. New York: Basic Books. $23.00.

MASTERS, ROGER D. 1996. *Machiavelli, Leonardo, and the Science of Power*. Pp. x, 366. Notre Dame, IN: University of Notre Dame Press. Paperbound, $24.95.

McKAY, DAVID. 2000. *Essentials of American Government*. Pp. xix, 425. Boulder, CO: Westview Press. Paperbound, $27.00.

MORANTZ-SANCHEZ, REGINA. 2000. *Sympathy and Science: Women Physicians in American Medicine*. Pp. xxxvi, 464. Chapel Hill: University of North Carolina Press. Paperbound, $14.95.

MUELLER, JOHN, ed. 2000. *Peace, Prosperity, and Politics*. Pp. vii, 296. Boulder, CO: Westview Press. $70.00.

PETERS, B. GUY, R.A.W. RHODES, and VINCENT WRIGHT, eds. 2000. *Administering the Summit: Administration of the Core Executive in Developed Countries*. Pp. xvii, 275. New York: St. Martin's Press. $69.95.

PETTEGREW, JOHN, ed. 2000. *A Pragmatist's Progress? Richard Rorty and American Intellectual History*. Pp. vii, 222. Lanham, MD: Rowman & Littlefield. $60.00. Paperbound, $24.95.

PIERSON, CHRIS and SIMON TORMEY, eds. 2000. *Politics at the Edge*. Pp. xix, 284. New York: St. Martin's Press. $75.00.

ROSS, ROBERT L. 2000. *Mission Possible: The Story of the Latin American Agribusiness Development Corporation (LAAD)*. Pp. xvi, 160. New Brunswick, NJ: Transaction. $32.95.

SCHELL, JONATHAN. 2000. *The Fate of the Earth and the Abolition*. Pp. xl, 173. Stanford, CA: Stanford University Press. $55.00. Paperbound, $19.95.

SCHEUER, JEFFREY. 1999. *The Sound Bite Society: Television and the American Mind*. Pp. 230. New York: Four Walls, Eight Windows. $23.95.

SNODGRASS, WARREN. 2000. *Swords to Plowshares: The Fall of Communist Germany*. Pp. xvi, 174. Huntington, NY: Nova Science. $34.00.

STOESZ, DAVID. 2000. *A Poverty of Imagination: Bootstrap Capitalism, Sequel to Welfare Reform*. Pp. xxi, 194. Madison: University of Wisconsin Press. Paperbound, no price.

TANG, JOYCE. 2000. *Doing Engineering: The Career Attainment and Mobility of Caucasian, Black, and Asian-American Engineers*. Pp. xx, 242. Lanham, MD: Rowman & Littlefield. $65.00. Paperbound, $24.95.

TESKE, ROBIN L. and MARY ANN TETREAULT, eds. 2000. *Conscious Acts and the Politics of Social Change: Feminist Approaches to Social Movements, Community, and Power*. Vol. 1. Pp. viii, 308. Columbia: University of South Carolina Press. $34.95.

TIEN, HUNG-MAO and TUN-JEN CHENG, eds. 2000. *The Security Environment in the Asia-Pacific*. Pp. xi, 355. Armonk, NY: M. E. Sharpe. $72.95. Paperbound, $24.95.

WAKEMAN, FREDERIC, JR. and RICHARD LOUIS EDMONDS, eds. 2000. *Reappraising Republican China*. Pp. viii, 209. New York: Oxford University Press. Paperbound, $24.95.

WEBER, KATJA. 2000. *Hierarchy Amidst Anarchy: Transaction Costs and Institutional Choice*. Pp. xiii, 195. Albany: State University of New York Press. Paperbound, no price.

WEINER, DOUGLAS R. 2000. *Models of Nature: Ecology, Conservation and Cultural Revolution in Soviet Russia*. Pp. xii, 324. Pittsburgh, PA: University of Pittsburgh Press. Paperbound, $17.95.

WEISSBERG, ROBERT, ed. 2000. *Democracy and the Academy*. Pp. xxvi, 247. Huntington, NY: Nova Science. $59.00.

WHITE, TYRENE, ed. 2000. *China Briefing 2000: The Continuing Transformation*. Pp. viii, 397. Armonk, NY: M. E. Sharpe. $74.95. Paperbound, $26.95.

WILLIAMS, JAMES. 2000. *Lyotard and the Political*. Pp. ix, 153. New York: Routledge. $65.00. Paperbound, $20.99.

YU, PETER KIEN-HONG. 1999. *Bicoastal China: A Dialectical, Paradigmatic Analysis*. Pp. xix, 200. Huntington, NY: Nova Science. $59.00.

ZAKARIA, FAREED. 1998. *From Wealth to Power: The Unusual Origins of America's World Role*. Pp. x, 199. Princeton, NJ: Princeton University Press. $29.95.

ZHAO, SUISHENG, ed. 1999. *Across the Taiwan Strait: Mainland China, Taiwan, and the 1995-1996 Crisis*. Pp. x, 306. New York: Routledge. $80.00. Paperbound, $24.99.

ZHOU, MIN and CARL L. BANKSTON III. 1998. *Growing Up American: How Vietnamese Children Adapt to Life in the United States*. Pp. xii, 270. New York: Russell Sage Foundation. No price.

INDEX

STATEMENT OF OWNERSHIP, MANAGEMENT, AND CIRCULATION
P.S. Form 3526 Facsimile

1. TITLE: THE ANNALS OF THE AMERICAN ACADEMY OF POLITICAL AND SOCIAL SCIENCE
2. USPS PUB. #: 026-060

3. DATE OF FILING: October 1, 2000

4. FREQUENCY OF ISSUE: Bi-Monthly
5. NO. OF ISSUES ANNUALLY: 6
6. ANNUAL SUBSCRIPTION PRICE: Paper-Bound Institution $375; Cloth-Bound
   Institution $425; Paper-Bound Individual $65; Cloth-Bound Individual $100

7. PUBLISHER ADDRESS: 2455 Teller Road, Thousand Oaks, CA 91320
   CONTACT PERSON: Mary Nugent, Circulation
   TELEPHONE: (805) 499-0721

8. HEADQUARTERS ADDRESS: 2455 Teller Road, Thousand Oaks, CA 91320

9. PUBLISHER: Sara Miller McCune, 2979 Eucalyptus Hill Road, Montecito, CA 93108
   EDITOR: Dr. Alan W. Heston, The American Academy of Political and Social
   Science, 3937 Chestnut Street, Philadelphia, PA 19104
   MANAGING EDITOR: Erica Ginsburg, The American Academy of Political and
   Social Science, 3937 Chestnut Street, Philadelphia, PA 19104

10. OWNER: The American Academy of Political and Social Science, 3937 Chestnut
    Street, Philadelphia, PA 19104

11. KNOWN BONDHOLDERS, ETC.
    None

12. NONPROFIT PURPOSE, FUNCTION, STATUS:
    Has Not Changed During Preceding 12 Months

13. PUBLICATION NAME: THE ANNALS OF THE AMERICAN ACADEMY OF POLITICAL AND SOCIAL SCIENCE

14. ISSUE FOR CIRCULATION DATA BELOW: SEPTEMBER 2000

15. EXTENT & NATURE OF CIRCULATION:

		AVG. NO. COPIES EACH ISSUE DURING PRECEDING 12 MONTHS	ACT. NO. COPIES OF SINGLE ISSUE PUB. NEAREST TO FILING DATE
A.	TOTAL NO. COPIES	4226	3651
B.	PAID CIRCULATION		
	1. PAID/REQUESTED OUTSIDE-CO, ETC	2098	2120
	2. PAID IN-COUNTY SUBSCRIPTIONS	0	0
	3. SALES THROUGH DEALERS, ETC.	423	430
	4. OTHER CLASSES MAILED USPS	291	2
C.	TOTAL PAID CIRCULATION	2812	2552
D.	FREE DISTRIBUTION BY MAIL		
	1. OUTSIDE-COUNTY AS ON 3541	100	100
	2. IN-COUNTY AS STATED ON 3541	0	0
	3. OTHER CLASSES MAILED USPS	0	0
E.	FREE DISTRIBUTION OTHER	0	0
F.	TOTAL FREE DISTRIBUTION	100	100
G.	TOTAL DISTRIBUTION	2912	2652
H.	COPIES NOT DISTRIBUTED		
	1. OFFICE USE, ETC.	1319	1026
	2. RETURN FROM NEWS AGENTS	0	0
I.	TOTAL	4231	3678
	PERCENT PAID CIRCULATION	97%	96%

16. NOT REQUIRED TO PUBLISH.

17. I CERTIFY THAT ALL INFORMATION FURNISHED ON THIS FORM IS TRUE AND COMPLETE.
    I UNDERSTAND THAT ANYONE WHO FURNISHES FALSE OR MISLEADING INFORMATION ON
    THIS FORM OR WHO OMITS MATERIAL OR INFORMATION REQUESTED ON THE FORM MAY
    BE SUBJECT TO CRIMINAL SANCTIONS (INCLUDING FINES AND IMPRISONMENT) AND/OR
    CIVIL SANCTIONS (INCLUDING MULTIPLE DAMAGES AND CIVIL PENALTIES).

Mary Nugent   _Sept 20, 2000_

Mary Nugent   Date
Circulation Manager
Sage Publications, Inc.

Rated among the *top ten* journals in both Political and Social Science.

*Source: ISI®'s Journal Citation Reports®

Politics & Society

Edited by
The Politics Society Editorial Board

. . . an alternative, critical voice of the social sciences that raises questions about the way the world is organized politically, economically, and socially. Presents engaged as well as rational discourse and reconstructs social inquiry through scholarship addressed to fundamental questions of theory, policy, and politics.

Recent Article Highlights

Aristide R. Zolberg and Long Litt Woon
Why Islam Is Like Spanish:Cultural Incorporation in Europe and the United States

Sanford Schram and Joe Soss
The Real Value of Welfare:Why Poor Families Do Not Migrate

Marc Schneiberg
Political and Institutional Conditions for Governance by Association: Private Order and Price Controls in American Fire Insurance

Claire Jean Kim
The Racial Triangulation of Asian Americans

Heather L. Williams
Mobile Capital and Transborder Labor Rights Mobilization

Quarterly:
March, June, September,
December
Yearly rates:
Individual $70
Institution $300
576 pages
ISSN: 0032-3292

SAGE CONTENTS ALERT

STAY CURRENT ON THE LATEST RESEARCH...
FREE.

Sage Publications is pleased to announce **SAGE CONTENTS ALERT** a pre-publication alerting service **FREE** to all subscribers. If you have e-mail, you can now receive the table of contents for any journal you choose, delivered by e-mail directly to your PC.

You can automatically receive:
- Future Article Titles and Author(s)
- Volume and Issue Number
- Journal Title and Publication Date

Plus:
- Calls for Papers
- Special Issue Announcements
- News from the Editor

Registration is simple – just give us your name, the journal title(s) you want to receive, and your e-mail address.

E-mail: <u>contents.alert@sagepub.com</u>
Visit Website: <u>www.sagepub.com</u>
Or mail to: Sage Contents Alert
Sage Publications
2455 Teller Road
Thousand Oaks, CA 91320

VISIT SAGE ONLINE AT: WWW.SAGEPUB.COM

Find what you are looking for faster!

Our advanced search engine allows you to find what you are looking
for quickly and easily. Searches can be conducted by:

- Author/Editor
- Keyword/Discipline
- Product Type
- ISSN/ISBN
- Title

Payment online is secure and confidential!

Rest assured that all Web site transactions are completed on a
secured server. Only you and Sage Customer Service have access
to ordering information. Using your Visa, MasterCard, Discover,
or American Express card, you can complete your order in just
minutes.

Placing your order is easier than ever before!

Ordering online is simple using the Sage shopping cart feature.
Just click on the "Buy Now!" logo next to the product, and it is
automatically added to your shopping cart. When you are ready to
check out, a listing of all selected products appears for confirmation
before your order is completed.

WE'RE ONLINE!

Visit our Web site at: http://www.sagepub.com